Roy Castle was born in 1932 and raised in Yorkshire. Known and loved for his great versatility, his career in show business spanned over forty years. He died in September 1994.

D0996027

ROY
CASTLE

NOW and THEN

An Autobiography

Foreword by Sir Harry Secombe
Epilogue by Fiona Castle

PAN BOOKS

First published in Great Britain 1994 by Robson Books Ltd

This edition published 1995 by Pan Books

an imprint of Macmillan General Books
Cavaye Place London SW10 9PG
and Basingstoke

Associated companies throughout the world

ISBN 0 330 34193 6

5 7 9 8 6 4

A CIP catalogue record for this book is available from
the British Library

Printed and bound in Great Britain by
Mackays of Chatham PLC, Chatham, Kent

Author's Note

I have written my autobiography in two parts – not to differentiate happy from sad, youth from middle age or any of the usual reasons you might expect, but because a couple of years ago something happened to me which fundamentally changed my life.

Up until early January 1992, I'd had a 'fun', successful career and a loved and loving life – a beautiful wife, four wonderful children, great friends and a strong faith. After that date, I could add something else to that list: I had the beginnings of lung cancer.

It isn't that the former list has changed – I still enjoy all those things – but the newest addition had, naturally, a devastating effect.

Thus it is that in Part II I have drawn heavily on my diaries, as it seemed the best way to communicate my feelings and the timescale of events.

Foreword
by Sir Harry Secombe

In the firmament of show business no star shines brighter than Roy Castle. He can sing, he can dance, he can act and now he has proved he can also write.

I first met him on the Royal Command Performance at The Coliseum in 1958 when I happened to be compèring the first half. This slim bespectacled lad went on stage as an unknown and came off as the hit of the show. I was waiting in the wings as he made his exit and had to push him back into the spotlight three times to bow to the tremendous reception from the audience. The expression on his face was one of utter disbelief that such a thing was happening to him. But it was and it continues to happen.

I have had the privilege of working alongside Roy for many years. We did *Humpty Dumpty* together at the Palladium, *Let Yourself Go* at the same theatre in 1961, and he played Sam Weller to my Samuel Pickwick on Broadway in 1965. I was best man at his wedding, and he is godfather to David, my younger son, my elder daughter Jennifer is godmother to Daniel.

All the time I have known him I have marvelled at his energy, his zest for life, and the sheer joy he brings to those of us lucky enough to be in his presence. Even when he goes out of a room he leaves behind a sort of 'afterglow'.

During the past year we have been together in the revival of *Pickwick* in which he played the father of the character he took on Broadway – Sam Weller's 'ancient' Tony Weller. When we opened in Chichester he was recovering from his first battle with cancer but no one would have known from his performance.

It is difficult to put into words the effect that Roy had on the Company and on the audience. When he took his call at the end of the show, there was such an outgoing of love for him that it was impossible to hold back the tears. The whole audience would rise to him every night and yet in his eyes there was still that look of disbelief that I saw all those years ago at the Royal Command Performance.

He has endured the agony of chemotherapy several times but has chosen to fight his battle publicly so that other cancer victims might take heart from his example. His lovely Fiona has been a wonderful support throughout his life and his family and his faith are a great source of strength.

Added to all the other attributes that Roy possesses must be courage in the face of dreadful adversity. He has taken the measure of his illness and accepted the challenge with equanimity.

I am proud to be his friend.

Harry Secombe

July 1994

Part I

1

The Little Boy
with the Big Voice

'Does a lamppost catch bronchitis in the winter,/Standing on the corner of the street?' I also remember the tune. I was six years old and standing on my first professional stage.

Mam and Dad had taken me to a pantomime at the Palace Theatre, Huddersfield. Wally Wood was the comic and was about to administer the song sheet – audience participation number. The whole house had tried it a couple of times and now came the invitation for boy and girl volunteers to rush the stage.

The surge didn't happen. People looked at each other with embarrassed smiles, *sotto voce* urgings began around unwilling children as Wally Wood put on his big-uncle attitude.

'Come on, kids, I won't hurt you.' He might have been selling second-hand toothbrushes by the reaction. He became a pleading uncle, then a grovelling uncle as the whole evening began grinding to a non-event. Finally, three girls from one family blushed their way to the stage.

'Right, now all we need is a challenge from the boys!'

3

Wally's confidence was returning. 'Come on, lads, you're not going to be beaten by the girls, are you?'

Mam looked at me, the only boy around as far as I can remember. People behind were urging me to make a spectacle of myself. My head swam as I found myself – the unwilling 'volunteer' – walking down to the stage. Reprieved multitudes applauded the sacrificial lamb.

First, the girls huddled together and floundered meekly through the song whilst twirling their nervous fingers in their cotton dresses and looking at each other for confidence. A generous round of applause rewarded their efforts as, asked to do so, they curtsied awkwardly. Wally then brought me forward rather like a dog handler, asked me my name and where I was from, then mocked my broad accent which got a laugh, then an '*Aah*'.

I had quite a big voice for such a small frame and launched into 'Lamppost' with nervous energy. As I finished, the house roared its approval and Wally walked forward and held out his hands for silence.

'Ladies and gentlemen, if the parents of this boy are in the audience, please give him every opportunity. He has a great talent and should have a fine career in this business.'

More applause, together with "Ere, 'eres'. As I walked back to join Mam and Dad, people were patting me on the back and giving me the thumbs-up as they do to the winning team ascending the Wembley staircase to receive the FA Cup. Mam was really proud and even Dad was smiling. The seed was sown.

I was born on 31 August 1932 in Holmfirth Infirmary. *Last of the Summer Wine* country. We lived in the small village of Scholes near Huddersfield. Dad was an insurance agent for Pearl and Mam was a mill worker. Our house was terraced on three sides. Nobody had a back door. When the houses next door and behind had fires, we didn't need one. We lived next to Grandma and Grandad, my Mam's parents, and shared an outside water closet. Known as a one-up-and-one-down, our home also had a back-bending attic and three stone steps down to a small cellar. Grandma's was twelve steps and much bigger but smelly and dank; no light, we had to go down with a candle or torch. Nothing was kept down there. The fireplace had to be blackleaded once a week and contained an oven and a fire backboiler for hot water. The zinc bath tub was a once-a-week occasion in front of the fire, but I never saw how Mam and Dad got around to it. Chamber pots were used in emergencies and, as I slept in the same bedroom as Mam and Dad I often heard Dad releasing the pressure during the night. Never Mam. I slept in the same bedroom as my parents until I was sixteen! No wonder I am an only child.

There were two square windows upstairs and just one downstairs looking across a very small piece of common ground for the surrounding families to hang washing (always on a Monday) or play games (*never* on a Monday). We had a functioning fresh-water hand pump and a well with crystal-clear water trickling on to mossy stones and newts. Sloping at a gradient of approximately one in five, this was our football and cricket pitch. Our dustbin was the stumps and a clothes post was the bowling end.

On the other side of this 'green belt' was the woollen mill. The constant clatter of looms and bobbins was an accepted noise that became the norm and was no longer heard by the locals, its permanence hiding it as a piece of grit in an oyster is coated in pearl. Coming home after a spell away, I remarked to Mam, 'How do you put up with that noise?' She replied, 'What noise?'

The high chimneys belched thick black smoke into the sky and our stone-built houses had long since lost their natural light grey colour as the rain brought the smoke down to dribble over and seep into the stone, turning it into a drab, dark grey and black ode to pollution which was accepted with a shrug along with middle-age spread. Our fires were fuelled by coal which was collected by the bucketful from our designated 'coalhole' at the end of the terrace. Ours was number 5 and we had a rather cumbersome lock to protect our investment. The fuel was dumped outside the door on the rough stony ground and we had to shovel it into our lock-up as quickly as possible. In our broad accent this place was known as ':' coyle hoyle'. 'Will ta go an' get t' coyle in?' We also had to get Grandma's coal in as she weighed around eighteen stones and was virtually housebound. Grandad was the village barber as well as being the bandmaster of a local brass band. He was also the solo cornet player and had no teeth. The joke was he used to *triple* gum. He had a fierce stare, smoked a pipe, had a ginger moustache and wore a flat cap ... *all the time*. I never saw him without his cap. He never went to church or I might have seen the mysteries of what was really under there.

My mother eventually became a ladies' hairdresser and moved into the wooden hut in the village to extend Grandad's business into a Ladies *and* Gents. I often popped in and swept up the dead hair for Grandad. I never quite made it to lather boy. As he shaved his customers, they were always complimentary about his brass band.

I spent most of my evenings with Grandma playing patience or rummy or snap. Snakes and ladders and draughts were also favourites. She always used to lick her thumb and forefinger before dealing cards which eventually gave them a grey blob on each top right-hand corner. Grandad did the same which hastened the discoloration. I always remember his toothless mouth gripping his droopy, Sherlock Holmes pipe whilst the acrid smoke hit the underneath of his cap before dispersing into the cramped room. It had nowhere to go until it found the chimney. Whenever Grandma beat him at rummy, he would throw his cards down on the table and walk away. Grandma would pick up his box of Swan Vestas and throw them across the same table defiantly. 'Two can lake at that game!' ('Lake' meaning play – I have no idea why, it was the word we used.)

The coal fire was always burning and the kettle forever simmering 'on t' rib'. Grandma also made the finest apple puddings in the world. Wrapped in muslin, the dough-cased apples, peeled, cored and sectioned, would sit alongside the kettle in a chipped blue enamel pan with the lid popping up and down as the steam built up pressure. This ejection of steam carried with it a promising aroma which had this young lad drooling all over his dominoes. The ceremony of unwrapping the muslin, then slicing into the boiled dough casing to let the steaming apples and juice come spewing out on to a thick white plate is still one of my dearest memories of Grandma's love.

Grandad had a Canadian organ jammed into the room. It had to be pumped up by means of two foot pedals which filled the bellows and slowly brought the instrument to life. There were a few organ stops to add volume and octaves etc. Nothing over-intricate but it certainly earned its keep. Weekends saw the family gathering at Grandma's. My mother was one of seven children, four of them boys, and my Dad was one of three, with a twin sister and an older sister. All but one of them was married and most of them had children. It was bedlam, but very happy bedlam. Each family member would bring their contribution to the feast. Pre-discussed, naturally, or we may have finished up with ten fruit cakes – and *nowt else*!

The organ took a real hammering on those days. Singsongs were a must. Uncle John played the organ alongside cousin Douglas. Uncle Alec played saxophone and violin, Uncles Harold and Reg played cornets. Mam, Aunties Annie and Marion sang (later with the Huddersfield Choral Society).

My Dad, although not really musical, sang as loud as any. What he lacked as a musician, Dad more than made up for as

an amateur mechanic. He mended watches and did his own
car repairs. We owned a Jowett, AKW 164, which was always
under repair. At one time I thought my Dad was a pair of legs
sticking out from under a car. It was forever in bits. Grandad
had a similar model and we went together for picnics or visits
to Sherwood Forest or Knaresborough – that is when both
cars were operational.

During the 1939–45 war, when a German bomber on his
way to annihilate Sheffield had been hit, he had to shed his
load and hightail it back to Hitler. The willy-nilly bombs hit
our beloved Pennines leaving a few harmless craters. Off we
all went to rubberneck and 'appen find some shrapnel. Primus
stoves were used to boil water for picnics but were many times
blown out on those windy hillsides, the same hillsides that
attracted us in late summer to pick bilberries for pies and
jams. They left your teeth purple but smiling.

We often watched the bombardment of Sheffield as it took a
pounding. The sickening rumbling as bombs exploded
relentlessly, lighting the distant night sky. We carried our gas
masks to school but, apart from the bombing, had no real
taste of war. Uncle Harold had served in the Royal Navy
during the 1914–18 war and had many big-brother tales to
tell. Uncle Alec served in the Army and Reg in the Navy
during the '39–45 war. Uncle John was not fit enough so
carried on with his plumbing and piano playing. He was a
great nature lover and spent many hours in a place called
Morton Wood. He told wonderful stories of the exciting
battles of survival in the animal kingdom. A freshwater
stream rippled and bubbled through the valley which was
thickly lined with many species of trees and shrubs. He
caught trout with his tickling fingers. On many occasions he
would point out a sighting – 'Did you see that?' I hadn't. It
took a trained eye to spot the lightning black shadow as it
darted from the safety of one big stone to another. For proof,
he would feel gently around the half-submerged stone as he

straddled the stream perched on two other boulders. 'Ah' meant he had found the two possible trout exits and deftly closed the gaps. As the fish moved around with the flow of the stream, he tickled its belly until it was suitably placed for his expert grip and out it came. More often than not, he would put it back unless he was actually shopping for tea. Occasionally he would build a bonfire and cook a trout for us. I didn't really enjoy eating the fish in those days, but the excitement of it all was an indelible experience. I learnt the art of the tickle eventually and thoroughly enjoyed the slippery challenge.

We were also quite 'genned up' on the wild birds in our district, and had collections of birds' eggs which we blew and set out in a presentation case. Once we were told the error of our ways, we waited for eggs to hatch and only collected the ones which had not fertilized. Our gang then became the local bird protection society. We took it very badly if we ever lost a nest to some of the mindless rogues in our patch.

Just down the road from our house was an orphanage named Lee Hall. All boys, and known to us as 't' Lee Hoylers'. They wore grey trousers, grey socks, grey shirts and grey V-necked pullovers, and always smelled of cod liver oil – grey cod liver oil. Most of them were OK with the exception of one or two rogues. They had to fight for survival and knew no other way to exist. Some of them were constantly in trouble and would no doubt have gone through the treadmill of approved school then graduated to prison. Many have made good, which has to be applauded unreservedly. Their orphanage was a small village of houses surrounded by a high wall which we had to pass on our way to the other wooded area. This was named Dobb Wood and had two trout lakes. All rather beautiful but not appreciated by us at the time. Just recently, the Morton Wood has been made into a sanctuary and beautifully preserved in its natural state.

Wonderful memories of damming the river to provide

wading pools. Ropes tied to outstretched oak boughs to simulate Tarzan's swing across the stream. Climbing the highest tree in order to qualify for the gang. Endless games of cowboys and Indians and commandos. Bonfires to roast potatoes which were always raw in the middle. Acres of bluebells in the spring. When I returned, everything seemed much smaller, as did the wall overlooking Grandad's minuscule garden. Although our patches were tiny, both households grew a few vegetables. Dig for Victory was the slogan of the day. One year Grandad was boasting about his peas emerging before ours, so taking up the challenge I scratched the top half-inch of soil away to expose our own crop. I was feeling quite proud of myself until Dad went mad, assuming a dog had done the damage. I proudly owned up and pointed out that we were now on a par with Grandad. That's the only time I remember my Dad really smacking me. Trousers down and big hand laid across pink bottom until it really hurt. I screamed as Mam was clucking 'That's enough, Dad' and 'After all, he told the truth'. I sobbed myself to sleep that night with Dad explaining the rights and wrongs of my amateur gardening. The peas survived and we ate them in August.

Scholes boasted a population of around one hundred people. Everyone's history was well known and one could be judged by one's ancestors! 'Don't trust him, his Grandfather was a wrong-'un!'

We had one Co-op store and whatever you spent there was totalled up just before Easter when they paid out the year's dividends. Enough to buy new clothes, which were often referred to as divi-suits or divi-dresses. The old clothes were cut into strips and threaded through hessian to make scatter rugs over our cold stone floors. The new suit was always hailed with a coin dutifully placed in the pocket from smiling Uncles and Aunties. Normally the first airing of new clothes was the Easter procession around the surrounding villages led by a brass band. Each hamlet would be treated to an Easter hymn as we all grouped around the band. Seasonal toys were small windmills on sticks which were motivated by waving them through the air. Some had whistles attached which added to the atmosphere if not the musical content. Our main Easter delight apart from the eggs was brandysnap. We also chewed on liquorice roots which were known as 'Spanish juice' for some reason or other.

After the Co-op, our village sported one pub named the Boot and Shoe, and two cobblers' shops attending to the many pairs of clogs worn for work. These workshops were great congregating areas for young lads watching the action and sometimes trying to help. Pulling off the old irons with claw hammers then handing them back to the professional for the new irons to be hammered in. These clogs lasted some people a lifetime. The uppers were dubbined and they were fastened by stripped leather laces. A shiny metal toecap completed the rather ugly but very functional footwear. I once started a poem about my childhood in Scholes which contained the lines:

Where dogs bark at night
And clogs walk to work before it's light

I must try and finish it sometime.

Scholes had the obligatory working-men's club. One snooker table; table tennis could be accommodated downstairs in an otherwise available function room, and a committee room which was always locked to us kids. We never did know what lay beyond that door but whenever the committee filed in or out they were always grim-faced. There was no liquor served there in my day. A later visit revealed how rapacious progress can be. Much noisier, smokier and boozier. There was a bar in our table tennis room. I didn't know anyone there and felt as if I was on foreign soil. I preferred to keep my childhood memories intact and left pretty quickly.

Our fish and chip shop was a lone-standing, stone-built establishment which backed on to a field. As far as I can remember, that field housed a single cow. The competition for food was a walk-over and being adjacent to a fish shop instead of a McDonald's accounted for the creature's smug expression. One single cow maybe, but it was still a great feat being able to cross that field blindfold without stepping in a cow pat. (Local term was a cow clap. Possibly alluding to the noise made as it plopped in the field.) The fish and chip shop itself was well known for miles around and queues outside were a common sight. Our notorious proprietress was named Sarah Anna and was a happy distortion of middle-age spread. Her ample bosom only escaped being immersed in the boiling fat by years of experience. Not being able to afford fish too regularly, my usual purchase was 'A penn'orth o' chips wi' bits on', the 'bits' being loose crumbs of batter which swam around the fish fryer gradually getting browner and browner. These bits sponged up lots of fat but, eaten with freshly cooked chips placed in greaseproof paper supported by newspaper, squirted with vinegar and 'peppered' with salt from a tankard-sized shaker, our penny was exceedingly well spent. The chips had to be eaten straight away whilst stepping out into the chill night air. At first, unbearably hot chips were held in the mouth whilst sucking in cooling air until a safe swallowing temperature was achieved. Fingers acted as amusement-arcade grabbing machines to transport the bits across the choppers and were then laboriously licked clean ready for the next helping. The screwed-up greasy papers made excellent firelighters next morning.

Across from 't' chip 'oyle' was a small grocer's shop; he was in direct opposition to the Co-op but he survived by adding a boiled sweet to our purchases free of charge. He was a small red-faced chap who was an enthusiastic member of the local amateur operatic society. He would often rehearse in his shop. I would like to meet him again today. His name was Fred Marsden. We lived about fifty yards down the road from his shop. My mother would often send me up to 'Fred's' for various groceries. One one occasion, I walked past our coal hole towards Fred's but sighted a big dog sitting outside the shop. I went back home and explained to Mam. 'Don't worry, dear, it'll be gone in a minute.' Next trip. Dog still there. 'Well, it'll be gone next time.' No, it wasn't. 'All right, I'll come with you.' As we approached Fred's, hand in hand, the 'dog' turned out to be a sack of potatoes. This was the first inkling she had of my short-sightedness. I was approaching seven years old and, having never seen any better, I assumed this to be the norm. I was amazed how clever the other kids were at school. Rattling off additions and subtractions from the blackboard. When I was asked, I just didn't know because I couldn't see. One teacher had a clock and asked us the time as she moved the hands around. I couldn't see the clock. Mum and Dad once took me to the cinema in Holmfirth. All I saw was swirling fog with voices. I wondered why on earth they paid for this!

I was seven when compulsory eye-testing at school came into being. When the optician discovered my short-sightedness, he hit every wall in disbelief. I was sent into Huddersfield for a further test. My glasses were ready shortly afterwards and a whole new world was presented to me. 'Hey! Look! A clock on that church spire. Hey! Look Mam! That bus tells you where it's going!' Mam smiled at my exciting discoveries. I quickly caught up at school and told the time as well as the rest of them.

This was about the time I was sent for tap-dancing lessons. I had often rattled away with my clogs on our stone floor for neighbours and relations. It must have been excruciating to everyone but Mam. Because of my thin legs, it was decided by the Monday washing union that tap-dancing lessons would 'thicken his legs up!'. My knees were the widest part of my legs, which needed elastic garters to support my woollen socks.

The tap lessons administered by the Nora Bray School in Huddersfield proved invaluable to me ... as a scrapper. Taunts from my schoolmates had me battling to save my sporting image and my specs were often bent and splintered in replying to jibes such as 'Haaa, are ya goin' for yer dancin' lesson? Ha-ha, do you 'ave to wear a ballet frock?' BANG-CRASH-WALLOP, leaving specs swinging from one ear. My glasses never actually sat comfortably on my face, they clung to it.

Having performed in local concerts at our Sunday school from the age of three, the tap-dancing added to my repertoire. I was now a song-and-dance man and was included in a Dutch number during one of the Nora Bray Dance School's exhibitions. My Mam made my costume out of silk. She made all my costumes during those early days. Having won a talent competition when she was very young and hearing the adjudicator say 'I wish she were mine, I'd make her into a star', she saw dreams for herself materializing through me. Being the fourth child of seven born into a poor family, she was whisked straight into the woollen mill when she left school at fourteen years old. There was no hope of her following a career in show business. Apart from Uncle Harold who wanted me to become a lightweight boxer, the rest of the family on Mam's side were keen for me to go for it.

When I was twelve, Mam spotted an advert in our local rag, the *Huddersfield Examiner*. 'Wanted. Young Talent.' She wrote in and an audition was arranged for me with a lady named Mildred Crossley who ran a dancing-school-cum-concert-party in a place called Elland. She was also the producer pianist. We travelled to Elland by bus from Scholes to Huddersfield, then by electric trolley. The journey took around one and a half hours. Plenty of time to keep running over the words of the two audition songs. The Dutch number was an automatic inclusion, no problems there. The other song was very topical at the time, 'Johnny Zero'. A story of a boy who was a dunce at school and got Zero marks. He then grew up, became a fighter pilot and shot down Japanese planes – Zeros. 'Johnny's got a Zero, Johnny is a hero', etc, etc.

We arrived in Elland and, after asking directions, found Langdale House and knocked delicately on the door. Mildred Crossley opened up, introduced herself and ushered us into her front room. A tap mat was rolled out by the piano and someone was getting changed ready to leave. We had brought the home-made costume and I got dressed behind a curtain. I performed both numbers whilst Mildred Crossley played my music and snatched glimpses. We were not left in any doubt as to the outcome. She accepted me there and then and promised to be in touch regarding her show.

Youth on Parade consisted of young girl dancers, a couple of comics in their early twenties, a boy soprano, an accordionist and a magician. The line-up changed as people left for colleges or jobs and that was the reason for the advert for new talent. I joined as their only boy tapper and was moulded into the show, which played in church halls, YMCAs, old folks' homes, clubs and schools. I worked in production numbers, comedy sketches and fitted in Johnny Zero as a solo. The Dutch number was made into a duet with Jean Midgeley, a young girl who was a contortionist. We also did a cockney duet together. A revue artist yet! I became rather sweet on this young lass, but she was unimpressed.

In the summer holidays, a pleasure park called Sunny Vale, near Brighouse, booked our show for daily performances in an open-air theatre. Early and late afternoons were show times and during our breaks we could take advantage of the boating lakes, helter-skelter, roller rink and maze. It was considered a plum engagement. If wet, there was an indoor equivalent. Of course there were drawbacks. Entry to the wooden forms was free and people could come and go as they pleased. Groups would often watch the show until it was time for their scheduled tea. Our boy soprano was halfway through 'Oh for the wings of a dove' ('Hear My Prayer') when the canteen lady appeared at the back of a full house and shouted 'Meltham Baptists! Your tea's ready.' The entire audience scuttled off and left our soprano singing to wood. 'She might have waited till I'd finished,' he sobbed.

I too suffered embarrassment in Sunny Vale. Whilst performing a military song and dance number, 'When the Sergeant-Major's on Parade', a wire-haired terrier ran on stage, snapped at my black silk trousers, tearing a great lump out, and ran off to a nearby tree where it worried the piece of silk. The audience watched the dog.

We were paid in Marmite sandwiches plus the redoubtable honour of playing in such a career-establishing arena. We performed in many venues, including a high-security underground munitions factory beneath Yeadon Aerodrome near Leeds. We all had to be signed in, frisked and ushered through unmarked doors along a labyrinth of corridors until we reached a huge dining hall seating hundreds of munition workers. It was their lunch break and we were their light entertainment.

The first full week's booking was at Bradford Mechanics Hall, a circular venue that could have housed a bullfight. Whereas most shows were in the evening, this time I had one problem – a Wednesday matinee. It would be necessary to get permission to miss school. It was refused. Our headmaster, Mr Brain, was concerned that this frivolous sideline was not doing my schooling any good and promptly had a medical inspection arranged. I was judged to be anaemic and banned from any outside activities whilst attending Honley Grammar! I won the 3½-mile cross-country run four years in succession, but wasn't allowed to tap dance because of being anaemic.

I can't say I was an enthusiastic scholar, I dreamed my way

through most of the lessons and couldn't for the life of me understand why history was important. I do now, but not then. I once got three per cent for my history exam. The only date I knew was the date of the test. One question was 'What was the occupation of the Stone Age man?' Answer: 'Long beards and frightening faces.'

Nil point.

I was quite good at maths, coming in the top three regularly. English was fair when a bout of enthusiasm hit. PT was a favourite as it didn't tax the brain too much. Playground football and cricket were a must, both played with the same bald tennis ball.

My best friend was a lad named Keith Jowsey. A well-proportioned red-faced lad with a broken front tooth. He was fearsome and became my bodyguard. The only time he left my side was during the cross-country run. However, he waited for me at the finish, having taken the short cut and been disqualified.

I suppose my school days could be classed as average and my hopes for good results when taking my School Certificate were rather long odds. However, the confrontation was not to be. When I reached fourteen, possible school-leaving age, Mildred Crossley was back in touch regarding a two-week booking at the Queen's Theatre, Cleveleys, near Blackpool. The regular summer show finished at the end of August and the theatre owner offered her the first two weeks in September as a type of audition for the following full summer season. A tough decision! I considered it for all of three seconds and accepted. Mam obviously was thrilled. Dad was less enthusiastic. 'Don't you think he should finish his schoolin'? Get some qualifications to fall back on?' Mam and I both knew the 'qualifications' would not be forthcoming and eventually talked him round. One of his well-remembered phrases was 'If you're 'appy, I'm 'appy', but there were undertones of 'Don't blame me if it comes to nowt!'

The two weeks' trial in 1946 were successful enough for the theatre owner, Fred Thompson, to take a chance on us for the following summer season. I left school and instantly became an out-of-work professional entertainer.

My Uncle Alec was now a travelling grocer, successful enough to have exchanged his horse and cart for an open-sided wagon. He would drive to the fruit and veg market in Huddersfield about 5 a.m., buy in, then drive the seven miles back to Scholes before starting his round. The hilly district had been quite demanding on his horse, but now the wagon helped him cover more ground.

He graciously offered me a job as helper when I was 'resting'. I would run in to the house-bound folks' homes, take their orders, then race back with their groceries. I was given my script. 'Groceries, Groceries. What would you like today?'

'What are your potatoes like?'

'Big as your fist and twice as tender.'

''Ave you any King Edwards?'

'No, he wanted 'em 'imself today! You can 'ave some Uncle Alec's!' Show business on wheels.

He also sold fresh fish. Those Pennines in winter were akin to Siberia. You had to be very careful cutting the cold fish in such icy temperatures or we could have had fish fingers before Captain Birdseye was a cabin boy.

Odd shows here and there began to dribble in, sometimes a week in one of the smaller provincial theatres. Our very first week was at the Grand Theatre, Byker, in Newcastle-on-Tyne. Our 'digs' were fair but our landlord not only had a thick Geordie accent, he stammered too. I never understood a word he said all week, but grinned obligingly whenever he spoke to me. The show was accepted quite well during our twice-nightly initiation and Saturday was quite a boost, so we left feeling our future was launched.

'Green groceries! Owt you want today, luv?' Another stint

with Uncle Alec, then Theatre Royal, Bilston in Staffs. Totally different local accent, equally difficult to understand. I often wondered what would happen if Bilston and Byker ever met. Our Bilston landlady's husband was a long-distance lorry driver and not often home, so our older lads were given noticeably bigger portions than ours. Served with a lingering, knowing look.

Our summer season at Cleveley's in 1947 was a big success. We changed our entire programme and costumes to accommodate three different shows in the week. This was a reasonable ploy to attract the same audience back and back during their week's holiday. It worked very well and our confidence grew. One of my big items was a sketch with our comedian, Tony Lester, as a dame. I was the son coming home from school. The routine consisted of jokes about homework, school, Father and, finally, food – which upset my 'mother' and reduced her to tears. The pathos ending had the audience blurbing and applauding at the same time. I sang 'This is my mother's day' with my metallic tenor voice. Game set and match. Today the audience would probably throw up, but these were naive days and very enjoyable.

In order to strengthen our show, Fred Thompson, the theatre owner, insisted we add a big name to our ranks. A black song-and-dance man named Fred Brand. He was billed as 'The Chocolate Drop from Dixie'. He actually hailed from Nottingham and was a brilliant artist. He sang songs such as 'There's a Blue Ring Round my Heart, Virginia', 'Mammy', 'Red Roses for a Blue Lady', 'When that Midnight Choo-Choo Leaves for Alabam', and plenty more. He dressed immaculately in tails and top hat. I found out later he made his own clothes. He once took an old tail suit to pieces and copied it. He showed me how to fix taps on to my dancing shoes by putting wet salt in with the screws. The salt then corroded the screws and kept them firmly established. Araldite was still a gleam in its inventor's eye. My tap dancing improved tremendously under his guidance. He really was a genuine star and influenced my work considerably. We kept in touch over the years. He lived to be 94.

After that first summer season *Happiness Ahead* (successor to *Youth on Parade*) toured the provincial theatres through the autumn and spring, broken only by pantomime over the Christmas period. My first panto role was Baby Bear in *Goldilocks* and the 'other two', and I got my first experience of the orange juice and nappy smell permeating from the audience. We performed a musical act as the bears, although trumpet playing had not entered my life at this stage. Just as well – those wirenetting, glue and imitation fur heads were impenetrable. A piece of gauze in the throat was all we had to see through and anyone to either side of us needed to know of our limited vision or the subsequent collision was to our advantage as we were the ones wearing the crash helmets. Footlights were a great help in finding our whereabouts. For the finale walk-down we always doffed our heads and held them underarm as we beamed at the audience as if to say 'It was *me* all the time'. What young children must have thought didn't really occur to us in our moment of glory. Next week at the Zoo they were entitled to think they could pull the bear's head off and discover who it really was!

Playing panto in Stockton-on-Tees gave us one of our biggest laughs. A little crude but absolutely true. The local dancing school always provided the 'babes' (child dancers to appear in crowd scenes and perform a little routine). The three-year-old who went wrong always stole the show. This Christmas, they opened the second half with a dance routine dressed as flowers. The stage manager was about to set the whole thing in motion when the dance teacher ran across to him in apparent alarm shouting in broad Geordie 'Mista Styage Manager – Mista Styage Manager – the curtain canna gan up!'

'Why not?'

'Little Hyacinth's just shit hersel'.'

The curtain eventually went up without Hyacinth who was heard only from the second floor, obviously in some distress.

Goldilocks ran for six weeks on tour then *Happiness Ahead* was reunited as the bears' heads were returned to the tea chests until next December.

While we played at the Victoria Theatre in Burnley, there was an added attraction in the form of a contortionist who performed with a boa constrictor. This was a snake and a half and although harmless, nobody tried to be extra friendly. Certainly the contortionist's dressing room was never broken into – by no human being, at least! Chubb Alarms take note.

Arriving at the 'Vic' one morning in search of mail, our contortionist (I think Karina was her name) was ranting and raving. 'WHO'S FED MY SNAKE!!!' The boa constrictor was curled up in the corner of the dressing room with a large swelling in the middle of its torso and a distinct smile on its contented face.

'Somebody has fed my snake and it won't work for a week now!' She was bursting with rage. It was hardly audible but the stage doorman's voice was heard, asking someone backstage, 'You haven't seen my cat, have you?'

For one week only, *Happiness Ahead* hit Darlington. The Hippodrome was pretty much the same as most of the 'number two' theatres. The digs were adequate and the local shops accepted our travellers' ration cards. Each item was listed on a specially printed piece of grey paper. As we bought soap, out came the scissors, snip, snip and the card lost a tooth. Ration swapping was rife as meat was exchanged for fish or butter. Vegetarians always had plenty of soap.

I was assistant stage manager in conjunction with my song, dance and sketch input. We had been down to the station earlier on this particular Monday morning and collected our scenery and costumes, loaded them into a truck and brought them to the theatre. We then carried the lot into the stage area via the dock doors.

Curtains and background cloths were then hung as ground. rows and flats were stacked.

Our stage manager was also our principal comedian, 'Sonny Roy, The Funny Boy'. Lighting plots were discussed as our travelling musical director attended to the band call. Afternoons were spent checking, mending any damage and preparing for the first house.

The show opened with a concerted item incorporating most of the cast, then our stage-manager-cum-comic made his entrance and trotted out a few warm-up gags whilst the scene was set behind the front runners. He then led into the first sketch in which he was the husband leaving for work. Exit husband, enter lover.

'Whose eyes are those?'

Wife: 'They're yours, darling.'

'Whose arms are those?'

'They're yours, darling.'

'Whose lips are those?'

'They're yours, darling.'

Re-enter the comic. 'When you get to the umbrella, it's mine!'

DBO.

DBO means Dead Black Out and leaves the audience in no doubt that this is the end of the sketch. I was in charge of giving the electrician his cue to throw the switches. He was a short, thin-set individual with steel-rimmed goldfish-bowl glasses and in need of a shave. He was wearing thick rubber gloves as he prepared to throw two ancient mains levers. He took great pains to clear the way behind him which had me quite bewildered. We reached the end of the sketch and I gave him the cue. He threw the switches and there was an almighty flash. As my eyes gradually returned to their normal duty, I saw no sign of our electrician. A groan from the back wall attracted my attention and there he was in a creepled hump.

He picked himself up; staggered back to his switchboard and flashed the switches back on. He was not thrown quite so far this time. I couldn't believe it, my chin was on the floor. 'Phew that was close. It really threw you back that time.'

He replied with a thick Geordie accent. 'Why man, it *always* does that!'

There were three more DBOs in the first half – and no safety net!

The Attercliffe Palace was situated on the outskirts of Sheffield. A small theatre, I believe it has since given way to a supermarket – doing much better business.

Sonny Roy and I had collected the scenery and costumes from the station and we were hanging the backcloths and curtains. Sonny was having a fag as he worked alongside the resident stage manager and a couple of stage hands.

Suddenly, a diminutive chap wearing a collarless shirt, belt and braces holding up khaki corduroy trousers which stopped a few inches short of his greying plimsolls, sidled up to Sonny and said, ''Scuse me, pal, would you mind puttin' that fag out?'

Sonny just looked at him.

He repeated his request with a little more attack. 'Put that fag out, pal, no smokin' on stage!'

Sonny gave him a stare which told him to go away in the worst possible terms. They glowered at each other for a few seconds then the little chap's chin slid forward like a drawer opening automatically as he growled, 'Right, mate,' turned on his heels and strode off.

Sonny carried on with his setting up. It couldn't have been more than three minutes before the little chap returned in full fireman's uniform, apart from the greying plimsolls. It was immediately obvious that it was not his own outfit. The real fireman must have been a much bigger chap. The concertinaed trousers draped over his plimsolls and the jacket sleeves swung well below his hands as the axe dangled around his ankles. His helmet rested on his nose as he shuffled up to Sonny (who had by now finished his fag) and asserted himself.

'Right, pal.'

He lifted up the front of his helmet.

'Put that ...'

He searched for the offending item and saw that it was no longer there. His authoritative attitude was slightly punctured as he turned and shambled off muttering, 'I'd have 'ad you there mate. Just WATCH IT.'

He returned to his changing room as we collapsed with laughter. Had I known then what I know now, I would have shaken his hand. If I could have found it.

All our scenery had to be fireproofed, by law, for obvious reasons. This was another Monday morning ritual as the local fire inspector performed the examination.

We had experienced no problems with our tour ... until we arrived in Lowestoft. It must have been the fireman's first time: 'Nip down the theatre and test the scenery for fireproofing.'

'Right, boss – what do I do?'

'Just see if it burns, if it does, don't pass it. Simple as that.'

'Right, guv.'

Normally, the fire inspector would hold a lighted match to a remote corner of each item considered inflammable. After a few seconds, if the material only smouldered, it was passed as safe. Should it catch light and burn, it was not accepted until it had been re-proofed, a messy and fairly expensive business.

The Lowestoft fireman arrived at the theatre, introduced himself and explained his duty.

'Go ahead,' was Sonny's confident invitation as he carried on with the set-up. Norman Teal was company manager in those early days and couldn't believe what he saw. This young fireman had brought a BLOWLAMP. It was already roaring away as he marched up to our most luxurious crushed-velvet curtains and stuck the blowlamp right in the middle of one of them. The pale blue flame went straight through, leaving a smouldering hole. Norman went bananas as he rushed over to the arsonist and, for a moment, I thought he was going to turn the blowlamp on the fireman. Our best curtains ruined.

'Do you know how much they cost?' is loosely what Norman implied.

The embarrassed curtain wrecker was given a comprehensive lesson on fireproof testing and left with his blowlamp in his ear.

As there were no Yellow Pages in those days an invisible mender was difficult to find so an 'iron on' patch was tried. It fell off in the middle of the umbrella sketch.

When working the Theatre Royal, Ashton-under-Lyne, I bought a new double-breasted brown suit and left it in my lock-up dressing room for the week. I had worn it a couple of times and left some chocolate in the jacket pocket. It seemed impossible, as the suit must have been three feet off the ground with nothing in between apart from a glossy painted wall, but a cunning little mouse somehow managed to get to my jacket, *and* to the chocolate by eating through the outside of the pocket.

Whether it formed a pyramid with its pals or had a mouse cannon or catapult I have no idea. A spider-mouse would have been fine on the gloss paint but once on the jacket the suckers would be useless. I've never left chocolate in a suit since.

Digs were an endless source of funny and horrific stories. In Mansfield, I could only get a last-minute single after the show. I was given supper of sorts and fussed by a Pekingese sniffler which had custard spilled all over it. I was in danger of contracting a ptomaine stroke. Managing to avoid custard contact, I was shown my room, a single bed in a corner. My landlady asked if I could manage without the light and left my door ajar. The custard Peke began nosing into the room so I had to close the door. I just *had* to. Now, I could see nothing. Nowhere to hang my clothes or even a chair to leave them on. Why couldn't I turn the light on? Surely it could do no harm. I fumbled on the wall by the door for the switch and eventually located it. As I turned on the light to find my whereabouts, I noticed a double bed to my immediate left. Peeping over the sheets were five little faces, wide-eyed with fear. I tried to look friendly and switched off the light again. As quietly as possible, I undressed and got into a cold, damp bed and kept the sheets over my head until the bedroom had cleared the following morning. As I carefully looked over my bedclothes, I was greeted by the Peke. The custard was now dry and hard. I didn't enjoy my breakfast and found alternative accommodation by noon that day.

While appearing as Baby Bear at the Regent Theatre, Rotherham, I managed to 'dig in' locally, saving on bus fares and shoe leather. Our 'Robin Hood' for that particular season was Rita Hunter, a beautifully shaped thigh-slapping principal boy who was later to make it big in the operatic world. Her opening line was 'Good morning everyone, I am Robin Hood and these are my three bears, Fuzzy, Muzzy and Wuzzy'. After a 'confidential' word from Norman Teal (Father Bear), she strode on stage and announced herself as Robin. '... and these are my three bears, Freeman, Hardy and Willis.' I was known as little Willis to the end of the run.

The digs were adequate, my bedsit was on the ground floor and I was paying for bed, breakfast and evening meal. The house also accommodated other people from various pantos and clubs around the Sheffield area.

During the week I became more and more curious about a series of thuds upstairs. Anything from four to seven bumps, then silence for half an hour or so. The first time it coincided with the presence of my landlady was about Thursday. I asked her about the mysterious thuds. She thought a while, then said, 'Oh, that'll be Burton Lester's Midgets – when they go to the lavatory they can't reach the chain and have to jump for it!'

The mind then wondered what happened when they did actually grab the chain and hung on. When to let go would be a major decision! *That's* why they always wore their wellies!

Some digs still had gas lighting which was pretty spooky for a young lad. Hot water was left outside the room when there was no wash basin. A three-pint jug and washing bowl, usually painted with pink roses and badly chipped. It's quite an art keeping clean water back for rinsing. A face cloth was essential on these occasions and washing hair verged on the impossible. How on earth the girls managed I have no idea.

Queues for bathrooms were a constant hazard and baths were charged for. Some of those gas geysers ran so slow, by the time you had enough water to bath in it was lukewarm at best.

Outside lavs were not uncommon, with notices by the chain pull: 'Pull twice – then surprise it!' One had 'No Solids'. Middle-of-the-night visits were to be avoided at *all costs*.

Latchkeys were distributed to anyone wishing to stay out late, if you were lucky. Some digs had the rule 'If you're not in by half eleven, t' bolt goes on!' Or 'Midnight – all t' lights go out!'

Gas meters, electricity meters, pay phones, buy your own coal … memories to cherish but hopefully never to return.

Most landladies liked to boast a ghost. Supper after the show then almost believable stories of manifestations of people murdered in your bedroom, or burned by fire, were hardly the recipe for a cosy night's sleep. After a particularly chilling discussion where no one dared go to bed, the awesome hour arrived and we all went wide-eyed to our rooms. I left my light on for a while then thought myself stupid for believing such pathetic nonsense. I got up and turned out my bare lightbulb and slid back into bed.

After a few seconds I heard a knocking around my wooden bedhead. It was regular tap of about two per second. It didn't stop. I lay there, petrified. I wasn't keen to open my eyes but finally had to. There was nothing there as I lay very still. The tapping continued. I jumped out of bed and put the light on. The tapping had stopped, and I looked outside my room in case it was a practical joker trying to faze me. Nothing out there, or under the bed. I tried to think what it could possibly be ... not a clue.

I got back into bed leaving the light on and lay still. The tapping started again. I sat up and it stopped. I lay down and it started again. I eventually discovered the wooden bedhead was a millimetre away from the wall and as I lay still, my heartbeat moved the bed that tiny distance and caused the knocking. *Phew*! Had I not discovered the reason, my story next morning would have added to the gruesome encounters with the supernatural. I pulled the bed away from the wall a touch and slept soundly – with the light on!

2

Training, Trimming
and Trumpets

Whilst playing the Theatre Royal, Castleford in 1950, I was
summoned to go for a medical with regard to National
Service. I had to go to Leeds. Norman Teal (company
manager and xylophonist supreme) went with me, hoping I
would fail!

We arrived at the medical centre with all the other
prospective mercenaries, most of whom were much taller than
me. I got the odd sneer which said 'I hope we don't have to
depend on thee, lad!' Forms had to be filled in. I already had a
healthy hatred of this pursuit which has developed into a
full-blown paranoia over the years. We were passed from one
dead-eyed person to another. The only glimmer of life came to
those curtained orbs when it was cup-of-tea time and five
o'clock. I suppose the existence was rather routine.

It seems we had all heard of the wheezes one could get up to
in order to fail the medical. Eating soap apparently made the
heart beat abnormally fast. From the look of some of them the
very *sight* of soap would have had the same effect.

I was finally consigned to my personal physician. I guessed
him to be in his late fifties, thinning hair and thickening waist.
Sallow complexion, jowly with wobbly, off-white cheeks and
a neck like a pelican that had caught no fish. He peered at me
over half-glasses or ADHs as we lovingly called them, after
Alec Douglas-Home. They were also known as peerovers,
half-moons and reading crutches. Stethoscope around his
neck and boiled-white-coated, he jerked his head telling me to
come in. The bottle was handed to me with 'You know what
to do with *that*' gesture. Although I was on my own and there
was no reason to be embarrassed, the mere fact that he was
waiting for some action jammed the tubes. I tried to think of
running water, trickling streams, Niagara! Just a dribble,
pleeeeese! There was more moisture on my forehead than in
the bottle. 'Get a drink if you're having trouble' came from
the other side of the screen. 'Ah – he's used to this
happening,' I relaxed a little. The emergence of the first
lonely drop evoked rejoicing of a very special kind.
Eventually, the bottle was about full and I was still in full
flow. Now I needed a tourniquet.

More embarrassment was to follow. After the knee hammer
proved satisfactory (I had a terrible urge to kick up the *other*
knee but thought better of it), it was time to 'cough'. This I
did whilst he held on to my most delicate items of
reproduction. 'Could we try that again' ... 'Again' ...
'Hmmm' ... 'Just once more'. 'Just wait there a minute.' He
left me to ponder reasons for his concern. On his return, he
had enlisted the services of a 'Second Opinion'. The coughing
routine was given another airing and a muttered discussion
followed between the two doctors, just out of earshot.

'Have you ever had any trouble down there?' asked Second
Opinion.

'No,' I replied with the slightest hint of a yodel.

'Sure?'

'Yes.'

Another huddled muttering, followed by shrugging of shoulders and a quick glance at the clock. I was ushered to the next cubicle clutching my report.

The upshot of this whole escapade was my being passed fit, Grade 1!

The concern of the 'cough' doctors turned out to be a double hernia which was operated on during my two years' service. Considering that my eyesight was hopeless into the bargain, my classification of Grade 1 unnerved me about anyone being south of Grade 2. Add to this the fact that the war was over and this little Yorkshireman can be excused for thinking he was leaving his beloved show behind for another farce with a guaranteed two-year run, all found and seven shillings per week to spend. Things were not to change so much after all!

On 29 November 1950 I made my way to Padgate to be kitted out.

Blue-grey, heavy material fashioned into a working outfit (bomber jacket and trousers with braces), a dress outfit (half-length coat with brass buttons!), the first sign of the *bull* everyone warned me about. The second, more ominous, sign was a pair of heavy black boots with a pimply surface. The lumps on the toe ends were going to take up quite a sizeable amount of my next two years. Red-hot pokers to burn the surface smooth, then the actual spit and polish whilst building up a fierce hatred of corporals, sergeants, officers and all forms of seemingly unnecessary discipline. Creases in trousers were effected by carefully laying them in position under the sheet, and pressing them whilst sleeping. If you could also work up a head of steam, all the better. A rough night resulted in corrugated trousers and three days' 'jankers' after the morning inspection.

During the kitting-out farce, all forms of complaints were met with stock answers.

'These boots are a bit big.' – 'You'll grow!'

'These boots are a bit tight.' – 'They'll sober up by tomorrow.'

'Shouldn't I have three shirts?' – 'How many you got?' – 'Two.' – 'Let 'em sleep together!'

All these retorts made without any form of eye contact or sympathy. 'Roll 'em in, kit 'em out, roll 'em out! Is it five o'clock yet?'

I thought that being in show business and being used to living away from home comforts would have toughened me up and fortified me with a resistance to being homesick but that first night, as I tried to sleep on my prickly horsehair mattress, I had a big lump in my throat that would have filled my kitbag. I heard plenty sobbing around me. These were the men chosen to defend our country. I think the biggest shock was the total lack of love. From 'Roy', I was suddenly 'Castle. No. 2498944'.

Next day, we were told where our six weeks' training would be. The 'in' name was square bashing! Self-explanatory but all light-hearted anticipation was quickly dispelled. I was to be shepherded to Wilmslow just outside Manchester. Wilmslow has never appeared in a holiday brochure and I was about to find out why. Rows of huts, each accommodating 22 recruits, around a parade ground the size of a football pitch. There was, of course, a cookhouse which was loosely connected with food as we knew it. All the jokes about bromide in the tea had probably been handed down through two world wars, together with some of the menus. You *had* to be hungry ... by Christmas time – we were! Up at 5.30, jostling for a washbasin in order to get a near-cold-water scrape over the chin. Shave just wasn't the correct word – there is something quite nice and satisfying about a shave with hot water and thick lather. This experience was one step away from plucking out the hairs one by one. The styptic pencil was an essential part of the shaving kit; little squares of newspaper were not easily come by. In any case, our drill instructors would much rather see blood than newspaper, seeing as none of them could read! Out on parade in the snow at 6 a.m., mug and irons (knife, fork and spoon) in left hand. March down to cookhouse. 'Halt! Di-i-i-i-issmiss!!' Shamble in to discover the culinary surprises. Kippers and prunes often on the same plate. Porridge that was either runny and lumpy or more resistant than anything Michelin produced. However, when hungry enough it was cordon bleu. Once armed with the two platefuls and a mug of retarding liquid, one had to walk the plank of the queue in order to find a seat. The next hand-me-down joke was everyone in the queue sticking their fingers in your tea. 'Is it hot? – Oh yes, it's hot!' Don't grumble! You've just done it to the others. This attitude repeated itself at lunch and dinner. So did the menu. This time the porridge passed as gravy, the kippers were thrust into sausage skins and the prunes rolled into bullet proof pastry to impersonate a fruit pudding. The custard was more like failed sago. The hot chocolate in the evening was mahogany sawdust. All of this was scoffed with gusto, once fond memories of home cooking had dimmed.

Blankets and sheets had to be folded up and arranged in a design resembling a TV set. Most of them with a bad reception, some with no aerial at all. Anything below standard was knocked about by our DI (Drill Instructor) corporal. Some even thrown out of the window into the snow!

Each billet had two stoves for heating purposes. Sticks were chopped up with penknives to get these potential smoke machines started. Coke was added at the discretion of the 'committee'. Damp coke takes a long time to actually burn. In some cases, six weeks. Halfway through the training course, one of our chimneys became blocked and consequently filled the billet with thick smoke, thereby threatening all brass attachments, clean clothes and, worse still, our corporal's room. Invention led us to tie our firewood sticks together, fix a piece of torn-off blanket on the end of this makeshift flue brush and clear the soot from our 'chimney'. The stovepipe was removed and yours truly was chosen to be chimney sweep.

At this point I must explain that whenever our corporal (or any other rank above ours) came into the billet, the first recruit to spot him had to shout 'NCO!' (non-commissioned officer) at the top of his voice. Upon hearing this, all recruits in situ had to spring to quivering attention and freeze.

I had just got our flue brush well into our chimney when in walks our corporal. 'NCO!' – Attention on the spot, directly under the chimney. He twigged what was happening immediately and paraded up and down waffling on about a lot of unnecessary guff while my flue brush was very slowly answering the call of gravity. Inch by inch it dropped ... until, finally, with our NCO watching from a safe distance, the contraption fell free of the chimney and I was covered in soot – still at rigid attention. After it settled, the NCO came over to me and stared directly into my face and bellowed 'Well – don't just stand there – sing "MAMMY"!' Our stove burned brightly that night but the drain in the shower was blocked.

Naturally we were unable to answer back or even make suggestions to our NCOs which resulted in the desired attitude for wartime: Do it! Don't ask why! Some of our NCOs took unfair advantage of their position. One being our very own. I found out later that he had conned a few of my mates. He called them into his room separately over the six weeks. Asked them did they think a man could stand on a glass of water at one side of a billiards table, jump over the table and land on another glass of water on the other side without spilling a drop?

The gullibles naturally said 'No chance'. Then they were asked if they would like to 'go in' with the corporal and gamble a few quid on this certainty. Once the bet was on, our NCO would get a piece of paper, signed and witnessed by another officer, saying the feat had been accomplished. I need say no more. As the corporals' mess was out of bounds to recruits, the signed note verifying the successful feat was produced with the open-palmed shrug of the shoulders. He took quite a few oncers from the lads in our billet. I'm glad I wasn't faced with the proposal. I would have *had* to have gone along or I would have been delegated as chimney sweep again!

At the end of our square bash, we were told where our next destination would be. I had not volunteered for overseas posting as I had secret hopes of being able to get away to do some shows once I got to know the ropes. As my name was called, I answered 'Sir 944!'

'Dyce.'

Dyce didn't mean a lot to me, a geographical turnip. I later found out it was an airport just outside Aberdeen. Not *quite* an overseas posting. Certainly a foreign language. Even to a Scot the Aberdonian accent is difficult. Granite City, here I come.

From Blackpool, the train journey was, at best, seven hours with the full walk along Princes Street in Edinburgh as I changed stations. Full kit draped about me, I swung to and fro in my scratchy trousers and unforgiving boots. Casting glances at Edinburgh Castle like a swimmer catching breath whilst doing the crawl. Princes Street seemed fifty miles long.

Thankfully, an RAF bus was at the station in Aberdeen and took me to what was to be my main home for the next two years. My billet was 25/7, known as twenty-five seven. It housed 22 Air Force men of various qualifications. I was to be a Storeman (Non Tech). Obviously requiring little or no expertise. My main duties were packing up all kinds of equipment, from huge crates containing engines to a couple of screws in an envelope, addressing them and setting them up to be collected. Then all the paperwork had to be done such as Internal Issue Vouchers (673), External Issue Vouchers (674), Internal Demand and Issue Vouchers, and for the first time in my life the most important part of the day was tea break at five o'clock! EEEK! I had become one!

Luckily, sport was a great diversion and I was in the soccer team, cricket team, table tennis team, badminton team, cross-country team and any other team going. There was not even a suggestion of show business on the camp so that part of me died.

I did, however, learn the basics of trumpet playing in my spare time. My Uncle Harold, the cornet player, decided it would be a bit daft to waste two years doing 'nowt but polishin' an' marchin' ', so he sorted out a cheap trumpet for me. It cost £10 but the valves worked and he got a tune out of it. Together with the Arbans cornet tutor book and a few tips on embouchure, he wished me luck with it.

Although my early attempts to get something sensible out of the instrument were excruciating to all the billets around, not many chaps complained for one simple reason. There was no barber on the camp and it became quite a costly exercise when the return fare to Aberdeen was added to the cost of a haircut. In those days it was two shillings and sixpence for the fare and a shilling for the haircut. Having watched my Grandad cut hair for many years plus picking up a few tips from my mother, I was well qualified to do a decent job. My charge of one shilling was most acceptable. Hence the lack of complaint about my trumpet practice. Grumble and you get a fancy haircut – or none at all.

One chap forced me to cut his hair as he was going out to a dance. I willingly obliged but left a crude word in longer hair across the back of his head. He couldn't understand why people kept slipping round behind him and giggling. Next morning he woke me and asked *nicely* if I would remove it ... before the parade and inspection? He even threw in that he thought my trumpet playing was improving.

My best pal during my stay at Dyce was a Geordie called Joe Fishburn. He was about 5-foot-8 and 12 stones, with a thick accent. As a soccer back, he could kick the ball the length of the field. He was a leg-break bowler and a

tremendous hitter of the ball. And he was highly rated in
Northumberland as a table tennis player, and very competent
with the badminton racket. We got along well together. We
worked in the same stores and filled in the same ledgers and
watched the same clock. He taught me most of the techniques
of table tennis. I would serve, he would flash an unbelievable
backhand flick followed by 'It's behind you, Roy!' We
practised a lot as the TT room was not as popular as the local
dance hall. A two-hour work-out, then egg and double chips
in the NAAFI, and the nights went by easily. We had a team
in the Aberdeenshire League and one of my proudest
write-ups was one in the local paper saying 'Castle still proves
to be the match winner for RAF Dyce'. Joe taught me the
backhand and forehand defence, the forehand attack and then
he was posted, so my backhand attack is still in need of
attention.

Our equipment section was headed by Flying Officer
Wilson who was also the proud owner of a St Bernard dog
named, for want of a little more thought, 'Bruno'. Our job
occasionally was to give this mountain of hair and saliva a
shampoo. It was like a car wash turned inside out. When
Bruno shook himself it rained in Inverness.

He was also allowed in the NAAFI and would sit at tables
staring diners eye to droopy eye with strings of saliva swinging
from his sagging jowls. A cross between threatening and
pleading, one felt either terrorized or sympathetically inclined
to give him a morsel. A morsel being half your dinner. As he
wandered from table to table, twenty-six half-dinners just
about sated him. I once watched a less than scrupulous diner
toss a piece of swiss roll to Bruno who watched it drop, sniffed
it, then ate it. The next piece got the same treatment. Next
was gobbled up without checking and from here on he felt
confident enough to try and catch the tasty morsel in mid-air.
Once he was catching the offerings with expertise, the cruel
diner threw a lighted cigarette end. Have you ever seen a fully

grown St Bernard with all four feet off the ground above your head? The NAAFI cleared quicker than a scramble at Biggin Hill in 1943.

Although most of my two years doing National Service seemed a waste of time, there were lots of laughs to compensate. We had a lad called Ken Smith who hailed from Blackburn, and discipline was a foreign word to him. He wasn't a hooligan, just unaware of rank or duty. He wandered into the pilots of 612 Squadron (out of bounds to the rank and file) and asked if someone would take him up for a spin. After many spells of jankers, he was given up as a bad job and awarded a post on the telephone exchange. His night duty absolved him of station routine orders and he was normally asleep during the day. On odd occasions he would wander into the countryside where he had a favourite fresh water stream. He would sit and contemplate – we shall never know what. He discovered trout in the seemingly well-stocked reach. He told us of the fish he had caught by hand and brought them back for the cookhouse to prepare. Of course nobody believed him. Determined to prove his story, he went down to his stream, caught a trout and raced back to the camp with the fish thrashing about in his dripping hand. He got it back to the billet, still very much alive, ran the cold tap in one of the basins in our 'ablutions'. Of course, not being subject to station routine orders, he was completely oblivious to the fact that this was a station inspection day. The rest of us had polished up the billet, including the ablutions. Our beds and blankets were made up with extra special attention and well blanco'd webbing laid out in accordance with the RAF blueprint, together with all brasses and boots in immaculate condition. We all stood to attention by our beds and awaited the arrival of our Commanding Officer. A big man with an ample, red face and a fearsome stare. Obviously his nerves of steel would see him supremely confident in any crisis. He was followed by the station Warrant Officer, known as the SWO.

The CO picked at bits and pieces of kit as he wandered along the rows of laboriously laid out trappings. Airmen standing to attention, the only movement being the eyes which widened as the inspection neared one's bed space. Naturally, young Smith's dishevelled apology for a bed space was explained away by the corporal in charge of our beloved 25/7. Nothing seriously wrong with our efforts, the only place left to pop a nose into was our ablutions. The CO gave them a cursory glance and then he saw the trout, swimming around as if he was always there at this time. I promise you, Oliver Hardy could not have done a better double take. First the dreamy scan through the place, then the jerk of the head into the full upright position, the eyes gradually widening, then the incredulous look back at the languishing trout. This man had obviously seen kit inspections for the best part of his life, lived through many scary battles during the war, probably limped home from bombing sessions with all but one engine on fire, but a trout in a wash basin during a station inspection had him totally speechless. I am sure he was unaware of his open mouth. He was transfixed. So was the SWO *and* our corporal. They reminded me of the fairground game where you have to try and throw a table tennis ball into the open mouths of a row of clowns.

The frozen action was eventually broken by the arrival of young Smith, breathless, standing with another wiggling fish in his hand. His eyes opened to the back of his head and without looking, he grabbed the other fish from the basin and made off to the cookhouse. The CO's face slowly relaxed from total horror to a schoolboy grin and he had to depart to save his dignity. We heard the suppressed laughter which was the release valve for all of us. Smithy had a fine breakfast that day. So did the cook.

I once had to cut Smith's hair when he was doing his first of many sets of jankers. This meant being on the six o'clock evening parade, wearing full kit, highly polished and blanco'd. Then heavy duties all evening, such as scrubbing out the guard room, washing out the huge soup vats, mowing grass but, lucky for him, washing Bruno was not on the list! He certainly wouldn't have passed the inspection with hair touching his collar. I had some electric cutters which did the job very well. Unfortunately, the electric light fitting was a little suspect. I had sheared halfway round his head when the fitting collapsed, the cutters jammed and I pulled some of the hairs out of his neck. He jumped up shouting 'You did that on purpose – Lawk! I'm late!' and ran out of the room, back pack and mess tin flying behind, and on to the parade ground ... with half a haircut! We all had visions of the orderly officer standing on one side saying, 'This man needs a haircut,' and the SWO standing on the other side saying, 'Oh no, he doesn't!'

Every couple of weeks, six of us had to take our turn on 'Security Patrol'. This entailed splitting into three pairs. The on-duty pair would patrol various locations of the camp according to a plan. The other two pairs would sleep in the guardroom until they had finished their two hours. They would then wake up the next pair who continued the patrol whilst the first pair settled down for four hours. A mug of strong tea with plenty of sugar and a bacon sandwich tasted fantastic at four in the morning.

This whole procedure was preceded by a six o'clock parade and inspection and the ceremony of saluting the flag down. The orderly officer would bring the six of us to attention, and salute as the RAF policeman, wearing a white cheesecutter hat (hence the nickname snowdrop), pulled down the flag on a looped rope. On one occasion, a young Alsatian had escaped from one of our corporals' quarters. As the snowdrop was reeling down the flag, this canine bulk of energy spotted the snake-like rope and decided this could be a good game. He grabbed the rope and hung on. As the flag came down the dog went up, writhing and growling. The dog had to be brought down so the flag went up again, together with the orderly officer's salute. The dog was shooed away, and the ceremony restarted. The dog, however, had not had enough of the game and grabbed the rope again. Eventually the flag came down. The dog was under the snowdrop's arm writhing furiously, and as the flag was finally brought to ground and unhooked, the dog made off with it. The shaking shoulders of the orderly officer again told us that this would be the talk of the Officers' Mess that night. We had a new flag the next morning. Good old equipment section (non tech).

The high point of pay-days was conducted in the dining hall. The whole station was crammed in and the CO, SWO and pay clerk were seated at a trestle-table. The SWO would call out a name. The 'name' would shout 'SIR' followed by his last three numbers. One lad's number was a clean thousand so he had always to call 'SIR, OH-OH-OH'. Mine was 'SIR, 944'. The next thing to do was march forward to the table, come to attention, salute and grab the money with one hand. The 'OH-OH-OH' chap had just had his boots mended and given new studs. His name was called – he responded, marched forward in his newly cobbled boots, came to a slippery attention and shot under the table. CO and SWO yelled out with pain and started rubbing shins, whilst his bodyless hand came up above the table and fumbled around trying to locate his money.

My pay was 21 shillings, of which seven were sent home to my parents who had by now moved to Blackpool, and seven put into a bank account, which left seven to grab on pay-day. Weekends normally saw everybody skint and the beginning of the week was either early to bed or playing cards for matchsticks. On occasions, one would even have to borrow matchsticks!

I was a little better off, being able to cut hair. I did the SWO's often, and eventually the CO's. They obviously paid me – and I took it – with one hand. Joe Fishburn and I were the only ones able to buy egg and double chips on a Wednesday.

I was once awakened in the middle of the night. An RAF physical display team had arrived and were performing that day in Aberdeen. They all needed a haircut. Fifty of them. It was a bleary-eyed but affluent Castle 944 on parade that morning.

My double hernia finally got troublesome thanks to the lifting of heavy packing cases in the equipment section so our station doctor sent me to RAF Hospital Cosford. The right-hand side first time, then a few weeks later, the other one. When I returned to camp I was considered to be on light duties which excused me from all parades, rifle drill and security patrol. I missed the 4 a.m. cuppa and bacon bap, but not *too* much.

When a hernia operation has just been done, laughing is out of the question. Far too painful. I was in pain most of the time. One of the nurses took charge of the travelling shop – a trolley laden with groceries, books etc. She approached an ageing airman in the next bed to me and asked if he wanted anything. He solemnly shook his head.

'Paper?'

Shake.

'Book?'

Shake.

'Magazine?'

Shake.

'Biscuits?'

Shake.

Getting desperate. 'Toothbrush?'

He looked at her and said, 'No teeth' with his gums!

Oh! that hurt. Try laughing without using your stomach muscles.

One visiting day in the summer, all our families had arrived and were chatting away. One sergeant had no visitors. Shame!

He was taken short and had to ask discreetly for the bed pan. Screens were draped around him and he was allowed to get on with it in private. That is, until a summery gust of wind coming through the open windows blew his screens down and left him sitting there grinning sheepishly. Oh, the pain!

My two years came and went and demob approached. Naturally, twenty-year-olds were not going to let this pass without a celebration. We pooled our money and decided to visit every pub on the way into Aberdeen. Then we were to have a curry, go to the ice rink and pick up whoever could handle drunks with ale and curry breath.

I don't think any of us got as far as Aberdeen. I certainly don't remember getting back to camp. I *must* have, because I didn't wake up in the guardroom – thereby prolonging my stay for another few days. Next morning I had to take a form round to all the different sections to be signed off, so to speak. I don't remember much of *that* either. I think I came to my senses on the train back to Blackpool.

3

Scandals with Randle

November, when I was demobbed in 1952, wasn't the ideal time of the year to re-enter show business. All the acts were just about to move into pantomime. The possibility of a place seemed hopeless and I was resigned to signing on for the Christmas dole when, out of the grey, came a possible part. Apparently, the regular cat in *Dick Whittington* had suddenly died. It must have been his ninth year. I was offered his part and the use of his skin. The cat suit was made out of hessian which was worked with thick wool in the fashion of a carpet. The head was more like an anorak hood with ears. Gloves for hands and plimsolls for feet. I had to make my own papier-maché mask which allowed my eyes to be 'live' and my chin able to miaow. The run was to be four weeks, three shows a day for six days a week, starting in Burnley and touring to a different town each week. For this I was to be paid the princely sum of £5 per week, and all the milk I could drink. Travelling between towns was paid by the company but we had to book and pay for our own digs.

Theatrical accommodation at the time was around £2 10 shillings for bed, breakfast and evening meal. The fiver lasted out quite well if one had a lie in, late breakfast (by prior arrangement), a packet of crisps between shows, maybe a cup of tea. A couple of letters home with a small donation towards upkeep. Stamps about tuppence-ha'penny.

Playing cat had its advantages. The skin would have been popular with any Eskimo. I was wringing wet after my first entrance and didn't have a long enough break to take the skin off during the whole show. The Shivering Fairy in her tutu was blue with cold. During the interval the poor old cat was expected to go out in the audience and play games with them whilst they peeled their oranges and ate their ice-creams and chocolates. I sometimes had my best meal during the interval. I often had some cat food left for me at the stage door! Had I still been in the RAF, I would have eaten it!

I did get a chance to take the wet suit off in between shows and hang it over the radiator, but it only kept the damp hessian and wool warm. It was not a pretty smell. Also, quite often, the stage doorkeeper would pop his head around the dressing-room door and apologize. 'We've got a couple of kids at the stage door wanting to see the cat.'

Here we go! Climb back into the clammy rag and pad down to the stage door to appease the kiddiewinkies. Of course, the cat-loving groupies were expecting a real cat! What trundled up to them resembled a mangy baboon. Much bigger than what they'd seen on stage from the upper circle. Their eyes would pop and then they would scream off in all directions, with mothers scuttling after them. Back to the dressing room to prise myself out of the soggy moggy wet suit.

I sort of enjoyed playing the cat for that short time, but handed the suit back to the wife of its rightful owner with no feelings of regret. I have not been tempted to play it again. Even by Andrew Lloyd Webber!

The following year's panto saw me playing Father Bear. Milk exchanged for sampled porridge and an unmade bed. *Goldilocks* was a good pantomime and one of our speciality acts was billed as 'SWIFTY: FUN ON WHEELS'. He was a comedy cyclist and did his bit in the forest glade. He performed all the traditional tricks on various cycles and unicycles. His *pièce de résistance*, dressed as a fairy, was skipping on a unicycle. He gripped the seat with his thighs and bounced around the stage whilst winging the rope around at high speed. Brought the place down.

We three bears shared a dressing room with him. He was about 5 foot small and quite a pleasant chap. We 'fairly new' members of the business regarded him as an old pro – term of endearment in those days. It so happened that halfway through our season, he developed diarrhoea. The scenario in the dressing room became, unfortunately, very funny. We bears would be getting in or out of our costumes, adding a little make-up for our walk down in the finale, the door would open very slowly and Swifty would creep in and gently sit down in the corner, look up dolefully and almost whisper, 'I've been again'. This performance continued for a few days until it became the password of the panto – 'He's been again'. Eventually he became so weak he had to cut out his skips. Swifty became WISTY: THE RUNS ON WHEELS.

I resumed my place in the summer show at Cleveleys as a mature 21-year-old war veteran. Highly influenced by Frank Sinatra, I had moved on from a boy tenor to a ballad singer – I thought! I sang 'Young at Heart' for our producer-pianist Mildred Crossley. As I ended my song there was a pause which I assumed to be the speechless attitude of a doting fan, lost for words worthy enough to express their appreciation of such depth of feeling. Mildred Crossley slowly looked up and said, 'It's a shame your voice didn't come back.'

It seems a fairly innocuous remark on the face of it but that ill-considered damning of my new passion and enthusiasm totally shattered my confidence in ballad singing and gave me a complex that was to stay with me for many years. I never forgave MC for her blinkered criticism and when she followed it with 'Some people have ideas above their station', I was prepared to jack it in, right there.

The audience reaction to my song renewed a little faith in my being Frankie II, but MC's scowling face whilst she murdered my accompaniment on the piano led to a few dry mouths. I later found out that she was none too pleased when I started doing well. 'They all have to come down again!' She was a chain smoker – maybe she should have smoked cigarettes instead.

Touring, between summer and panto, was beginning to suffer owing to the introduction of TV. Anyone who owned a television set had many friends. Theatres were closing all over England and only the big drawing names were surviving. *Happiness Ahead* seemed doomed to extinction along with many other touring shows. One week's work, then six weeks out (or 'resting'). One famous variety act put an advert in the theatrical paper, the *Stage*. All dates from February to December were listed as available apart from two weeks in August which were earmarked 'holidays'!

Work was becoming difficult and the title *Happiness Ahead* was not representative of our future. Regular visits to the labour exchange. Fatherly advice from the civil servant behind the counter. 'If you had a proper trade I might be able to place you. I'm not sure if you are actually eligible for dole money. I can't really place a tap dancer. Tap fitter, yes – but tap dancer! No call for one.' I got this, or a similar routine, every week. He even attempted the tap-dancer-fell-in-sink joke.

Just as the repartee was wearing very thin, Norman Teal rang to say we had an offer to put a musical act into Frank Randle's Show, *Randle's Scandals of '53*. He was a Lancashire comic who was coarse but very funny. I remembered watching him as a boy at the South Pier Blackpool. He said something which really tickled my sense of humour and I laughed and laughed on my own. He said, 'Who let that kid in!' Now we were to be in the same show. We hastily formed a musical trio consisting of Norman Teal on xylophone and bass fiddle, Marjorie Kendall on trumpet and toe taps on point à la ballet and me on trumpet and high hat cymbal. We started out as clowns and quick-changed into brown tails for our big finish – the Lost Chord with two trumpets and soft hammers on the xylo.

Acts never auditioned for Mr Randle, he put you into the show saying, 'The audience is the best judge.' We stayed with the show for two years, enduring some of the weirdest experiences we could imagine.

Frank Randle was totally unpredictable, some said he was ruled by the moon. He would often disappear for a couple of days then show up with no apology or explanation. Because he was such a crowd puller and always played to full houses, nobody took on the onerous duty of challenging him. He had been a trapeze artist as a young man so had no fear. He worked with no teeth. His first entrance would be *with* teeth, he would say, 'Good evening', flashing his ill-fitting choppers, then snap his fingers. On came a page boy with a satin cushion. There would be a drum roll and Randle would take out his false teeth and place them on the cushion, and the page boy would walk ceremoniously off stage whilst Randle would splutter, 'That's better', and launch into his bawdy stories. He was the first person to tell the story: 'Passing a pub the other day and a dog came out and started savaging my leg. I shouted to t' landlord, "Hey, can't tha see, thy dog has just savaged me leg!" T' landlord said, "He can't bite thee, he's got no teeth!" I said, "Well by heck, he's given me a nasty suck!" ' Delivered by a master this gag got a roar.

He was renowned for having a big supporting company. The Dagenham Girl Pipers, Hal Mack and his Dancing Demons, the Ben Abdrahaman Wazzan acrobatic troupe from Abyssinia, the Bouncing Dillons, our trio and a big group of

Neapolitan singers who also played in his sketches. This group featured Gus Aubrey who will still be remembered by some people. He finished up selling ladies' underwear in Lewis's, Manchester.

Randle had a stranglehold over this last set of people. He knew they wouldn't get a job with anyone else and gave them all a very hard time. He often called us all into his dressing room after the second house and ranted and raved about agents, other performers, income tax inspectors etc, whilst consuming many bottles of Guinness but offering none to anyone else. He had a habit of reaching the climax of his wrath by holding a half-empty bottle menacingly above him and letting the contents pour on to his head and trickle down his face and on to his yellowing vest. These sessions could go on as late as 1 a.m. until he either fell asleep or got violent enough for us all to leave in self-defence.

Barrow-in-Furness was the location of a memorable event. Business had been dropping off around the country, but suddenly in Barrow, there were queues around the theatre clamouring for seats. Randle was in an 'I'm still the bee's knees' mood and quite pleased with life. A chap came backstage to speak to him, said he wanted to know if Randle would bring a few people over to the Town Hall on Friday and give a charity performance for the NSPCC fund. The normal Randle would have booted him out of the stage door – but *no!* – he was in his Uncle Frank character and promised them a cabaret after our show. We gently mentioned the fact that we would miss our meals at our various digs. Randle assured us all would be taken care of, adding a few remarks about landladies ruling the roost. He then had a bright idea of: 'In case things are not to our liking, I shall blow this whistle. You will then all fall in line behind me and we shall march out!'

The evil hour arrived. Curtain down on a packed house of cheers and standing ovations. The final bow, then the house curtain falling and muting the orchestra as they played the audience out. The mad scramble to get to the Town Hall in full costume and make-up. We had to dismantle the xylophone, lump it into a van, carry it up three flights of a spiral staircase and set it up again. A quick 'talk through' our music with the local trio of piano, bass and drums.

The audience of Barrow-in-Furness's upper class was quietened by the MC and we were introduced as the warmer-uppers! We started with 'Lady of Spain'. First chorus in B flat and the second chorus in E flat. The trio played both choruses in C. A great start. It sounded more like Lady of Pain. We motioned to the trio to leave it to us for our other two numbers. 'The Lost Chord' would never have been more aptly named. The Ben Abdrahaman Wazzan troupe followed but had no room for their better acrobatic routines. The pyramid had to be cut as the top man would have had his head in the chandelier. Our singer sang with no accompaniment and wandered through quite a few different keys. However, it was now time for the Top of the Bill. 'Ladeees and Gentlemennn! The Great Frraank Rannndle!'

The aged microphone provided was fossilized. A square frame with a spring coming from each corner suspending the actual microphone in the middle. The sound it created was that of a very old station announcement. A peg over the nose accompanied by a constant crackle.

Randle started into some of his tried and true gags but halfway through his first woofer, the worst possible thing happened. A posh voice from the audience shouted 'Speak up, we can't hear you!'

Randle glared in the heckler's direction – for a long, chilling time – then he grabbed the microphone stand, banged it down behind him sending the springs quivering in an extended diminuendo. He shouted through glistening gums, 'If you can't *bluddy well* listen, perhaps you'll watch!' He then did his mime routine showing the difference between a woman

and a man sewing a button on a shirt. No laughs. He was
getting more and more contemptuous of the fidgety audience.
He finished and marched straight through the icy crowd
shouting 'Where's the food?' We tagged along and were
ushered to the Mayor's parlour. The door was unlocked and
we were allowed in. The carpet had been covered by
newspapers which made us feel like assumed ill-mannered
louts. There was a trestle-table with plates of sandwiches, one
plate containing about six greasy sausage rolls and some cup
cakes, most of which clung to the corrugated greased paper. A
large tea urn was surrounded by cups and a jug of milk and
bowl of sugar. For twelve of us! We made noises as if to say
'*See!* Told you!' having missed out on hot meals in the digs.
Randle called for the Mayor who eventually rattled in and
asked naively, 'Can I help?'

'If you were a chef you might,' Randle rumbled. 'What the
hell do you call thissss?' his toothless, sibilant hisses growing
in length. 'My artisstss have given up a hot meal to do your
bluddy charity. How much did this lot cost you?' He took a
wad of notes out of his pocket and slung two pounds on the
table. 'That should cover it! I'm going to start a new charity
... The National Society for Prevention of Cruelty to
Artisstsss.' His fiery eyes then focused on the plate of greasy
sausage rolls. Remember, we were in the Mayor's parlour.
The walls were festooned with carefully lit original paintings
of past mayors. Randle picked up the plate of sausage rolls
and started firing them at the portraits. 'By Jove, I'm in fine
fettle tonight.' Greasy sausage rolls slowly descending from
the mayors' faces. One hit fair and square on the nose slowly
became Cyrano de Bergerac. Then Pinnochio. The Mayor was
frothing at the mouth and perspiring profusely from every
pore. 'Mr Randle,' he pleaded, 'if you could give us a few
minutes we could arrange a hot meal.'

'What – like hot cup cakes? Not bluddy likely. It's too
bluddy late now.' Randle then stopped stock-still, transfixed,

staring into space as if some divine plot was hatching. He slowly and deliberately reached into his pocket, pulled out the whistle and blew it with all his toothless puff. We all jumped into line behind him and off he strode out of the vandalized Mayor's parlour, along the thickly carpeted corridor and on to the spiral staircase. Round and round he led us. Down and down with the Mayor, cloak flailing behind him, pleading with Randle to reconsider. Obviously Randle couldn't change his mind now. He was hurt. He had failed his 'artissstsss' and had to make a big show for our benefit more than anything else. I don't think even a crate of Guinness would have coaxed him back. As we all spilled out of the Town Hall into the chilly night with empty bellies, we peeled off in the various directions of our digs, savouring the thought of perhaps a cold greasy sausage and sagging chips. Hot toast might save the day if we had a shilling for the meter.

Next morning, of course, Norman Teal and I had to return to the Town Hall to pick up the xylophone. Luckily, it hadn't finished up being used as a trolley for collecting empty glasses!

Which reminds me ... whilst we were still with Randle, playing Rochdale Theatre Royal, Norman's xylophone was always left in a backstage corner with a big dust cover over it and a notice stating it was a 'musical instrument, please do not put anything on it'. We always went to the theatre after breakfast to collect mail, rehearse, meet up for coffee, etc. On this particular morning, we were looking in the letter rack and exchanging pleasantries with other cast members. The sound of sawing didn't arouse any alarm as the stage staff were often doing repair work or building scenery ready for incoming productions. It wasn't until we wandered on to the stage that the unbelievable scenario had Norman Teal's ears popping. One of the carpenters had removed the cover from the xylophone and was sawing a plank of wood on it. Norman went bananas. 'What the XXXXXX do you think you're doing! That's a xylophone. Three thousand pounds' worth of musical instrument.' The ageing carpenter looked over his sawdusted glasses and explained, 'It's all right, I'm judgin' it between t' notes!'

One slip and the note in question would have gone sharp and would have to be replaced, which could have taken days if not weeks. It's just as well he hadn't knelt on the plank otherwise he would have bowed the instrument into the bargain. We may have had to change the musical act into a comedy trampoline speciality.

Whilst we were in Rochdale, not doing the kind of business Randle was used to, he decided to end it all. With hooded eyes, he announced to the cast and press that he started in Rochdale (another good word with no teeth) and he was going to finish in Rochdale. He planned to burn all his scenery, costumes and props on the one-time cattle market across the road from the theatre. However, the council wouldn't allow it as that area was classed as a smokeless zone! So we carried on with the tour.

We were once due to work at the Empire Theatre, Oldham, but when we looked in the *Stage* the week before, there was no sign of us in 'Who's where next week'. Oldham Empire had a variety bill planned with names like Ken Frith – piano player, and Jeffrey Lenner – smart young comic, and various other acts. Naturally we challenged Randle on this turn of events. First of all he didn't believe it. Someone found his reading glasses and prodded at the 'next week's attractions' section. As he read, saliva began to escape down his quivering lip, his eyebrows dipped over his steely stare and he growled a deep rumbling which must have registered on the Richter scale and alarmed scientists in all parts of Lancashire.

'The BASSSTARDSSSS!'

His mind was visibly racing through all possible reasons why this could happen to him. To *him! Frank Randle. The biggest draw in the North for many years. Ousted by a*

TUPPENCE-HA'PENNY VARIETY BILL! He certainly
was not going to let this happen. Especially to his artissstsss.
His reputation was on the line – so too was his place in the first
division. Was he now on the slippery slope to number two
theatres and oblivion? 'Didn't you used to be Frank Randle?'

After more ranting and raving, he decided to buy the
variety bill and put our show on as well!

At this time variety had gone continuous – we performed a
twice-nightly programme but the customers could come in at
any time and stay until they had had enough. It *was* possible
to sit through the whole thing twice if you really had nothing
better to do, or didn't know anyone with a TV. So Randle
decided that everyone should cut their act in half. This should
result in the shows coming down to time. Simple!

The first house at Oldham on the Monday opened to a very
sparse audience which gradually thickened to almost full
during the second half. Likewise, the first half of the second
house was full and slowly dwindled until the last turn
worked to very few. It evened out in a rather bizarre fashion.
The final curtain came down about 12.30 a.m.!

On Tuesday, it was decided that everyone would do their
full act once and we would give Oldham a show the like of
which they had never seen before or were ever likely to see
again. It was rough on the opening and closing artisstss but
that's show busssinessss!

We still finished around 12.30 a.m. I got paid three quid
that week. Just as well VAT hadn't started.

As Randle's popularity teetered he became more and more
difficult and unpredictable. So much so that a special clause
was written into his contract protecting the theatre in case he
didn't show up. In the event of his absence, there would be no
pay for that particular show.

One night at Doncaster Grand, we were well into the
second half when the company manager realized there was no
Frank. He rang the hotel who finally roused him out of a deep

sleep, and informed us he was on his way. 'Keep the show going till he gets there.' We were approaching the final item and there was no Randle. 'Who can do something until he gets here?' the company manager was near hysterics. Norman Teal volunteered, 'Roy can tap-dance.' 'Great! Have you got your tap shoes?'

'Yes.'

'Right! Quick as you can.'

Rita Shearer played organ on stage and was invaluable when the show ran late and all the pit musicians had 'gone for t' last bus'. Shoes on and organ in place, no time for rehearsal, out I went and started tapping. I was going great guns for four or five minutes. I kept looking off stage to see if Randle had arrived. 'Keep going' signs spurred me on. We went through all the traditional tap numbers. 'Chinatown', 'Limehouse Blues', 'Top Hat', 'Bye Bye Blues', 'Bye Bye Blackbird', 'The Saints', 'Putting on the Ritz' – Rita Shearer knew them all. The audience were now more than a little confused, verging on the restless. It was obvious once Rita had to start repeating 'Chinatown' and 'Bye Bye Blues' that we were struggling. My legs were beginning to complain and my pleas to the side were just met with shrugs. Then! A sudden burst of applause and a cheer. I looked around and saw Randle's face, unshaven and a little pinker than normal, sticking out of the prompt side. Mackintosh draped over striped pyjamas and untied plimsolls. He waved and the audience cheered, then settled down expectantly. Randle's head then spoke. 'Well, that's taken care of the contractual obligations.' He looked at me and said, 'Well done! Carry on, son,' and went to his dressing room. I walked off to the sound of my own feet. The finale got one applaud as people were getting up to leave amid disgruntled mutterings.

That same theatre had swing doors in the circle that were badly in need of attention. As anyone entered or left, the doors would bang loudly as they shuddered to a quivering close. One second

house, as Randle was delivering his final comedy routine
('The Hiker'), we were late as usual. People had to catch last
buses and were leaving, many from the circle. The swing
doors were working overtime. It's not easy to get a routine
across with this kind of distraction. Randle, for once, cut
short his *pièce de résistance* and fumed off the stage. The finale
walk-down followed, or as Eric Morecambe always termed it,
'The Who's Best'. Randle came down last in blue jeans and
his off-white short-sleeved vest with the rubber buttons (they
don't break in the mangle).

He walked forward, as one does, to make his speech. The
audience hushed as he stared hard and long at the circle. He
then went into a new routine. 'Tomorrow, I shall get out of
my bed earlier than usual. Eat a hurried breakfast, then get
into my car and drive into the heart of Doncaster and find a
parking space. I shall then ask a pleasant passer-by where I
can find Woolworth's. Upon finding this reasonably priced
store, I shall find the correct counter, take this right hand of
mine, turn it in a sideways position pointing downwards.
Slide it into my pocket, pick out a few modest coins' – pause –
'AND BUY SOME RUBBER STOPPERS FOR THOSE
BLASSSTED DOORS!'

Wood Green Empire in North London was the scene of the
most outrageous experience. *Randle's Scandals* wasn't doing
very good business. He never was the superstar south of
Birmingham and was not taking kindly to the lukewarm
reception he was getting. The show was running late as usual
and the interval of the second house was nudging eleven
o'clock. Randle was getting some stick from the audience so
he rose to the occasion and spat back. In the end it seemed he
questioned the valid parenthood of the entire audience such as
it was. The manager of the theatre immediately ordered the
curtain to be dropped and to the relief of most, the show was
over for that particular Wednesday evening. In fact, it turned
out to be the end of our 'week' in Wood Green. Next day, we

were informed that the show was being replaced by a variety bill that was rehearsing in London prior to a provincial tour. We were barred from the theatre during the day to avoid a confrontation which would have interfered with the new show's rehearsal. We were allowed into the corridor backstage once they had started, but we were not allowed in the dressing rooms to collect our make-up and costumes until the end of the show. There was not much point in going out again with no money and insufficient clothing for such a cold and rainy night.

Norman Teal and I were waiting outside our dressing room when Malcolm Mitchell, star of the 'new' show, came out with his guitar and said that 'on no account' must we go in there and let his dog out. Norman was incensed by this and as soon as Malcolm had disappeared, he went in to get our things. The dog, a Jack Russell, shot out of the dressing room and followed the sign 'To Stage'. The tannoy relay system was blurting out backstage to let other acts know whereabouts they were in the programme. Call boys had long since been made redundant. From the music coming through, we assumed the pit orchestra was playing for either acrobats or jugglers. *The Ritual Firedance* by de Falla was the classic hurry-hurry music. Also the curse of all trumpet players. It would be repeated *ad nauseam* until the blood ran down the chin. We assumed it to be the music for a juggler as the Jack Russell padded proudly back to the dressing room with an Indian club in its mouth and proceeded to chew it into several pieces. As we scuttled through the stage door, a Spanish voice was heard ranting and raving in its native tongue, apart from a very distinguishable 'Dog' every few words!

Nobody got paid that week.

The ensuing court case was handled by Randle himself in his own defence. He explained that 'As the item was a medley of Italian songs, he addressed the audience in Italian: *'Basta, basta'* means 'enough, enough'! He got away with a small fine, got lashings of free publicity and had very good houses at the 'Met', Edgware Road the following week.

Pit orchestras were also a source of amusement in retrospect. They would often wear dinner jackets, bow ties – and jeans (if the pit rail was high enough). When the comic was on, they would scramble out of the pit door, under the stage and pop out for a quickie. If the comic was dying and finished early he would often end with his song accompanied by a violin and saxophone.

During the Randle days, Norman Teal and I opened our musical act with *Blue Skies*. I ran on with a high hat cymbal whilst he came on from the opposite side with a bass fiddle. We arrived at the centre mike together and started into the song.

'Blue skies –' short phrase from the orchestra.

'Shinin' at me –' short phrase from the orchestra.

'Nothing but blue skies –' short phrase from the orchestra.

'Do I see –' short phrase from the orchestra, but a little longer, and so on to the end of the number. Simple enough.

We were playing the specially opened Hippodrome Theatre in Accrington and the band call was fine considering it was a hastily assembled bunch, due to the theatre being dark for quite some time. As we sat through the rest of the band call, the cornet player, during any lull, gave us a rendition of *Carnival of Venice*. Sometimes with variations, then his proud red face would slowly rise above the pit rail as if to say 'That was me'. Normally during a lull, the musicians would read the paper, do the crossword or peruse a magazine. Not this chap. He was obviously the pride of the local brass band and rightly so. His reading of the music was immaculate, but he didn't 'swing'.

Halfway through the week as Norman and I were changing for the start of the show together with the Ben Abdrahaman Wazzan Troupe and Hal Mack and his Dancing Demons, we became aware of this cornet player framed in our doorway. He was well rounded and seemed to lean slightly to one side. Not quite Mr Blobby, more like a red balloon in a dinner jacket. He smelled of moth balls and aftershave as he coughed to gain our attention. We couldn't ask him in as we were too cramped. He inquired what type of trumpet I was playing for openers then launched into the real reason for his visit.

'I've been studying this "rebop" stuff.'

'Oh yes?'

'I was wondering ...'

'Yes?'

'Well,' he went slightly redder, 'I was wonderin', er well ... er ... you know in *Blue Skies* we just have a few bits to play?'

'Yes?'

'Well – er – I was wondering if you'd mind letting me loose.'

Norman and I exchanged glances. I left the decision to him.

'Sure, help yourself.'

'Thanks.'

He gave me a wink and was gone.

We had forgotten this episode by the time our act was due and ran on as normal.

'Blue Skies'. Then it happened. He waded into a machine-gun attack of totally unselected notes which bore no relevance to the chord structure whatsoever. His idea of rebop was 'play 'owt' as fast as you can. It was excruciating and to top it all, he looked up halfway through the chorus and gave us a big wink as if to say 'How about that, pal?' We couldn't sing the rest of the number so played along with him. Almost.

We had to explain to him that we didn't think 'Accrington was ready for such adventurous stuff yet'. He reluctantly agreed and played the original dots for the rest of the week. As we looked down from the stage we could see him thinking 'I'm wasted 'ere!' *Wasted*!

Norman Teal taught me the basics of orchestration and I started to write my own 'charts' for small pit bands – which was economically necessary in those days. A few years later I was performing solo at the Grand Theatre, Bolton.

Michael Holliday had just had a big hit with *Story of My Life*. So I wrote out a set of parts and introduced it into my act. I got a little carried away with one of the phrases for the trumpet, wondered if I should, then decided to write a simpler version in red ink.

During the run-up to band call on the Monday morning, the trumpet player had singled this particular phrase out and was having a 'stab' at it. He couldn't get near it so I went over and pointed out the possibility of playing the red notes if he felt more comfortable.

'No, no, I like a challenge.'

He didn't get it at rehearsals so asked me if I minded him 'takin' it 'ome and gettin' to grips wi' it?'

'Not at all, help yourself.'

'Do you mind there bein' a crease in it? I shall have to fold it to gerrit in me pocket. I'm on my bike.'

'No problem.'

He made brave attempts at the phrase twice nightly through the week. Always different. Always wrong. I kept making a mental note to tell him to play the red notes but, once I came off, forgot.

By Friday night, second house, I was approaching the phrase thinking, 'Oh no, I've forgotten to tell him again. What are we going to get this time? Steel yourself.'

The moment arrived and he played ... nothing. Total silence. I had to look down. He was counting his wages!

I wrecked my own opening song but *had* to say it: 'That's the first time you've had the right notes all week.' I lost my audience but the trombone player went hysterical.

The Musicians Union ruling at one time stated that at least three musicians must be locally hired. Especially when summer seasons were in full flow.

I was playing the Winter Gardens in Margate and

performing my 'How High the Moon' routine which incorporated my orchestra build-up before launching into the song.

The local musicians were bass, trombone and drums. The drummer had an old-fashioned kit with temple blocks and a sunset painted on black velvet draped over his bass drum. He was a nice chap but didn't read very well. My build-up started with him, and sounded something like 'TSH-T'T'-TSH-T'T'-TSH-T' meant for his high hat cymbal. He just bashed on his bass drum pedal: 'Dump-Dump-Dump-Dump'.

'No TSH-T'T'-TSH-T' on the high hat.'

DUMP-DUMP-DUMP-DUMP

'I tried to show him but he couldn't manage it. TSH-T'T'-TSH-T' – DUMP-DUMP-DUMP.

I was getting slightly agitated when he looked balefully at me and said, 'Listen, mate, I'm delivering milk at five o'clock in the morning.'

I had no answer. 'Oh well … why didn't you say before.'

I started the routine with DUMP-DUMP-DUMP-DUMP and we got along fine.

I had a singing routine which involved my tapping a tuning fork on the microphone stand and singing to the note it produced. I would then be joined, first of all by the bass fiddle player. I had written his music which went quite high but not unreasonably so. Most players had no difficulty and it normally sounded fine so it was quite a shock when one chap started into his bit but, when it came to the higher notes, dropped down an octave which took the excitement away. I asked him, 'Why?'

'Eee, lad. I've never been that far up t' neck! I nearly 'ad me fingers on t' bridge.'

Many memories of Frank Randle float around in these hazy recollections of days long gone. His fiery battles with Josef Locke. His shooting practice – empty bottles lined up on top of his caravan whilst his wife was washing up inside. His late-night crash with a Blackpool tram which wouldn't move out of his way! His great artistry when on form. His successful films. His eventual slide from stardom. The last time I saw him he was well-dressed in a dark blue sports coat with shiny buttons, grey, neatly pressed trousers, white shirt and tie and highly polished shoes. He was carrying a Bible under his arm and trying to spread the message to anyone who would listen. Although this was a courageous move, coming from him with his background so well-known to the whole country, it rather seemed like a naughty boy saying sorry to the teacher just before he received his punishment. It reminded me of that well-known saying 'Many people, planning to repent at the eleventh hour, die at ten-thirty'!

4

Roman Candles
and The Windmill

As the Randle Band Wagon shuddered to a halt, we found ourselves 'resting' again. Back to the labour exchange and the tap jokes. As my place in the queue reached the counter my careers adviser's eyes lit up. He was just about to come up with a derisory gem but I beat him to it with 'I've heard it'. Being totally humourless, he said, 'You don't know what I'm going to say yet.' With hooded eyes and resigned acceptance of defeat, I waited for his 'told you so', but to my amazement he confided his daughter's decision to 'take up tap-dancing', and would I 'like to assess her potential'? I asked him if he was 'offering me a job'? His enthusiasm returned to normal. I took my money and wished his daughter success. 'Maybe we'll be in the same show together one day ...' then as I made my exit, 'or the same dole queue.'

A rather distinguished gentleman named Walter Cartmell was a regular visitor to the Queen's Theatre. He was a fish merchant who lived in Blackpool and had a flourishing business in Fleetwood. He became very interested in my career, offering to help me if I would like him to. I thought, 'Yes, I know, I've heard *that* one before.' He then said he was very friendly with Val Parnell. The *B-i-i-i-g* man in show business at that time. I was still not impressed. This guy was obviously bloated with his success as a fish flogger and, like many wealthy businessmen, fancied his chances as a talent spotter and possible impresario. I thanked him and said a hollow, 'Sure, go ahead.'

The next day ... I went to the labour exchange, got my money and carried on 'resting' as I made some new wooden gates for our house and practised the trumpet. Tap-dancing came easy. The odd game of golf when funds allowed.

When I arrived home, Dad said, 'There's been a chap on t' phone for you. Says he's arranged it wi' a chap in London.'

'Was it Mr Cartmell?'

'Ay lad, I didn't ask 'im.'

'Did he leave his number?'

'No.'

'Oh no!'

'He said it were all fixed up or summat.'

There were not many Cartmells in the directory and only one fish merchant, so Dad's shortcomings as a secretary were not too debilitating.

The deal was on. I was to get down to London, turn up at the Hippodrome, Leicester Square and perform for *the* Val Parnell. An audience of one, and his secretary. The Hippodrome probably seated around two thousand five hundred people. A bottle tester if there ever was one.

Armed with trumpet, tap shoes, stage suit and Jerry Lewis wig plus the extra fortification of a pocket sewn into my vest by Mam – 'You can't trust them Londoners! You hear such funny stories!' – I tried not to be fazed by the occasion and boarded the train at Blackpool with an outward confidence. The butterflies grew bigger and bigger as I neared my come-uppance. All the previous desire to show the world what

real talent was began to dissipate with every revolution of the
metal wheels. The more I thought of my act, the more puerile
it seemed. I became that little boy from Scholes showing my
wares to the god of show business. In private! Would he even
know Jerry Lewis? Of course, he's the man who would *book*
Jerry Lewis!

I don't really remember the journey from Euston to
Leicester Square. London should have been exciting but the
pressure of my impending audition was causing those roman
candles to explode in my head. Suddenly I was looking up at
the Hippodrome. The stage door was well-hidden around the
back. I pushed it open and lumped my trappings inside. The
stage doorkeeper was a man of few words.

'Yes?'

'Er, I'm doing an audition for Mr Val Parnell.'

'Name?'

'Er, Roy Castle.'

'Carsell?'

'Er, yes.'

'Right. Pop on the stage, round there. The pianist's waitin'
for you.'

I shambled towards the stage, peeped round the prompt
side. The vast auditorium was dark and very empty.

'Roy Castle?' The voice came from below me.

'Yes?' I yodelled to this bodyless aproach. As my eyes got
used to the lack of light, I saw a chap sitting at the piano in the
pit.

'Have you got your dots?'

'Oh … yes.' I tugged my piano parts out of my trumpet case
and handed them down to him. We walked through, then
rehearsed my three numbers. 'The Whole Town's Talking
About the Jones Boy', vocal and trumpet. Jerry Lewis
singing 'Never Smile at a Crocodile', then tap-dance finish
'Bye Bye Blues'. Halfway through the latter, a lady came from
the back of the theatre and informed me that Mr Parnell had

arrived and was ready to see my act.

Roman candles!

'You needn't change into your suit.' Meaning Mr Parnell is a very busy man.

'Relax! Pretend you've got a full house.' That must have been Val Parnell himself! My mouth was dry. In this stage, singing is just about possible but trumpet playing is a mega No-no. Try and muster some saliva from somewhere. I went off stage, the pianist started into my intro and this was it! Blow it now and all is lost. How could I tell Mr Cartmell?

On I went and plunged into 'The Jones Boy'. Vocal OK. The trumpet, luckily, sat well on my lips and I managed to play a half chorus and finished on the vocal. No applause.

'Good,' Val Parnell said. 'Have you anything else?'

I did my Jerry Lewis and the lady laughed. My tap-dance went through easily and I made my exit.

Not knowing what happened next, I went back on stage and peered out.

'Could you come here, please,' the lady said.

The pianist pointed out the steps into the auditorium. I made my way to the assumed area of the man himself. He was a very big man in every way. Tall, wide, deep-voiced, and immaculate.

'Walter was right! You have plenty of talent. Go and see Sydney Grace at Lew and Leslie Grade. He'll handle you. Good man. Give my regards to Walter!' He muttered to his secretary and left us. I was given Sydney Grace's address and told how to get there. *Wheeee*! This is it! I'm in!

London was not so threatening as I emerged from that stage door. Even the pianist was enthusiastic. I hailed a taxi and gave the driver the address. 235 Regent Street. I had hardly the time to wrestle my money out of my vest pocket before we were there. My trappings were much lighter as I mounted the spiral staircase to the fourth floor. Lew and Leslie Grade Ltd, Theatrical Agency. I eased my way through the door and met a man with some documents in his hand, well-dressed with a bow tie and gold-rimmed glasses.

'Can I help you?'

'I've come to see Mr Sydney Grace.'

'He's not in today. Come back some other time.'

I was totally confused and deflated, and too green to say 'But I have an appointment.' I accepted the fact that Sydney Grace wasn't there and I had to get back to Euston and home. Totally devastated by the unreality of the weird experience.

The truth of the situation was that Burton Brown, a lesser agent, was shielding Sydney Grace from me, a probable chancer, when Grace was, in fact, waiting for me to see him with regard to representing me on the recommendation of Val Parnell. As far as he was concerned, I hadn't turned up. Possibly unreliable. End of story.

I was shattered to have been raised so high then smashed down without knowing why. Maybe Val Parnell was just being nice for Walter's sake, but the real word was that I was a 'no hoper'. This roller-coaster experience was going to happen to me many times as I threaded my way through show business. It's supposed to sort out the men from the boys. Get up from the floor and start punching again. However, this particular experience was heavy going.

On my return home I found there had been a telephone message from Norman Teal. Apparently, as there was as yet no TV in Scotland, live theatre still had a pulse left in it. A Scottish booker had seen our musical act with Randle and offered us a couple of weeks in Dundee. Marjorie Kendall had taken work elsewhere so we had to cobble together a double act. We renamed ourselves Teal and Castle Instru'mental'ists, jumped on the train to Dundee, found some digs and presented ourselves at the Palace for Monday morning band call and rehearsal. The top of the bill, a big name in Scotland, was Tommy Morgan, a gravel-voiced man of about 65 but well loved by his many fans.

Our act went very well. Well, well enough to be offered a longer run at the Palladium, Edinburgh. This time our bill topper was Johnny Victory. His main contribution was a specially written monologue incorporating current affairs. He was a bombastic type who always sported a dewdrop on the end of his amply nostrilled nose. He owned a few Rolls-Royces which he seemed to fill with large hungry dogs. No one was likely to break into his motors and that's for sure. The Palladium run lasted ten weeks and was organized like a repertory company. We changed our acts each week, which meant performing one show at night, rehearsing the next show during the day whilst thinking of material for the show after that. Everyone joined in sketches and production numbers. Back to *Happiness Ahead* really.

We had to try and speak with a Scottish accent on many occasions, it must have sounded pathetic to the real Scots in the audience. I had to make an entrance to warn some gamblers of approaching policemen. I was instructed to say, 'Look out, it's the *pawliss*'! I said, 'Are you sure?' 'Just say it, son,' said Johnny V. It got a huge laugh and I still don't know why. Maybe my brave attempts as a Yorkshire Glaswegian was funny, as in Bernard Manning dancing a *pas de deux*. I've tried it many times since, but not a titter.

We became reasonably popular and stayed in Scotland almost two years. It was quite exciting playing the Tivoli in Aberdeen, having been to many shows there whilst doing my National Service. The bill toppers were 'Clarke and Murray', a well-loved Scottish man-and-wife comedy duo. On the same bill was an up-and-coming young comic called Andy Stewart. We played the Pavilion, Glasgow with Lex McLean, probably Scotland's answer to Ken Dodd. Throw in the Gaiety Theatre, Leith for a few more weeks and I had to thank Scotland for lots of experience and keeping my career alive. After this run, Norman and I managed to land ourselves a pantomime in Newcastle upon Tyne. The theatre was the Palace, known locally as 'The Dirty Alice'.

One stand-out memory from that pantomime was the poor old witch. Quite an ageing old soul, she had to be harnessed up for a Kirby wire. (Kirby being the experts at 'flying' people around *à la* Peter Pan.) Our green-faced, black-toothed witch with sequins on her eyelids was to deliver her lines from the right-hand side of the stage, the handlers would then pull her up into the air and she *should* take off and swing to the other side of the stage whilst on the rise. As she got to the left-hand side a rope was waiting for her to grab. She delivered her chilling lines to the principal boy and girl, finishing with, 'I go now, but rest assured, I will be *back*!' The Kirby team pulled her up in the air and she 'flew' on her broomstick off stage left. Unfortunately, she made a grab at the rope, missed it and swung back. She now had less momentum and her second swing didn't take her as far as the rope so she was condemned to swing back and forth over the rest of the scene. 'I *told* you I'd be back' was all she could offer. The Kirby team decided to keep her up there rather than lower her to stage level and have her slouch off with her broomstick dragging behind. The harness was none too comfortable and her suppressed cries of agony had us all in fits.

During this run, Mam had to phone me and gently break the news that Dad was in hospital. When they moved to Blackpool, Dad had become a railway porter. He had cycled to the station in gale conditions, a distance of around two miles, and collapsed on arrival with a serious heart attack. 'He's doing well and will be able to come home soon, so don't worry,' Mam told me. I suggested coming down, but she assured me it was not necessary as I only had a few more days to go.

After the panto, work was very sparse – non-existent in fact. Norman decided he would like to go into management, and we wrapped up the act, which had taken early retirement anyway.

For me it was back to Blackpool with the labour exchange as my agent once again. With Dad laid up, times were somewhat gloomy.

However, a short time later, I ran into Walter Cartmell, who suggested I go back to London to see Sydney Grace. This was quickly arranged and off I went again. No brush-off this time. I was ushered in to see Mr Grace who had organized an audition for me at the Windmill Theatre in London's West End, famous for its boast 'We never closed', referring to the war years 1939–45, and rephrased by many 'We never clothed' alluding to the girls who danced in next to nothing and attracted the traditional men in mackintoshes. A pretty sordid affair. However, many star names had made their first breakthrough at this venue.

I assumed that the audition was a foregone conclusion and just a case of going through the motions as I breezed in full of confidence. London was my oyster and I felt as if I towered over all the other auditioners there. Some had tried regularly to pass the test without success. 'Nothing much else to do at this time of day. You never know when your face might fit.'

'Poor fish,' I thought as I donned tap shoes and oiled trumpet valves. My friend was called and off he went on his hopeless mission. My turn! As I prepared to enter, my friend was leaving. 'Any luck?'

'Face didn't fit again! See you at the next one.'

'Poor fish.'

My music started and on I jumped, brandishing trumpet. I landed, establishing that I was also wearing tap shoes. I sang and played 'The Jones Boy' as well as I have ever done it. Great. Now for my Jerry Lewis.

'Thank you,' came from the dark auditorium. The notorious Vivian Van Damm.

'But I haven't finished yet.'

'*Thank you!*'

'But …'

'Not suitable for this theatre, THANK YOU!'

Another voice shouted 'Next' and I was on my way. *My* face didn't fit either. I walked out of the stage door totally bewildered again. The buildings seemed to sneer at me. Back to Euston Station and home ... and the dole ... Poor fish!

5

'Are You Puttin' it Around that I'm Barmy?'

My Dad's sick pay eked things out, topped up with my dole fortune. We ate meat twice a week. One of the criteria of social status.

Just as my show-business horizon seemed bleak, the phone rang again. Peter Webster ran a children's talent competition on the Central Pier Blackpool during the summer months. Unbeknown to me, he also took on the onerous duty of booking the star attractions for the main show in the theatre. He had watched me on many occasions during our seasonal shows at the Queen's, Cleveleys. He didn't want to step out of line but heard through the dole vine that I was now a solo entity and may be available for offers. I pretended to be semi interested. The deal was to provide a solo spot of five minutes and feed Jimmy Clitheroe. In other words play the straight man to this dwarf comedian who looked like the eternal schoolboy. The money involved was £10 per week, but it was a wonderful showcase for me. I took it. My digs were cheap and with little walking either end, the trams ran me door to door.

My five minutes allowed a shortened version of 'The Jones Boy' and I fused the Jerry Lewis impersonation with the tap-dance. Together with the two spots with Jimmy Clitheroe, I got a fair airing in one of the main summer season towns in the UK (extended by the illuminations!).

The bill topper was Ken Dodd supported by Jimmy James the comic genius together with his stooge, 'Our Eli', Denis Spicer, one of the outstanding ventriloquists of our day, a few speciality acts, two singers and a chorus line. This was a big bill which was necessary considering all the other shows in competition for the holiday-makers' yearly spending spree. Most people booked up for the shows in advance, paid the landladies on arrival, then what they had left had often dried up by Tuesday. Rainy days left them dragging wailing children around shops they could only look at and their imaginations were stretched to the limit explaining why ice-cream and lettered rock was bad for them.

'It wasn't bad for me on Monday!'

'Too much in one week and your teeth'll fall out!'

'So the tooth fairy will owe me a fortune!'

'Shut up.'

The answer to all problems. 'Shut up!'

The show was a big draw and our theatre was packed. My short spot went well and I enjoyed working with Jimmy Clitheroe.

I had heard much about Jimmy James from other pros and was not disappointed. He had been attributed with the longest laugh ever recorded at the London Palladium. It was during the Second World War years, and London was taking a pasting from the German bombers and doodlebugs. The sirens were droning their ominous warnings with sickening regularity. Defiantly, the shows went on.

One of Jimmy's acts was a 'discovery spot', where he would introduce Our Eli as his new 'discovery'. On this occasion Our Eli was a whistling contortionist. 'He whistles "Bird

Songs at Eventide" and does the splits at one and the same time.' Jimmy paused to take a quick drag, but just before the fag got to his mouth he added, 'And if the sirens go, he'll probably do *three*!'

In Blackpool the year I joined them, Eli, dressed in an ill-fitting suit and a Davy Crockett hat, was introduced as 'The Singing Skunk Trapper'. The sheer lunacy of the situation, presented very seriously, had 'em rolling in the aisles.

Eli had a stammer and, occasionally, Jimmy would receive letters complaining about taking the mickey out of the afflicted. He replied explaining that Eli really *did* stammer and should he sack him? Complaint withdrawn.

Halfway through the season I had a phone call to say that Eli was ill and couldn't perform that night – 'would you come in straight away and rehearse with Mr James?' I didn't need to rehearse, I knew the thing backwards having watched it every night. I turned up and went straight through it. Mr James was very complimentary and thanked me for being such a quick study.

So, now I was doing my own five minutes, two spots with Jimmy Clitheroe and two spots with Jimmy James – a great showcase, and an extra £10 per week from JJ! Eli was ill for the rest of the summer season so I played the Singing Skunk Trapper for some eleven weeks. The poor fish bites back. We ate meat four times a week and I was able to buy a television, which helped Mam and Dad to pass the time during his convalescence.

Alas, the season ended, but the show was booked for a short tour. Jimmy Clitheroe was to tour for a couple of weeks, but on the last night of the second week I was apologetically told by the company manager, Bert Myers, that my services would no longer be required when the show – minus Jimmy Clitheroe – went on. Apparently Dave Forrester, an agent who was also producing the show, didn't feel my act was necessary and did the indecent thing. However, Jimmy James was none too pleased with this and asked me to stay on with him as his second stooge. By this time Our Eli was better, so the Davy Crockett hat was no longer mine, but, as JJ had been used to working with two stooges, he asked me if I'd consider being the 'other' one. I had no idea what the following 'knowing' wink meant ...

On the following Monday we opened at Bristol Hippodrome. Jimmy Clitheroe had been replaced by Kenny Baker, Britain's number-one trumpet player for years on end. My act was cut, but I still had my stooge part. The costume was ferreted out of JJ's hamper: a full-length beige overcoat with dark brown cuffs and collar, a long-haired wig and a battered felt hat pulled down well over the eyes. In those days it was considered outrageous – it would probably be admired as new gear today. My handed-down-through-the-ages-of-variety catchphrase was the beloved, 'Are you puttin' it around that I'm barmy?'

Later on that Monday morning, the company manager came to me and said, 'Could you do your act without the trumpet?' I grabbed at it. I could cut 'The Jones Boy', replace it with 'Crocodile' after a couple of gags and still do the tap-dance as Jerry Lewis. 'Fine, kid!'

Apparently when JJ had heard that my act was cut he was furious, sent for Dave Forrester and asked 'Why?' Forrester was a typical agent with ill-fitting glasses and a half-gravel, half-whispered voice. He seemed to be talking confidentially until you realized that this was his full volume. His open-palmed shrug accompanied most of his conversation. He always wore a pained expression in case anyone asked for more money.

'Well, Jim,' he drawled, 'we're a bit pushed for time.'

'How much are we over?' JJ asked.

'About eight minutes,' wheezed DF.

'Then you haven't got a problem, Dave,' JJ said with

confidence. 'How long are my two spots? Let's see, twelve minutes in the first and eighteen minutes in the second. So there you are, Dave, that saves you a half an hour!'

DF cottoned on and shrugged, 'Jiiiiim! You wouldn't do thaaat.'

'Just watch me. I'll have the doctor's note for you this afternoon.'

DF put my act back in and it stayed for the rest of the run.

That week in Bristol, I played no trumpet in the show but practised during the day in my third-floor dressing room. One day Jimmy James got the stage doorkeeper to come up and say, 'Kenny Baker says would you mind not practising 'cos people might think it's him!' This was one of the few snatches of the fun-loving legend I had been told about. He was obviously getting a little older and, I suspect, a little cross with himself for having lost all his money at the race track. Extremely well paid for many years and once, in the 1930s, having won £30,000 on a seven-horse accumulator, he was now an undischarged bankrupt and owed more to the income tax man than he could ever earn. This meant his *having* to work theatres he could otherwise have been a little more choosy about. For instance, the *Glasgow Empire*!

A beautiful theatre, the Glasgow Empire, part of the Moss Empire circuit, had all the hallmarks of the first-class venues in each major city. I was thankful to Jimmy James for pulling me up from the second-class variety halls into this, the first division of the theatre world. The 'Mecca' was the London Palladium, followed by Finsbury Park Empire which was the 'nearly there' achievement. The Glasgow Empire, though, sent violent shivers down the spine of every English comedian. Much has been written about the comics' graveyard and its reputation was fearsome, but, if you were fortunate enough to get the Moss tour, Glasgow Empire was part of the package.

Having played the Pavilion Theatre in Glasgow with

Norman Teal a few years earlier, I felt quite warm towards the locals and booked into my usual digs. So far so good. I set out early on the Monday morning and put our band parts down in order of arrival. The orchestration pad nearest the centre microphone rehearsed first and were assured of their music being accepted. Anyone after that who had the same tunes was obliged to change them. That was the unwritten law of the theatre. Negotiations could be made but it was a first-come-first-served arrangement. Naturally if Frank Sinatra was topping the bill and the jugglers used 'My Way', there would have to be a discussion – albeit a short one!

Whilst the different artists were awaiting their rehearsal time, stories were rife and the comedians talked to each other as if they were on death row. Acrobats, jugglers, dancers and singers were not so concerned. They could just get on with it and conceal their nationality. For English, especially London, comics – no chance! The orchestra pit was covered over with chicken wire for ominous reasons.

Band call over, back to digs for an attempt at lunch then a walk around Sauchiehall Street which still had trams rattling people to and fro. I know it was all in the mind, but everyone seemed to be looking at me with that menacing *'See you!'* look. The clock whizzed round and suddenly it was time to get ready for the first house. Jimmy, his brother Peter, and Eli had arrived and were in a sombre mood. Jimmy was going through half a cigarette with one drag. He was not known for bottling out but there was a definite tenseness that I had never noticed before.

The orchestra started and made my temples throb with the extra surge of blood forced around by a pounding heart. The dancers were on and I was next! Check trumpet valves, tap shoes, for any proud screws, hair, teeth … flies! Right! – here we go.

I was genuinely surprised that I got a fair hearing. I suppose my Yorkshire accent got me off the hook. They adored my

Jerry Lewis impression and, coupled with the tap-dance, I got away with it. Very well, in fact. That really was a big relief and took a lot of the weight off the rest of the week. However, I now had to change into my policeman's outfit for Jimmy's 'First Night' sketch which closed the first half. Again, the audience were polite, they didn't laugh much but neither did they heckle. It was the same for the second sketch in the second half which immediately preceded the top of the bill.

Slim Whitman was a Country and Western cowboy singer with some big hits behind him. The hot one at the time was 'Rose Marie', which he performed with a yodel on the MaRIE bit and played his guitar left-handed. He stormed 'em.

In all honesty, the week went by without drama … until second house on Friday. This was the notorious house. One of the reasons being the Scottish licensing laws. After the interval there would be no more booze available that night. The pubs were shut before the end of the show and, barring private deals, that was it! Consequently, that second house interval was the last-ditch watering hole. The heavy boozers would have trays piled high with whiskys and double chasers – 'Same again, hen'. And again. And again…

By the time the second half started, they were glowing with confidence and their tolerance level was seriously diminished.

I had gone really well with my single act, to the extent of cheers and whistles and our first sketch had been endured in comparative silence. I was quite confident about the second half until I saw JJ giving me a knowing look which said his experience of previous visits didn't allow any room for celebrations at this point. He was mentally putting in my gum shield and handing me shin pads and crash helmet.

The aforementioned interval was taking place out there while I was changing into the long overcoat, hat, wig and locating various necessary bits of paraphernalia.

Jugglers opened the second half and were received politely. Jimmy's music, 'Liebesträume', set this classic show-business experience on its way. He ambled on stage with his cigarette and faltering walk and started to talk. Even with his Stockton-on-Tees accent he was now an intolerable sassenach and 'We came tae heeerr Slim Whitman!' was heard from the audience.

Eli's entrance meant nothing and the atmosphere was quiet but hostile. There were a couple of unintelligible hecklers which froze the audience even more. Then! it started. A hissing from the upper circle which permeated through to the circle ... then to the stalls. Two thousand five hundred people hissing. Jimmy went through the dialogue like a racing commentator and my cue, which was normally eight minutes into the sketch, came up in one! 'The lodger got more meat than your father got!' On I went in my outrageous outfit. They gave us a fleeting chance then started the hiss again ... augmented by a slow hand clap. Although it could be explained as impatience to see Slim Whitman, the hostility of the moment was matching up to the worst stories we had heard about the place. We finished an eighteen-minute routine in four minutes flat without missing a word! Our exit was jeered and we omitted a second bow.

The way back to our upstairs dressing room was past the only one on ground level. The Star's room. As we filed past it, out came Slim Whitman in just his cowboy shirt and cowboy socks. His wispy legs bore out the reason for calling him Slim. We passed by under his nose, Jimmy first with a half-smoked cigarette when he normally went through two, Our Eli lurching behind him, six-foot-nothing and three stones wet through. Me in my long coat and wig, followed by Jimmy's brother Peter with his single leg and crutch. Whitman's eyes widened and he demanded, 'Hey! What's going on here?' JJ took another drag at his fag and answered, 'YOU are!'

We slunk back to our rooms and made all the 'never again' promises to ourselves.

Next day, even the old warhorse himself had almost lost his

voice. We soldiered on through the two performances and avoided the fearsome hiss and slow hand clap, but had the hamper packed and into the car and away before Slim had got anywhere near 'Rose Marie'.

Unbeknown to us, that was our last performance at Glasgow Empire. It was later demolished in favour of an office block.

I have visited the location many times since and relieved that awesome four minutes, resisting the temptation to sing 'I'm still here' in case a passer-by dropped a wee bawbee into my hat! It's the one and only time I've been cheered and jeered in the same show. I don't recommend it for anyone with a dodgy heart.

Apart from that incident, I never saw Jimmy James get flustered at any time. That was one of the things that impressed me. No matter how the comedy was going, he carried on with apparent confidence. He would say, 'I know it's funny, you know it's funny, last week it was funny, last night it was funny, so if they don't laugh tonight, *they're* wrong!'

He also developed his own language. If a nutter visited the dressing room (and there were plenty) he would size him up and say, 'My, my, you're tall enough to be a policeman, aren't you?' This meant to us 'This chap's a nutcase.' The visitor would take it as a compliment and no harm was done.

When boring visitors came and settled in, he would say to Peter, 'I'm just going to check the hamper,' and leave. This meant 'Get rid of 'em.' Peter would then usher them out with his untrained diplomacy and again there was no bad feeling.

On stage, he was forever exploring new avenues of comedy and we two stooges had to try and go along with him or 'How are we going to discover new material if we don't try?' When an exploratory probe led us nowhere and he decided to abandon it, he would look at me and say, 'How are you keeping? All right?' This meant 'Where are we?' I then had the task of bringing us back to the script.

The famous box routine started as a two-minute gag told to Jimmy by Dickie Valentine in the dressing room. Jimmy immediately took up the idea and sent Eli for a shoe box. The two-minute gag grew and grew and became a classic piece which lasted up to twelve minutes of beautiful nonsense and is still very funny to this day.

The premise of a supposedly sane man trying to sort out two weirdos and finally becoming the daftest of all three was a great recipe for laughs. One critic wrote, 'The humour of Jimmy James and Co. came over the footlights in suede clogs.' A poignant assessment of the way JJ and Co. appealed to all classes of audience.

We also collected many strange digs stories whilst touring the Moss's. In Brighton, Eli, Peter and I were sharing the same bedroom. Three single beds. First morning there was a knock on our door and the landlady came in. Unfortunately she picked on Peter's bed and asked him what he wanted for breakfast – twice. (Peter was rather deaf.) In our half-sleep we heard him say 'I'll have some porridge, luv.' She replied, 'Sorry dear, we haven't got porridge, but we've got cornflakes, Rice Krispies, Weetabix, Shredded Wheat or All Bran. Then there's eggs, boiled scrambled or poached, sausages, bacon, fried bread, toast, fruit juice, tea or coffee, so what would you like?'

'I'll have some porridge, luv!'

That woke us up.

The very same digs had an outside lavatory, to get to which you had to go through the kitchen. Eli was unfortunately taken short in the night and had to find his way downstairs and through the kitchen, but the door was locked. He tried a few times to open it but no luck. He spent the rest of the night in agony. The next morning the landlady gave us all our marching orders. 'One of you three tried to get into my bedroom last night.' Eli almost exploded, if you'll pardon the expression.

Our greatest digs experience was in Liverpool. We were playing the Empire for a week and it was my job to take band call on Monday morning and set up the dressing room, then fix my accommodation. On this occasion, Eli asked me to fix him up also as he and the others were only going to arrive in time for the show. Jimmy, his wife Emmy and his brother Peter were all fixed up at the Lord Nelson Hotel nearby. After the band rehearsal I asked the stage doorkeeper where I might get some decent accommodation and he sent me to a Mrs Darcy just up the road on Lord Nelson Street. Off I went and found the correct house, only about a hundred yards away, and knocked on the door. Waited. It seemed pretty lifeless. Knocked again. Checked I had got the right number. Yes. Looked up and down the terraced row as a double confirmation. I definitely had the correct address. As I was about to return to the theatre and start again, I heard a sound from the house. It was a sort of slap-slap-*cough*, slap-slap-*cough*. The door latch clicked and slowly, the door opened. A lady's face peered through the three-inch gap allowed by the safety chain. The cough dislodged the ash from the dangling cigarette as she asked:

'Are you looking for rooms?'

'Yes. I'm appearing at the Empire this week.'

'All right, luv, you can have number nine.'

'There will be another chap coming later; can you fix him up as well?'

'He can have number ten. Have you eaten?'

'No.'

She wrestled with the chain and let me in. The slap-slaps were made by carpet slippers which had the heel backs trodden down turning them into flip-flops. The head scarf wrapped around curlers completed the cartoonist's idea of a typical landlady. She showed me into a fusty sitting room with a small table and an open fire.

Three pieces of coal were trying valiantly to support one

struggling flame but William Hill would give you a thousand to one against.

I sat down to write a letter home and was feeling pretty lonely when the landlady came into the room and asked, 'Are you looking for rooms?'

I wasn't sure if she was winding me up. Alas, she wasn't.

'Yes, you said I could have number nine.'

'Yes, you can.'

'And the other chap who's coming later.'

'He can have number ten. Have you eaten?'

'No. I thought you were making something.'

'All right, dear.' She slapped out.

I carried on writing whilst the fire lost its battle.

She brought in a plateful of something with dumplings. I think there was a bit of tomato there amongst the gravy and some sort of meat – or fish. The dumplings were the last experiment before Blu-Tack was discovered. Grease rings floating in the gravy were pretty but stomach-churning. There was nowhere to get rid of it. The fire was out and I hadn't been shown the geography of the house in order to flush it away. It may have been possible to dig it into the potted palm's earth but the plant was already struggling, possibly from previous meals. If only there had been a dog. I finished my letter and decided to post it. As I left the 'dining' room I was met by her ladyship, who asked, 'Are you looking for rooms?'

'Yes, I'm in number nine ... and my friend's in number ten.'

'Have you eaten?'

'Yes, but you overfed me.'

I left and posted my letter, had a wander around some shops and went to the theatre for some trumpet practice.

Jimmy, Eli and Peter arrived as it was almost showtime. I explained to Eli about the digs and wondered if we ought to try somewhere else. Eli was happy to take a chance. The shows went well and we set off up Lord Nelson Street to find our lodgings. The house was dark, not a suggestion of a light anywhere. I knocked and we waited. It was a perfect re-enactment of my first encounter. After a good five minutes a light came on and the slap-slap-*cough* routine assured me of the right address. Face and fag through the slightly open door. 'Are you looking for rooms?'

'Yes, I'm the one who came earlier and you said I could have number nine.'

'Yes, that's right, dear.'

'And my friend is in number ten?'

'Yes, dear. Have you eaten?'

'No, we've just finished the show at the Empire.'

She fiddled with the chain again and let us in. We went into the dining room and my dinner was still there. The fire was still out and the potted palm had wilted further.

'Would you rather come into the breakfast room? The fire is still going.'

'Yes, please,' avoiding the explanation of the untouched entrée.

We sat and chatted as we heard the crackle of frying from the kitchen. She emerged with two plates containing one fried egg each. The fat turned them into spirit levels. You could tell which way the table leant. 'I'll bring you some bread to dip in the fat.'

We actually ate the eggs and eventual fried bread having had nothing else all day.

'Good night, luv!'

'Good night.'

I found number nine, two flights up, and opened the door. I fumbled for the light switch and was aware of somebody snoring away under a heap of blankets. There was a pair of huge boots on the floor and a smell of diesel oil. I closed the door quietly and came face to face with Eli.

'There's somebody already in my room,' I whispered.

'W-w-wait t-t-till you s-s-see mine.'

We went into number ten and it was empty. But I mean *empty*. No bed, no chairs, no carpet. Nothing, but bare floorboards.

I went downstairs to check with the landlady.

'Are you looking for rooms?'

I explained our predicament and she gave me some clean sheets! All we needed now were beds and mattresses. No chance.

We attempted sleep sitting with our backs against the wall, then rolling up the sheets for pillows, lying on the boards and using our towels and pyjamas for pillows. None of these ploys worked for long. Sheer exhaustion put us out for a while, but she came in at 5 a.m. to ask us what time we wanted calling in the morning. We said, 'The chap in number nine wants waking now,' then jammed our door shut.

This marvellous fiasco was explained the next day when our landlady phoned the stage doorkeeper and complained that he hadn't sent anybody. Apparently, her daughter had taken over the boarding house when Mum's marbles had wandered a little, but was on holiday and the stage doorman hadn't been informed. Mrs Darcy, we love you! Have you eaten?

Whichever town we played, JJ & Co. liked to drive home after the show on Saturday night, no matter how far. At the end of our week in Brighton, everyone piled into his American Dodge, a big powder-blue limo which had a Mafia ring to it. Tinted windows, ostentatious grill and white wall tyres. Bugsy James and Co. piled into it and roared off towards Stockton-on-Tees, three hundred miles away. Jimmy would drive first and Eli would take over if necessary. On one particular occasion, in foul weather, Eli was negotiating his way through Peterborough in the early hours of the morning. He couldn't find his way through in a northerly direction and had passed the same place a couple of times. There was no one about as the rain was coming down in a way that would have started Noah buying wood. Tempers were rising when Eli spotted a sole pedestrian walking hunched-up to avoid the collected rain in the brim of his trilby pouring down his neck. Eli swung the big Dodge over to him and wound down the window. "S-s-scuse me ... c-c-could you t-t-tell m-me how t-to g-g-get on the r-r-road n-n-north?'

The sodden stranger looked at Eli long and hard then stammered back, 'A-A-A-A'. Eli wound the window up and said 'F-f-f-forget it!' and roared around Peterborough twice more.

Peter with his one leg and crutch always sat in the back with Jimmy's wife. Jimmy and Emmy's son was James Casey, head of light entertainment for BBC Radio Manchester, who was responsible for the *Clitheroe Kid* series, Les Dawson's series, Ken Dodd, and who later on did a few series with me and of course many more, writing most and co-writing others. He wrote most of his father's scripts for radio but sadly had just had a very serious car accident and almost died. Working too hard and driving home to Liverpool every night caused him to have a momentary lapse of concentration and he went off the road and was concussed for a few hours before he was found. He had lost a lot of blood and was in a critical condition for quite some time.

This had shaken his family and friends, and falling asleep at the wheel was high in everyone's mind. No one more than Peter. Each time the 'home run' was attempted, he would keep tabs on the driver, whilst clinging to the straps that cars used to have for aiding passengers as they pulled themselves out of their seats – one in his right hand and one in his left, almost swinging in the centre of the back seat ... whistling! His was a tuneless whistle, no recognizable melody whatsoever. A wide vibrato ranging over three notes at best, repeated and repeated. Rather like a badly played musical saw. Two hours of this was no great help to a driver, but Peter thought he was playing his part in keeping him awake. After two and a half hours of this monotonous warble, JJ said over his shoulder, 'Can't you whistle us that other one you know?'

In his deafness, Peter often came out with some cracking lines which bore no relation to the situation or to what was being said. One day I was playing my guitar in JJ's dressing room, Peter had brewed the tea and Jimmy and Eli were discussing the racing form for the next day's meeting. Jimmy looked at me and asked what tune I was playing. ' "Swingin' Shepherd's Blues".' Peter had missed it and raised his eyebrows which meant 'What did you say?' I repeated ' "Swingin' Shepherd's Blues".' Peter muttered, 'Crikey, have they opened that place up again?' (The Shepherd's Bush Theatre had been closed for some time.)

On another occasion, in a restaurant, Jimmy noticed the polished maple floor and said, 'You could hold a dance here, couldn't you?' Peter replied, 'No thanks, I've had plenty!'

Having had only one leg for many years, Peter had acquired a friend in Northampton who had lost the 'other' leg and was the same shoe size. They used to buy a pair of shoes between them. 'I'd like to try a pair of brogues this time – do you fancy some?'

One of the few times Jimmy was in the theatre for a Monday morning band call was at the Gaumont Southampton. Petula Clarke was top of the bill and was in her dressing room. Her band parts were last in line and it was our turn to rehearse. I caught the twinkle in JJ's eyes as he winked at the resident conductor and handed out Pet's music. In his own inimitable style he busked through 'Shoes to Set my Feet A-Dancing', 'May Each Day' and was about to launch into her latest hit, when Joe 'Piano' Henderson, her accompanist, came frothing over, followed by a tearful Petula.

'Mr James, you're doing some of our numbers.'

'Pardon?'

' "May Each Day", "Shoes to Set my Feet A-Dancing" – they are Pet's big hits.'

'Ah well, you see, our Eli's got himself into the pop scene. I thought you knew. He's in his dressing room now, recovering. The fans have just ripped all his clothes off at the stage door.'

The penny still hadn't dropped. He discussed the situation 'seriously' and eventually agreed to relinquish Eli's strangle-hold on the pop market and return to his 'Bless This House' 'B' side.

Pet caught on when she noticed her band parts were already in the pit and did the 'You-you-you' bit. They cuddled and I saw the impish grin of the prankster I had heard so much about.

Incidentally, one of the other songs Jimmy suggested in his act was 'I'll Walk Beside You'. He would then take one look at Eli and hastily add 'Maybe not! If I walk beside him I'll be on my own coming back!'

During these two years of touring variety I met up with Don Smoothey, part of the Smoothey and Layton double act. Don had kindly invited me to stay with his family if I was ever down in London. He didn't sound *too* surprised when he answered the phone to this little Yorkshire voice informing him that 'I'm in London for a couple of days and I wondered if …?'

'Sure, mate! We'll set a bed up for you.'

I stayed with Don and Joan spasmodically for around two years and became part of the family. I shall never forget their selfless generosity.

My musical roots: Grandad (*middle row, fifth from left*), bandmaster and cornet soloist supreme, 1913.

The proud parents: Mam and Dad on our front step in Scholes, 1932.

I revisited our old house many years later – 't' coyle hoyle' was still there too!

'By a Dutch Canal' with the Nora Bray School in 1943. Mam made my suit.

'Tantalizing Mother' with Tony Lester as the Dame at Cleveleys in 1947.

With Mam during my first summer season at Cleveleys.

Another sketch in a 'mam-made' suit!

Uncle Alec's greengrocery wagon – which kept me going whilst 'resting' in the early days – revisited.

Happy days with great and talented friends.

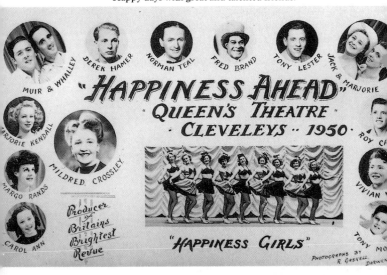

MUIR & WHALLEY · DEREK HAMER · NORMAN TEAL · FRED BRAND · TONY LESTER · JACK & MARJORIE

"HAPPINESS AHEAD"
"QUEEN'S THEATRE"
CLEVELEYS · 1950 · ROY CL

MARJORIE KENDALL · MILDRED CROSSLEY · ROY CL

MARGO RANDS

CAROL ANN

Producer
of
Britains
Brightest
Revue

"HAPPINESS GIRLS"

VIVIAN

TONY MO

PHOTOGRAPHS BY
R. GASNELL
DARWEN

'Castle, 2498944!' (*front row, second right*). Glory days in the RAF, first in Wilmslow, then in Aberdeen.

Out of the RAF and into a cat suit! *Dick Whittington*, 1952.

Great days with the incomparable
Jimmy James and Our Eli.

Walter Cartmell, a Blackpool fish
merchant, played a big part in
forwarding my career.

Sunday Night at the London Palladium, re-guesting as stooge to Jimmy
James with (*left to right*) musical director Cyril Ornadel, Bruce Forsyth,
J J and Our Eli.

With Dickie Valentine (*left*) and Billy Butlin at a Variety Club lunch.
It was through Dickie, a great pal, that I got my first big TV break on
Saturday Spectacular.

After my first Royal Command Performance, 3 November 1958, Eartha
Kitt rewarded me with a kiss on the cheek.

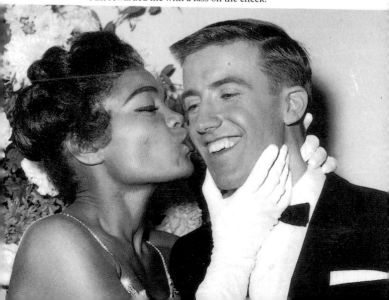

A headline writer's dream: 'Roy Castle Opens in Cape Town'!

6

The Poor Fish Bites Back

Towards the end of my stay in JJ & Co. we worked on the bill with Dickie Valentine. He was *the* big home-grown star at the time. As a singer in the Ted Heath orchestra, alongside Lita Rose and Denis Lotis, he had many hits and also did a stint of impressions whilst the young dancers would clamour around the stage and go quite wild with ecstasy. He eventually left the Heath band and went solo, topping the bill in all the major theatres and packing them in everywhere. JJ & Co. were booked to appear with him at the New Theatre, Oxford. I had watched Dickie many times at the Winter Gardens Ballroom, Blackpool, and even the Beach Ballroom, Aberdeen, whilst I was in the RAF. I was a fan!

I knew he impersonated Jerry Lewis and had already planned my four minutes without it. He asked to see me on the Monday morning and very gently broached the subject of impressions. I told him I wasn't doing any and although surprised, he was relieved at not having to play the heavy. In fact, it was a great favour to me because I was forced to come out from behind the mask and try my own personality, such as it was.

Dickie became a great friend and encouraged me with my singing. He had heard me doodling in the dressing room and was impressed. I couldn't help remembering Mildred Crossley and 'It's a shame your voice didn't come back'. The vocal healing process began right there.

Dickie was about to star in a TV special called *Saturday Spectacular*. It was live and still in black and white. He mentioned my name to the producer, Brian Tesler, who was the bright young director of the day and has since proved his talent all the way to the top. He came to Oxford to see the show and immediately offered me a spot in the *Saturday Spec*. I was given seven minutes for my own solo to be followed by a four-minute duet with Dickie. Eleven minutes' exposure in the prime slot of the week. This was what you could call *the* big break. It could equally possibly be *the* big flop. Memories of being turned down at the Windmill kept flashing across my mind.

We rehearsed for a few days prior to the show and I was introduced to a whole new world of show business. During the meal breaks I was ooohing and aaahing as I recognized well-known television faces who were eating and drinking just like ordinary people. Dickie introduced me to many as a bright new talent which scared me a lot. I was feeling the pressure of having to come up with the goods for the first time in my life.

Saturday morning brought band call and another wonderful experience. The conductor was Jack Parnell, a tall, laid-back musician who played drums with the same Ted Heath Band in which Dickie sang and performed. Jack also had a bass baritone voice and occasionally sang jazz/swing numbers of which I would have been happy to have heard much more. He was now a conductor and was to remain so for a long time.

The orchestra included big names such as Kenny Baker, Eddie Blair, Don Lusher, Phil Seaman, Lenny Bush, Jackie Armstrong, Dave Goldberg, Stan Roderick and all the great names of the day. After rehearsing all week with Kenny Powell, a brilliant pianist who rolled his own in a sort of liquorice paper, the band suddenly brought a whole new dimension to the show. It remains one of the biggest thrills of my life.

I was doing my tuning-fork routine. 'Play your own accompaniment' as my fictional Yorkshire Grandad had advised me. 'Play your own accompaniment, then you're not fast to nowt nor nubdy' (nothing nor nobody). I tapped my tuning fork on the mike stand, as usual, placed the vibrating point on the mike itself to produce the humming note to which I was going to sing 'I Got Rhythm'. This had worked well in the theatre, but in the TV studios the first 'hum' had all the technicians who were wearing headphones screaming with pain. 'What have I done?' The whole studio seemed to have developed a violent headache and I was stepping over prostrate bodies in a vain attempt to find out what had happened. The bodyless voice from the control room explained, 'It's all right, we weren't expecting it, we'll be all right now – carry on.' Totally unnerved, I carried on with my routine, causing no more damage to the future of ATV.

Being 'live', the appearance received instant reaction, and another rung of the ladder had been negotiated. Apparently the theatrical impresario Bernard Delfont had seen it and was impressed enough to offer me a spot in a two-week variety bill at the Prince of Wales Theatre in the West End. Kathryn Grayson, the American singing film star, was to have been top of the bill, but she was taken ill and the second choice was none other than Dickie Valentine – which took a lot of the pressure away from my first West End appearance. Having had those two abortive auditions within a stone's throw of the Prince of Wales, this could be third time lucky.

Jimmy James was most gracious in letting me go, and I felt a great sadness in leaving the illustrous set-up which had given me tremendous experience and many memories. Our last performance together was at the New Theatre, Coventry, and Dickie Valentine recorded our 'act' from the dressing room tannoy system. The sound quality was atrocious but it was the only memento I ever had of our two years together in an actual theatre.

The Prince of Wales stint was very successful for me and I received good crits and sometimes, in restaurants, I heard people mention my name without knowing I was there. 'Did you see this kid Roy Castle? He's certainly got it!' I was very happy to have 'it' whatever 'it' was. After the reception I received on the opening night I was approached by the Grade Organization 'with a view to representing' me. My sole and personal manager was to be? ... Sydney Grace! Not even a mention of an audition at the Windmill! I was *in* again. Experience kept me cautious and I dared not let my hopes get ahead of me. Syd and I talked and terms were agreed. Really, it was an offer I couldn't refuse: he would not take a percentage of my wages unless I earned £100 or more per week. So – if I earned £99, I got £99 ... if I earned £100, I got £90! The future certainly looked rosy. Topping all this was the temple-bursting news that I had been chosen to appear in the next Command Performance at the Coliseum, attended by Her Majesty the Queen and the Duke of Edinburgh – it was roman candles time again.

Meanwhile, I had a couple of weeks' provincial variety with my single act, now promoted up the bill a little. The second of these weeks was at the Sheffield Empire, where one night I came near to wrecking the whole of my future. One of my show-off steps during my tap routine was a walking step which took me from one side of the stage to the other tapping four times with each foot. It was an applause getter and as the audience showed their enthusiasm, and as I was looking out front giving them the Jerry Lewis laugh, I bumped into the proscenium arch, which got a roar. Good show business. However, first house Monday, I found I had misplaced my

contact lenses and had to judge my 'walk' by the footlights –
no real problem, but during the rehearsal I failed to notice
there was a slight cutaway where the stage met the 'pros arch'
and as I hit the side of the stage and stepped back, there was
nothing there. The next thing I knew, the pit drummer was
looking down at me. I had landed in his lap, missing all those
cymbal stands and accessories which could have gone through
me like a kebab stick. All I sustained was a sprained finger,
but the funny moment was when the drummer looked at me
as if to say 'You're not going to be doing this every time, are
you?' Six weeks' rehearsal couldn't have perfected the
manoeuvre any better. I found my lenses for the second house
and half expected the drummer to be wearing a hard hat!
However, that could have put paid to my Command
Performance, indeed my career. I often get cold shudders
when I remember it.

The big day arrived – 3 November 1958 – and my emotions
were in the jangle box again. I had been given my band call
time and warned not to be late as this would inconvenience
the whole operation. I just about made it and was in a fair old
froth as I finally found the stage door. Clinging to guitar,
trumpet, suitbag and gripper, I bundled through and
introduced myself to the stage doorkeeper. He thumbed
through some papers and arrived at my name, 'Carsell', and
directed me to the allotted dressing room. On my way there
an official wearing headphones approached me.

'Roy Castle?'

'Yes.'

'Would you like to come on stage, we are ready for your
rehearsal.'

'Certainly.' Heart starts to rev up!

I followed the young chap to the stage and was introduced
to the conductor, Cyril Ornadel. He asked for my music
which was in my trumpet case together with my towel and
pyjamas. All had to come out in my haste. As the pyjamas

came out, there was a big laugh from an unlit auditorium. I didn't know it, but most of the other performers were sitting out there, chatting or waiting for their turn. I was pink about the gills as I started into my tuning fork routine. Managing to overcome this unnerving start, I rehearsed almost normally and got enthusiastic applause from some of the cream of showbiz. Had I known who was out there, I would have gone to pieces, I'm sure of it. That little lad from a one-up-and-one-down in Scholes mixing with the likes of Eartha Kitt, Pat Boone, Harry Secombe, Tommy Trinder, Bruce Forsyth, Max Bygraves, Norman Wisdom ... and many many more. They were all very nice to me and welcomed me as a fellow performer.

We were taught how to take our bow to the audience, one bow to the Royal Box, then off. The finale ensemble had also to be rehearsed, then it was time to relax, trying to avoid the jitters. Comics were all wandering around muttering their routines to themselves, jugglers were practising feats they had worked for years as the pressure of the approaching public examination neared. A long wait, then *one* crack at it. Of all the testing times so far, this was easily the worst. The number of times I oiled my trumpet valves escapes me. Check Jerry Lewis wig in jacket pocket – six times; run through song lyrics – ten times. Tuning fork in pocket? Guitar in tune? Plectrum in pocket?

I had arranged a ticket for my mother in the Royal circle about ten yards from the Royal Box (Dad was still not well enough to travel). Uncle Alec and Aunty Bessie had brought Mam down and, although I couldn't run to two more tickets, they stayed in order to take Mam back the next day.

'This is your half-hour call, show goes up in thirty minutes, ladies and gentlemen.'

Check trumpet valves again, taps, guitar, accessories in pockets. Song lyrics. *I'm not ready, I need more time.*

'Fifteen minutes.'

Roman candles.

'Five minutes.'

Check everything again. Mouth is dry. What were those words again? *Help!*

'Overture and beginners, please.'

Over the dressing-room relay system we heard the orchestra play 'God Save the Queen' and the show was under way.

My spot was in the second half so the tension was unbearable. Through the suppressed anxiety, we heard Max Bygraves getting laughs. All other comics were listening intently in case there was any clash of material. My turn got nearer and nearer the edge of the cliff. Second half under way and all the performers who had been on were relaxed and relieved and saying things like 'They're great out there, they'll love you.' This didn't mean a thing. *If one of my trumpet valves doesn't come back up again, I'm dead. (Better check them again.)* I followed Antonio, a big star flamenco dancer, very popular at the time. Max Bygraves went on as his applause was finally fading and introduced me. This was it! *'If the parents of this boy are in the audience...?'* Echoes of Wally Wood and the lamppost song at Huddersfield Palace. *Mam was out there.*

I walked out and was completely fazed by the magnificent Royal Box housing Her Majesty and the Duke ... looking at ME. The audience also threw me as I had never seen a huge house full, in formal dress. No one had ever mentioned this; it was a wonderful but awesome sight. Time to sing as the conductor looked at me expectantly – 'The Whole Town's Talkin' About the Jones Boy' – I remembered the words and the trumpet sat pleasantly and the valves came back up again. Generous applause. My guitar 'bit' involved a little humour and I was one of the first to dare to guy Elvis Presley and the rock 'n' roll bunch. My remarks were centred around the three-chord trick and the gyrating hips. At one point, Prince Philip guffawed all by himself. The whole audience looked at him, then back at me and then laughed. I am certain it was that very moment which launched me into the big time. The rest of that short routine got good laughs and my Jerry Lewis tap routine fairly sizzled. I finished to solid applause as I took my bow to the audience and one to the Royal Box and off I went in a blue haze. The other performers in the wings were all applauding as I staggered through them. I floated back towards my dressing room in a completely drained but thankful state, when Harry Secombe raced after me, grabbed my arm and dragged me back to the stage. 'Take another bow, son, they love you.' He eased me back out there and I had to take another bow to audience and Royal Box ... and *Mam was out there.* The little girl who won the talent competition but wasn't able to pursue her career, finally watched her son perform for Royalty. Melodramatic, I know, but for me, it meant everything. I was asked to join the line-up after the show and was introduced to the Royals. Whenever I'm asked by interviewers what my greatest moment in show business was – look no further. It would not be possible to have such a big leap forward ever again. 'You *shall* go to the ball.'

I was besieged by journalists and photographers after the presentation and I was in dreamland. 'What did the Queen say to you?' 'What are your plans for the future?' 'Had you any idea you were going to go so big?' Posing for photographs whilst other artists slapped me on the back. Eartha Kitt kissed my cheek – *click!*

My Mam was able to come with me to the showbiz party afterwards at the Talk of the Town which had been reconstructed into a plush night-spot from the old Hippodrome Leicester Square. The very place I had originally auditioned for Val Parnell. We sat with Bruce Forsyth, his wife and friends, Bernie and Diane Coral. It was a treat to watch Mam's face as well-known stars came over to hand on congratulations. 'Aren't you proud of him?' etc.

Next day, the press were still very interested and

photographed me, Mam, Uncle Alec and Auntie Bessie celebrating, mainly for the *Huddersfield Examiner*. The snap of Eartha Kitt kissing my cheek was on the front page of the *Daily Mirror*. We wallowed in reading all the accounts of the show and kept quoting bits as we discovered them. Self-indulgence was rife but, to us, it was unbelievable.

However, the fairytale was to be short-lived as the future unfolded.

Brian Tesler had booked me for a TV series with the title *New Look*. A revue type of show with musical numbers and sketches featuring hitherto unknown or little-known talent. Bruce Forsyth was to have been in it but had just had a tremendous success as compère of *Sunday Night at the London Palladium*.

New Look included Joyce and Lionel Blair, Joe Baker and Jack Douglas, Gillian Moran, Stephanie Voss, Ronnie Stevens and me. Jack Parnell was our musical director.

We had a load of laughs and enjoyed every minute of the series which was well received. I was mainly used as a song-and-dance man but had my fair share of sketch work too. Good television experience. This led to my being offered my own show for ATV, 'live' from Hackney Empire which had been converted into a TV studio. Alec Fyne set it up and booked Joyce and Lionel as regulars and included Irene Handl as wardrobe mistress-cum-stage doorkeeper. We were to have a special guest each week. Our title? *Castle's On the Air*! We were all very excited about it and I thought it was going to be the ace in my career pack.

The show turned out to be a pale version of *New Look* and was not received well. My association with Jimmy James led many people to believe I was a comic which I certainly wasn't and never had been. The dance routines were mostly with Joyce and Lionel, which made them into production numbers, our bits with Irene were exactly that – bits – and accommodating our special guest took a chunk out of the show. In all honesty, the show didn't need me! It didn't seem to get anywhere and was a non-event. As the Royal Command wasn't televised when I did it, this was the first chance the public at large had to see me as a solo performer and it was a great disappointment. My bubble burst.

Within ten months of my greatest high, I was having my deepest low. Phrases like 'Not star quality' were ringing in my ears. 'You should specialize' was one fairly regular criticism. My best talent really was ballad and jazz singing. Jack Parnell was very impressed when I sang in *New Look* and even *Castle's On the Air* but rock 'n' roll, Elvis Presley and Bill Hayley had blown that kind of singing right out of the water. I made one single for Pye Records entitled 'Mr Music Man' and written by Joe 'Piano' Henderson. It was a good song and the lyrics were about a lovesick youth in a 'Play it again Sam' mood. I gave it my best heartrending treatment. The Artists and Repertoire man, Michael Barclay, came down from the control room and asked me to put some life into it. 'Give it some zing! Smile through it. Be happy!' The lyrics were:

Mr Music Man
Your song is breaking my heart
Mr Music Man
Your love song tears me apart, etc.

How can anyone sing those lyrics and be jolly? It's like saying 'Hooray, I've got beri-beri!' It wasn't a hit or even a near miss. Joe Henderson was hidden away listening to it and stayed hunched up as he left.

'Shame your voice never came back!'

My confidence was now at the bottom of all twelve steps in my Grandma's cellar. A flash in the pan. *'They all have to come down again!'*

Sydney Grace had booked me into the pantomime at London Palladium, and rehearsals started at this time:

Humpty Dumpty, starring Harry Secombe. I was to be Simple Simon. The show was peppered with stars such as Alfred Marks, Paddy O'Neill, Gary Miller, Sally Smith, Svetlana, and many more.

I turned up imagining the worst. Everyone would have witnessed my pathetic TV series and flop recording. I was cowed and embarrassed.

Harry Secombe welcomed me like a long-lost brother and when I started apologizing for myself he steam-rollered over my whingeing by telling me how often he had gone through similar troughs. 'They don't last long, Jim!' he said in his high tenor voice and gave me a mental rubdown with last week's edition of the *Stage*. His generosity and warmth put life back into me and I shall never forget how important that was. He could easily have said 'Tough! That's show business' and left me in deeper distress.

Humpty Dumpty – directed by Robert Nesbitt, the number-one man for most of the big shows, including the Royal Commands – proved to be one of the finest and most successful pantomimes the Palladium had ever produced.

I had a solo spot in which I found a clown's basket on stage, took out his costume and props and finished up doing his act, playing a cornet solo, wearing the leaning boots and finishing with a big boot dance and falling back into the basket. It was a tremendous hit, and put me right back in the driving seat. I even got a good mention from Milton Shulman!

Little did I know, but a certain young lady watched that show who was to play the most important part in the rest of my life.

One of the hernia operations I had had during National Service misfired and I had to have it re-done at the Hammersmith Hospital as soon as the panto was over. I was then booked for a tour of South Africa and Kenya. This was before the trouble really started and the Equity ban had not been imposed.

It seemed a good idea to travel to Cape Town by boat as the fourteen-day trip would help me to get over the operation. Geoff Sanders, my pianist, came with me and we boarded the *Stirling Castle* at Southampton. Life of luxury, here we come. Oh really? Ever heard of the Bay of Biscay? We had a thirty-three-degree list and for two days could only lie in our beds with a bowl of apples on the floor between us. The curtains swung out into the room as the apples rolled to one side of the bowl, then smashed against the porthole as the apples changed sides. Our cabin attendant had very little to do as the mère lifting of the head from the pillow set the whole world flying around like a released balloon.

Once Biscay had been negotiated we settled down to calm seas and sunshine which amazingly burnt the tops of our feet. Only amazing to first-time travellers, of course. We had the great man himself on board. Field-Marshal Viscount Montgomery of Alamein, who strutted about the ship with a book under his arm. He seemed very much in command as he paced up and down with straight back and piercing stare. One afternoon I was playing a German scientist at chess and Monty came by, stood to attention and observed the strategy. I moved my pawn and he said 'Hmmm, you've moved your pawn!' I was grateful for his advice. He didn't stay long but upon leaving he threw in his catch-phrase: 'Always win your battles, always win your battles.' I lost the chess game, albeit narrowly. I did, however, win the table tennis competition and had to receive my plaque from Monty himself. 'Always win your battles' was uppermost in my mind as I walked through the applauding cruisers and I was feeling quite proud to have won something in his eyes. He shook my hand and said, 'Table tennis player, are you?'

'Yes, sir.'

'Sign of a misspent youth!'

There was just no way of winning with the man, no wonder Rommel packed it in!

Approaching Cape Town at 5 a.m. on a sunny morning is breathtaking. Table Mountain with the cloudy white tablecloth hanging over it had all the cameras clicking. It was truly a sight to behold. As we docked and passed through customs, the press wanted to interview me but 'Could you wait until we have finished with Mr Montgomerree?' 'Certainly.' It was rather humid and sticky, but no matter. Once Monty was done, the photographer asked me to follow him to a special location a few yards away.

'Remember you had a photograph jumping over the railings at King's Cross Station as if on your way to South Africa?' This was true. 'Well, we'd like to follow it up as if you had jumped over Table Mountain.'

'OK.'

'Good. Would you like to stand on that wall and jump in the air, it will look as if you had jumped over the mountain from King's Cross.'

'OK.'

I got up on to this four-foot wall and on the other side was a 24-foot drop on to some railway lines. *Don't panic or show any kind of fright! Monty might be watching.*

'OK. Jump!'

I jumped, bringing my knees up – but the humidity had struck and instead of my trousers slipping over my knees, they clung on and wouldn't give. However, the stitching around the crutch did. I heard it go – then the camera snap – in that order! I landed and mentioned this to the photographer. He assured me: 'It will be all right, we'll touch it up in the dark-room.'

Next day the untouched-up picture appeared on the front page of the local newspaper with the headlines: 'Roy Castle Opens in Cape Town!' We did good business.

Cape Town, Johannesburg and Durban were all successful. I did a couple of Town Hall concerts for mixed audiences, as the trouble, although rumbling gently, had not really gathered any momentum. There were plenty of jokes with some of the waiters, like 'Come de uprisin' I'm havin' your car', but that was 34 years ago.

On our way home, we stopped off in Kenya for a two-week stint at The New Stanley Hotel in Nairobi, where they billed me as a 'FUNSTER'. How was I going to live up to *that*? There was also a military establishment a couple of miles down the road, and naturally, we were invited to pop in and give 'em a turn. No problem. After the noon performance at the military base, we were ushered into the Officers' Mess where they had organized some fish and chips to make us feel at home. A pint of beer each and that was our payment. Fair enough. Geoff downed his pint quickly and was immediately offered another which he gratefully accepted. The tee-hee joke being – this next pint was half whisky. Geoff drained most of it before he realized this, and the damage was done. Back at the hotel, he fell on his bed and was out. Eyes rolling and groaning, finally snoring.

As show time approached he was still in hibernation. I had to try and get him into his dress suit which was worse than trying to play giant bagpipes in a bath of spaghetti. 'I'll be all right', he grunted with closed eyes. In order to set up, he had to carry my guitar and trumpet through the diners and on to the stage, and place them under the piano; then we would be ready to begin. He made an attempt at this simple manoeuvre and bashed the first table's host with my guitar. As he apologized to him he clumped a lady on the other side of the aisle. All the way to the stage he left a trail of devastation, people clutching ears and wiping wine from dresses. He arrived at the grand piano and shovelled my instruments under it, then slumped on the stool. The piano lid was shut and he appeared to be sleeping.

The young MC wearing blue-tinted glasses and a thin moustache, announced the 'Funster from England – Roy Castle'. Geoff sprung into life, lifted the piano lid and played perfectly. I went wrong twice worrying about him. After the show he went straight back to sleep. I carried my own guitar back through the audience.

We returned to England in a real boneshaker of a plane which took ages.

Nineteen-sixty brought the summer season in Brighton Hippodrome with Frankie Vaughan topping the bill and Tommy Cooper second. The three King Brothers and I were somewhere in the middle. I was asked to play straight man to Tommy in a sketch called 'Look at the Buffalo'. It was total nonsense but Tommy was extremely funny in it and the experience was invaluable – one of the things I learned was that this class of comedy was completely out of sight for me. His build and facial expressions wewre unique and those water-blue eyes defied anyone to keep a straight face.

His entrance was a classic. The dancing girls opened the show dressed in shocking-pink and wielding ostrich-feather fans. To end their routine a staircase was revealed and they presented this figure in top hat and tails with his back to the audience. The orchestra struck up with 'Gimme the Moonlight'. Frankie's fans all screamed and stamped. He slowly turned around and, of course, it was Tommy. He came down the staircase and sang the song using the cane in an *almost* professional manner, bouncing it on the stage and catching it – desperately – with both hands. He threw the topper up and tried to catch it on his head, hit himself on the nose and spent a few bars feeling his snitch to see if he had drawn blood. To end the routine, he threw the cane from hand to hand eventually missing it and racing after it off stage. It took a whole chorus, and was hysterical.

Halfway through the summer, as I was hearing the show in my dressing room, Tommy's opening number stopped abruptly and there was a silence broken only by one of the musicians laughing. '*Ha!*' (That's all you get from musicians.)

Apparently what happened was due to a bit of stage joinering. When acts came to the theatre using apparatus such as trampolines or trapezes, holes had to be bored in the stage so the hooks could be inserted, and the fixtures tightened to make the apparatus safe. At the end of the week, the stage carpenter bunged the holes up again with, in those days, fish glue.

Tommy started 'Moonlight', bounced his cane on the stage, hit one of these bungs flush in the middle and knocked it through into the band room. The stick followed the bung and disappeared! Nobody in the audience laughed because Tommy was a magician and they thought this was a trick. But he had lost his prop for the rest of the routine.

I heard him coming up the steps and popped out to see what had happened. He told me: 'The stick just went through the stage. Straight through. Through the stage. Like that! ... I did a great ad lib.'

'What did you do?'

'I just pissed off!'

He tried out a new sketch he was going to perform on TV the following Sunday. It was about the husband coming home late, drunk, trying to keep it from his wife. Singing loudly outside. When she lets him in he has to try desperately to appear sober. Each time she leaves the room he goes legless again. It was just a series of being drunk and sober according to whether his wife was in or out, the tag being:

Wife: Darling you look tired, what you need is a good stiff drink.

Whereupon he was to do a straight back pratt fall. End of sketch, draw the tabs (curtains).

Tommy, in his wisdom, didn't employ an actress for the part of the wife. Instead, he asked one of the chorus girls to do it. She was thrilled but nervous.

Tommy had just paralysed 'em with his hat routine, so felt confident enough to plough into this new try-out sketch. It died. He didn't get a titter anywhere, try as he might – nothing! Everything hung on the tag. The girl prepared to deliver the line and Tommy prepared to fall back.

Wife: Darling you look tired. What you need is a good *soft* drink.

Tommy was halfway in to his fall and had to check himself. He looked at his 'wife' with disbelief and shouted '*Tabs*' out of the side of his mouth. The curtains closed to nothing and he had to get Frankie Vaughan to apologize for it in the finale!

Maybe that was the time he and his wife, Dove, found what was to be their favourite restaurant in Brighton. Apparently for many years they would always drive down there from their place in Chiswick and have Sunday lunch. However, one Sunday, they had a blazing row and Dove jumped in the car and drove down to Brighton on her own. She was seated in the middle of the restaurant by herself and just about to start the main course when a cab drew up outside and Tommy emerged wearing only his trousers. He walked through the diners and stopped at Dove's table and said, 'Where's my shirt?'

Eric Morecambe told me of a time he and Ernie spent a whole afternoon with Tommy Cooper discussing ad libs and heckle stoppers. They had gone through all the well-known stock answers and invented a lot more.

'Stand closer to the wall, that's plastered as well.'

'Why don't you put your teeth in backwards and bite your throat?'

'Close your mouth, they're looking for a third airport.'

'No school today?'

And so on.

That night, Tommy was working at a night club in

Manchester called 'Mr Smiths' and the lads were at the Palace. After their show they went to see Tommy's late night cabaret. The place was packed and Tom was roaring away when a waiter with a tray full of drinks tripped right in front of him and the lot went crashing to the floor with an almighty wallop. The crowd gave the traditional cheer while Eric and Ernie watched every possible ad lib pass through Tommy's mind. They waited for his 'put down' as he stared at the apologetic waiter. He took his time, and came up with

'That's nice.'

The lads went hysterical.

Tommy often gave tips in envelopes. 'There you are, have a drink on me.' When the recipient opened the amply filled envelope, it contained a tea bag.

After a late-night card game following a show at the London Palladium, he and his pals left through the stage door around 4 a.m. There was still one little hunched figure waiting for his autograph. Tommy gladly signed it as he looked up and down Great Marlborough Street, then said, 'Bit of a slight isn't it. Only *one*!'

His classic remark to Her Majesty the Queen after a Royal Variety Show is well known, but if you haven't heard it...

ER: Fine show.

TC: Thank you .... Thank you .... er, Your Majesty .... I recognize you now .... I don't quite remember the face, but I never forget a hat!

Then he did the unforgivable as she moved on to the next person. He called her back!!

TC: 'Scuse me, Your Majesty?

ER: Er, yes?

TC: Do you like football?

ER: Not particularly.

TC: Well, can I have your tickets for Wembley?

The rest of us would have finished up in the Tower for that one.

After the 'Look at the Buffalo' routine in Brighton he gave me a present. It was a pen with 'Look at the Buffalo' inscribed on it. When I took the cap off, there was no writing end inside. Joke or oversight, it is still one of my most treasured possessions. When he died in the middle of a television performance, I was watching him from my couch and I thought something was amiss as I had worked that particular routine with him and knew there was more to come. It must have been very hard for Dove but I don't think even Tommy could have thought that one up. In front of millions, most of them still laughing. A very special talent indeed.

More variety dates and TV shows followed that magical summer in Brighton, before I travelled to Manchester to repeat *Humpty Dumpty* at the Palace with virtually the same cast. Harry Secombe was again topping – in every sense. He was also booked for the following summer season at the London Palladium and I was approached with a view to being a part of the 'supporting cast' (you bet your boots). During the panto I worked on a possible running gag for the summer. The idea being to keep dashing on at different intervals, try and play 'The Flight of the Bumblebee' on my trumpet, mess it up and run off. Towards the end of the show, run on and play it straight through. Should be good. In between matinée and evening performance of *Humpty* I practised and practised the 'Bumblebee' until everyone was heartily sick of it. We were kept informed as different performers were added to the Summer Show. Marion Ryan, Ronnie Corbett, Jeremy Hawk, etc., but the second top hadn't yet been fixed.

I finally had 'Bumblebee' ready and only needed a bit more polish as that final 'name' was announced.

'EDDIE CALVERT! So you won't play your trumpet will you, Roy?'

Justice was done, though. After the opening night went

really well, Harry gave Eddie Calvert a congratulatory hug and broke two of his ribs. For six weeks he played 'Oh Mein paPPAAAAHHH!'

It also did me a big favour as I was forced into doing something different and a new routine evolved during the Season. No one could have written it, it just developed, like Jimmy James's box routine.

I started with 'How High the Moon', singing each part to different sections of the orchestra as I built up the intro then sang the song. Scat choruses led into a few snatched impersonations which eventually became a complete nonsense routine with my fingers. Impossible to describe but Spike Milligan liked it and that'll do me, folks.

This routine got me an invitation to go to New York and guest on the award-winning series *The Garry Moore Show*. Coast to coast. Roman Candles again. America! *If the parents of this boy are in the audience...*

7

'Our Talented British Friend'

In the US my versatility was accepted much more readily than at home. Almost everyone there was a 'triple threat': singing, dancing and acting was the norm. With my bits of humour and trumpet playing as well, I was hailed as 'Our talented friend from England'. I eventually guested on *The Garry Moore Show* forty-two times, working regularly with Carol Burnett who was a permanent member of the team, but destined for great things. Alan King was a guest on many occasions but my favourite show was when I was asked to duet with Mel Tormé. We sang a version of 'Let's Call the Whole Thing Off' as we decided our different pronunciations wouldn't work, so we sang scat in thirds. That was another one of my fondest memories and I was sorry when it was over.

Keely Smith was a guest on one of the shows and had just split from her husband Louis Prima. He was a trumpet player and she sang with his outfit in Vegas and the Catskills for many years. Now she was on her own. She smiled at me very nicely and asked me 'if I fooled around'. Being completely and utterly naive, I replied, 'Yes, and I play trumpet and tap-dance too!' She looked at me long and hard, then muttered, 'I just got *rid* of a trumpet player!' I shall never know what I missed.

I trotted back and forth to America whilst continuing my career at home featuring a few of my own TV shows. One of these included my guests Morecambe and Wise. We had been friends for many years hailing way back into the dark, unknown days and had many great times together. Once we were playing the Coventry Theatre along with Arthur Askey and the popular and sexy singer, Yana. The six-week run was highly successful and equally hilarious. Eric was staying with me and my pianist, Geoff Sanders, and we shared a large bedroom over a pub. Many times, the humour over supper wouldn't subside, and continued to erupt as we tried to sleep. All it took was one suppressed snort and we all exploded again, eventually not knowing what we were laughing at. The determined effort to calm down and try to sleep was high-tension stuff and any sound whatsoever would prolong the agony. Arthur Askey had told us a rather cheeky story about a 'bowser'.

A chap was having his hair cut opposite the Windmill Theatre in Soho and noticed these wig-like contraptions in plastic containers. 'What are they, then?'

'Well, sir, they are used by the strippers across the road. Wearing such scanty clothes, they have to shave the rude bits but, when they get a date, they use one of these bowsers.' The customer paid for his haircut and ordered two 'bowsers'.

'Shall I wrap 'em up?'

'No thanks, I'll eat 'em here!'

Pretty crude stuff in those days but it led to the reason for the follow-up. In the show, we were doing a sand dance based on Wilson, Keppel and Betty. Eric and I were to be Wilson and Keppel and Arthur was to be Betty. We wore sheet loincloths, fezzes and big Pancho moustaches. These became known as Bowsers. It was opening night and the lads had just done one of their routines, the karate sketch. 'Get out of that – you can't, can you?' followed by a short production number, then Wilson, Keppel and Arthur. It was a very quick change for Eric and I was helping as suit was flung off and sheet was hastily tied around him. The moustache was proving difficult to stick on.

'It's not gonna stay *on*!'

'It'll be all right, just leave it.'

Half of it sagged and he pressed it back.

'It's gonna go! Where's the glue?'

The production number was nearing its end.

'Come on – we're on.'

'It's not *safe*.'

'It'll be OK. Try and keep your lip still.'

Our music started and Eric and I made our closely assembled entrance. Hop-slide. Hop-slide. Hop-slide. Hop-slide, with arms in the teapot position. We then had to do a smart about-face. Eric's mouth was almost in my ear as he whispered, 'The Bowser's gone.'

We didn't get to sleep for quite some time *that* night.

Saturday night saw us all high-tailing it home for the weekend and, as I was leaving the stage door, Eric was being sung to by a short, stocky, sixtyish-year-old man created by 'Giles'. His wife was equally rotund and from her glowing expression, in seventh heaven as she listened to her husband's serenade. Eric caught my inquisitive gaze and gave me, as only Eric could, the 'The man's a fool' look. He then broke into the recital with 'Roy! Come and hear this song. It's a beauty! Just right for the next record.' He dragged me into the scene and instructed the chap to start again. This dumpy, toothless ballad singer turned out to have written a song about Yana, the singer in our show. 'It came to 'im overnight,' explained his 'agent'. Eric disappeared as the pair encircled me and he started to sing.

'Yana, wonderful Yana
Why do we all love you?'

Eric waved from his car as he shot off into the night wearing that supercilious grin.

As Arthur Askey emerged from the stage door, we re-enacted the scene. 'Arthur! Come and hear this song. Just right for your publishing company.' The minstrel started again, holding Arthur in a half-nelson arm lock. I waved goodbye as I screeched into the night trying to match Eric's parting grin.

The song turned out to be a well-established one referring to Amy Johnson's solo flight across the Channel, 'Amy Wonderful Amy'.

'It came to 'im overnoight!'

Yana dared not come out!!

When playing the Pavilion Theatre in Torquay in the early sixties, David Hughes, a ballad and operatic singer with a powerful voice, was top of the bill. The lads and I were in support, along with the jugglers, dancers and acrobats. Quite a big cast.

At the Monday morning band call, David approached Eric, Ernie and me with a request for a little help. 'I've introduced an Elvis Presley impersonation into my act and it goes a storm. The problem is, I have to do a quick change in the wings and needed someone to do a couple of minutes whilst I get ready.'

We looked at each other with a 'what kind of lumber is *this*' exchange. Eric pushed his glasses to his nose. 'Such as?'

'Well, last week the three King Brothers did a quick song.'

'A quick *song*?'

'Yeah – it worked a treat all week.'

'Ernie? Do we know a quick song?'

'We could sing "Near You".'

'Will "Near You" be all right, Mr Hughes?'

'Yes. I'd really appreciate it.'

'Say no more.'

Eric looked at us with his 'This could be fun' stare and we

carried on with our various band calls and unpacking.

The King Brothers were three smart young lads who played piano, bass and guitar and sang very well, but seriously. Ideal for the quick change. Our trio was a little different. As we were announced by David, I was dressed as a clown tramp with my cornet, Ernie was a lollipop-licking schoolboy and Eric was wearing a massive sombrero and carrying an untuned guitar.

The laughs were rolling in before we started the song. Eric gave us the 'chord' and we sang 'There's just one place for me'. Here we stopped whilst Eric fumbled around for this piece of paper, showed it to both of us and then we sang 'Near You'. And so it went on. David was now changed into his Presley outfit and was making 'OK, I'm ready' signs. We were roaring along and still had the guitar, cornet and lollipop chorus to come.

David was getting a little agitated on the side. 'I'm *ready*.'

'He's ready.' We carried on.

Suddenly, David must have leapt five feet in the air and landed almost by us, clutching his own guitar and posing for the recognition impact. Nothing!

We looked at him, Eric whispered, 'He's ready.' Handed the piece of paper round.

'Near you.' Big laugh.

David thanked us which meant 'That's enough', and we shuffled off. After the first house finished, David came to the room and said, 'It didn't quite work, did it?'

'Didn't it? Oh! Sorry.'

We were excused from repeating our little trio for the second house and all got home early.

'Pity, I thought we'd got a good little turn going there,' mused Eric as he pushed his glasses up his nose and left through the stage door into the Torquay night.

One day, during the week's rehearsal for my TV show in the

early sixties, Eric pulled me to one side and said, 'I'm bringing a fan of yours to the show on Sunday. She's a friend of the family and would like to meet you. All right, Sunshine?'

He pushed his glasses up on the bridge of his nose.

'Certainly,' I agreed.

'Be nice to her, she's a grand lass. She's in *The Sound of Music* at the Palace. She's a nun.'

No more was said until the day of the show at the studios in Wood Green – the old Empire – from which the Frank Randle show had been ejected, and I had the dressing room which housed Malcolm Mitchell's dog.

As I prepared for the countdown, there was a knock on my door. 'Are you decent?'

'Yes, come in.'

Eric came in with a young lady. I was expecting a shy young girl, perhaps with braces on her teeth, who would sit in the corner and giggle nervously. Not a bit of it. This elegantly beautiful young lady with blond hair swept back into a pony tail stood upright in fifth position – she was also a ballet dancer.

Eric announced, 'This is Fiona and she's in love with you!' then left.

We stood, transfixed, for ages it seemed. All we needed was the string orchestra in the background. Fiona blushed to the roots of her hair and smiled. No teeth braces. I was very struck, but had a show on my mind and can't honestly remember what we said. I just know I was very impressed. This was the young lady who had seen me as Simple Simon in the Palladium pantomime of *Humpty Dumpty*. Apparently while she was watching TV with the Family Morecambe, I had appeared on the programme, and she had said to Eric, 'If ever you get a chance to introduce me ...' – de-dah de-dah. Eric said, 'How much is it worth?' de-dah de-dah.

After this historic meeting Fiona rejoined Eric's wife and

sat in the audience. Following the show I invited everyone to a meal at the Lotus House in the Edgware Road – the 'in' place for showbiz folk at the time. My parents had come down from Blackpool so I thought I would make it a big night for them. I sat opposite Fiona and found myself making all the stupid heady young male remarks. She smiled with a sophisticated confidence which again scored points. I had flirted around in a small way compared to my mates, and never had serious thoughts of anything permanent, but my ears were definitely popping this time. However, I didn't make a move. I didn't want her to think I was a conquest merchant whose next approach would be 'your place or mine'.

The following week, I was in the Morecambe and Wise dressing room and Ernie, as a reciprocal gesture, invited me out to dinner with his wife Doreen, and would I like to bring my girlfriend?

'I don't have one at the moment.'

Eric was already dialling. 'Is that the Palace Theatre stage door? Good. Can I speak to Fiona Dickson, please? … Eric … Eric Morecambe … suit yourself. Hello? Fiona? You're going out to dinner. Get over here as soon as you can.'

The four of us ate Italian food, drank a little wine and I took Fiona back to her flat in Lennox Gardens. It was now the right time to ask her out as a duo. Our romance blossomed and I knew immediately that this was it for me. I told Fiona of my feelings but perhaps shouldn't have done as she must have suddenly felt threatened. Shopping is great fun until you have to make up your mind what to buy. I backed off a little to give her space. She was eight years younger than me but that didn't put me anywhere near the sugar daddy category. I was 30, she was 22. As I kept trotting off to America, I wrote to her most days and often beat the letters back. The cast of *The Sound of Music* got to know me as I became a stage-door Johnnie waiting for Fiona to come out. The *Evening Standard* got wind of the budding romance and I was accosted on the golf course by a reporter wanting some news. Next day blazed 'Wedding Bells for Roy?'

'Oh no!' Disaster. This could wreck the whole of my hopeful plans. How am I going to explain this to Fiona? Will she understand? Who let the cat out of the bag anyway?

I was waiting at the stage door with the paper under my arm and no idea how to broach the subject. I realized she must know when some of her dressing room mates came out whistling 'Here Comes the Bride!' I felt sick.

Fiona was a while coming out and when she did, she was wearing an accusing look which could be referred to as tight-lipped.

'You've seen it!'

'I certainly have.'

'I couldn't help it, they were determined to get *something*. I was reluctant to talk but you know what it's like.'

'No? Tell me.'

'Weellllll, I could have denied it, but that would not be the truth.' (Afterthought:) 'No comment sounds like guilty anyway.'

'I'm not too bothered for myself, I can handle it, but what about my mother and father? *Some*body is bound to see it and tell them.'

Fiona's parents were retired and lived in Speen just outside High Wycombe, Bucks. Father was from Belfast, a GP whose main practice had been in West Kirby, Cheshire. Mother was a most elegant lady – from Yorkshire but her high-class accent did not give this away. As yet, we had not met. Fiona suggested this be rectified a.s.a.p. From my point of view, this at least proved there was a spark of intention lurking, although the mere thought of another audition lit the blue touch-paper again.

Fiona phoned them and explained the 'article' and arranged a meeting at her flat the next day.

The fourth-floor walk up had them panting a little, but I

was more breathless just waiting for them to arrive. I had dressed as soberly as possible for the doctor and his wife. Fiona introduced us and my temples throbbed as I tried to speak at their level. No doubt they would have rather been introduced to a well-heeled son of a company director with fortunes to be inherited eventually. The doctor assumed I was a 'pop star' with no qualifications or prospects. I wasn't even *that*!

Fiona had made coffee and we sat around making point-scoring conversation. I tried to appear relaxed but found my hand creeping up the wallpaper. I crossed my legs and became aware of my foot flapping around as if it were waving goodbye. I don't think they were impressed. Correction! *I know* they weren't impressed.

As they left I felt a numbing thumbs-down was on the way. For the first time I was aware of my humble beginnings. I was a strolling player with fly-by-night prospects trying to steal their youngest and extremely precious daughter. How could it last? How could I keep her in a way to which she was used?

Fiona had two elder sisters, Liza and Maureen, and big brother Tony who was most amused that she had chosen a Tyke!

The days went by and a couple of my TV appearances were accepted – with reservations. Our tastes were miles apart in both music and dancing. Humour was a nonstarter. I was a complete moron as far as classical music and ballet was concerned. To them, tap-dancing was simply a flippant offshoot of the dancing world and Frank Sinatra was a hooligan. This was going to be a tough hill to climb, but if *that* put me off, then I wasn't much of a suitor. A new world was opening up for me.

Finally, I asked Fiona if she would really like to take me on officially and go for it. She went a little pink and her blue eyes seared into my head as she accepted the challenge. I just floated around as if I were Gene Kelly in the rain for the rest of the day.

Next day, I was about to train it to Liverpool, when Fiona rang and apologized but had 'had second thoughts'. I was destroyed. However much I knew I loved her before doubled. I was sick, torn apart having found the one I wanted, won her, then lost her again. Isn't this a load of shmaltz? But it really was as bad as that.

The private show at the Adelphi in Liverpool for Littlewoods Pools executives and their wives included Al Read, Tommy Cooper and two lady singers. Al Read insisted he should go on last as the star. I asked him if he was sure he wanted to follow Tommy? He was! Wrong!

Tommy destroyed them and they were all aching with laughter when I introduced Al, who might have been giving a party political broadcast on behalf of the exceedingly dull party.

I was in no mood to console him as I needed all the pity that was available. Tommy made us all laugh a lot at the supper afterwards, but I kept returning to my thoughts of emptiness.

'Just a moment, young man! Do you love her or don't you? Don't sit there whingeing. *Do* something about it!'

I sent a telegram. 'See you in Speen tomorrow!'

Fiona had already had second thoughts about her second thoughts and was feeling as empty as I was. The telegram did the trick. We met in Speen and everything was on again.

Soon afterwards, I felt I should do the right thing and ask, in true old-fashioned style, the doctor's permission to marry his daughter. Fiona and Mum made themselves scarce and busied themselves in the kitchen next door. Dad didn't make it easy for me to broach the subject as he chatted about gardens and his sit-upon mower problems.

Eventually, during a short pause, I jumped in with my prepared request. He listened intently to my future prospects as Fiona and Mum pressed wine glasses to the kitchen wall in an attempt to hear what was going on. I ended my case and waited for the verdict. He looked at me for what seemed an eternity, then said, 'Welcome to the family.' He glanced at his watch and jumped up. 'Good gracious, look at the time!

We're missing *The Archers*!'

Fiona and Mum heard the whole thing and came to join us straight away. Once *The Archers* was finished, out came the champagne and the ordeal was over.

We became very close over the years and they took me to their hearts – so much so that mother-in-law jokes were a definite no-go area!

We were officially engaged during the pantomime season in Brighton 1962/63 and set the date of our marriage: 29 July 1963 at St James's Church, Gerrards Cross. Fiona's sister Liza lived there so Fiona could leave a suitcase under the bed in order to qualify for the banns being read for three weeks. They were also read in Fiona's local church in Lacey Green. We attended one of the services and preened as the banns were announced. The vicar then went on to lambast the evils of show business.

This was the first time I had been to church with my future in-laws and I was hoping I would not disgrace myself. It always got to me when people made the first attempt at pitching the note of each hymn and reminded me of Jimmy James trying to get the note from the pianist in the pit orchestra:

FAH   FA   HEY FAH   FA
    FAH   AH   AH

'Is that piano damp? You'd better get it fixed before Josef Locke comes here.'

I was standing next to Fiona's father as the organist reminded us of the hymn tune, then that awful pause that comes before the congregation make valiant but cacophonic prods at the first note. I had to steel myself at this point and think of something sad in my life. A sideways glance at Fiona who was in on my plight almost had the adverse effect but, happily, I saw the moment through and settled to the hymn.

It wasn't my day. Dr Dickson being in the medical profession was keen on hygiene and not too happy with flies. He was certainly not pleased with the large bluebottle which landed on his hymn book. He took a swipe at it. Missed. It returned. Pow! The hymn book was on the floor and the fly was on his bald head. It was unfair to this young Yorkshireman who was trying so hard to control himself. Fortunately, Fiona and Mother were giggling also.

The days leading up to the wedding were drizzly and overcast, so we prepared ourselves for a wet one. However, the actual day started rather hazy then cleared revealing wall-to-wall blue sky. We were very fortunate to have Harry Secombe as the best man. 'And the biggest, Jim!' The cast from *The Sound of Music* jammed the church and sang magnificently: 'Dear Lord and Father of Mankind', Psalm 121 and 'Praise My Soul the King of Heaven'. No faulty starts. The Reverend Gordon Harrison took us through our marriage vows beautifully but held a rather lengthy pause, I thought, over 'If anyone knows just cause...'. We promised to love, honour and cherish. 'Obey' had been replaced. Then the mighty 'Those whom God hath joined together let no man put asunder' was very powerful.

The reception was a most happy affair, although the caterers let poor Dad down slightly. They thought that plying everybody with champagne and strawberries would disguise the fact that food was rather sparse. But a lot of our guests had travelled down from the North – 'We need summat to fill t' belly, lad! Summat to drive home on!' Skipping over the state of famine, the atmosphere was magnanimous and the speeches went well. Harry was in great form, the bridesmaids were well toasted when he'd finished. Colin, one of my brothers-in-law, was a fluent speaker, being a barrister who later took silk. His recollections of little Fiona wrecking his and Liza's canoodling days were priceless and when he'd finished, he had all the pros shouting 'Follow *that*!' I got by with remarks like

'Don't think of it as losing a daughter, more as gaining a weekend gardener,' and we cut the cake. A great day. We changed into our 'going away' outfits and were bounced along the church drive in a little Ford Popular covered in all the usual regalia and dragging empty tin cans. We drove it half a mile to Liza and Colin's place where we said a final farewell and drove to The Polygon Hotel in Southampton. The following day we were scheduled to sail on the *Statendam* to New York. I was booked for another *Garry Moore Show* and the rest of the time was spent as our honeymoon.

One of the sponsors of the show was Oldsmobile cars. They loaned us one of their models as we drove up the East Coast through New York State, Massachusetts, New Hampshire, Vermont and up to Bar Harbour Maine where Garry had a holiday home overlooking the Atlantic. The name of his hideaway was 'Serendipity' – and it certainly was a happy and unexpected discovery. We stayed a couple of days and sailed on his 40-foot yacht, then moved on, stopping at a place called Lake Kenebago for a couple of days. Log cabins surrounding a trout lake in a large forest where wild bears came and scavenged through the garbage at night. Atmospheric barbecues and lakeside walks were extremely romantic. By the time we awoke for breakfast our log fire was already roaring. The return journey through Vermont as the leaves were turning red, orange, yellow and brown was every bit as idyllic as any song could capture.

Back to New York for another *Garry Moore Show* which also featured Fiona 'Our talented English friend's new and beautiful wife'. My cup runneth over. We then spent a couple of weeks in Bermuda whilst I played in cabaret at the Forty Thieves nightclub. There were many Brits on the island and the *Garry Moore Shows* were seen there.

This was again paradise. A honeymoon cottage by the warm pale green sea, pink sand and blue sky. On the other side of our cottage was a swimming pool shared with a few other

people. There were cooking facilities and a maid to do the
hoovering and bed changing (mustn't get too used to *this*!).

The nightclub was a big success and we were invited out
incessantly. Eventually we had to take a day off and just flop.
We were happily dozing away when we became aware of a
scratching. It was coming from underneath a small
free-standing cupboard by the bed. The scratching was loud
enough to be more than a cockroach. What on earth could it
be? We had to do something about it. All we had was a
carving knife. I fetched it from the kitchen and, with Fiona
standing on the bed, I lifted the cupboard. A huge crab
scrambled out and came straight for me. In a wild rush of
self-defence I took a chop at the attacker and cut it straight
down the middle and it ran off to opposite sides of the room.

One night at the nightclub, we were asked out to meet some
rather influential customers who normally wouldn't have
patronized the place. The club owner was being rather
gushing when Fiona spotted a huge cockroach rattling along a
sill behind them. She almost shrieked with horror. The club
owner, not wishing to draw attention to this unwelcome
guest, grabbed it and put it in his pocket! He then slapped his
pocket whilst saying jovially, 'Well! *So* glad you're enjoying
your evening.' He was wearing a different jacket the next
night.

8

Elation and Disappointment

On the strength of the *Garry Moore Shows*, Jack Entratter, the owner of The Sands Hotel in Las Vegas, booked me for three weeks the following February (1964). The headline was 'George Gobel to make you laugh'. Second top was 'Tommy Sands to sing for you', and 'Roy Castle to dance for you'. Some of Fiona's relations lived in California. Her father was one of ten brothers and most of them had emigrated from Ireland many years ago. Uncles Alfie, Hally and Ernest and their families made us very welcome as we spent Christmas in shirtsleeves amongst them all. Alfie had two married sons, Jim and Hal; their wives, respectively, Peggy and Nancee. Hal and Nancee were married at the same time as we were so we had plenty in common and we have all remained close friends ever since.

Jim and Peggy came to see the show in Vegas. I was working in the main room for the diners. The Sands was known mainly as a comic's room, hence George Gobel starring. He's the man who once went into Garry Moore's dressing room before a TV recording and produced a bottle of Scotch. Garry said, 'No thanks, I never drink before a show.'

Gobel replied, 'You mean you go out there *alone*?'

After our show, Peggy, Jim, Fiona and I decided we would 'do' the Strip. Entertainment was throbbing in every hotel along this dazzlingly ostentatious jewel in the middle of the desert. We started with a gentle drink in the lounge of our hotel, where there was a trio for entertainment or background music.

We noticed a tall chap slide down from his stool at the bar and walk over to the pianist, whisper in his ear and slap a ten-dollar bill on the piano. Immediately the pianist stopped his song, played an arpeggio, and sang 'I left my heart in San Francisco'. This scenario was re-enacted twice more whilst we were there. We left The Sands and worked our way along the Strip visiting most of the entertainment venues, returning to our hotel around 4 a.m. 'How about a nightcap?' 'OK.' The pianist was still playing and the same tall chap slithered from his barstool like a drunken snake, staggered over to the pianist, gave him a knowing look and fumbled for another ten-dollar bill. The pianist broke his song, played an arpeggio and sang 'I felt my cart in Fran Clan Biscay'. The punter smiled and became a bendy toy, as he melted on the floor. A fitting climax to a great day.

Our three weeks at The Sands was followed by *Dean Martin and Partner*. The 'Partner' was obviously Frank Sinatra and, as his daughter Nancy was married to Tommy Sands at the time, Frank came to watch our final show. We were invited to join his table in the lounge afterwards, where his mother also was. Fiona sat next to him for well over an hour, and he was the perfect host, contrary to his public image. I was really impressed when a little old lady broke through the bodyguards and asked him for his signature. She produced a soft paper napkin and an ink pen. It was almost impossible to sign his name without ripping the napkin into pieces. I expected 'Get lost', but he laboriously signed his name almost in a series of dots and handed it back with a smile. He talked to us about a new film he was doing as if he really valued our opinion. I told him to go ahead with it!

A jazz trio was playing in the background and he suggested I go and get my 'horn and have a blow'. An offer I dared not refuse. I collected it from my dressing room, realizing this could be my Waterloo as I was only a busker and didn't know what to play with three total strangers. They suggested ' "I Got Rhythm" in B flat?' Phew – relief! I played it adequately but, because I had come from Frank's table, I got a standing ovation led by the man himself. *'If the parents of this little boy …'* Surely nothing could surpass this!

Earlier in the Vegas stint I flew to New York to do an audition for an advertisement for Knickerbocker Beer. All I had to do was play a white-faced clown in the corner of the screen and react to the commentator's dialogue in mime. 'Smooth, rich, strong, thirst-quenching' etc. From around two hundred auditionees, I got the part, guaranteeing around fifty thousand dollars a year for five years. I had also been given the leading role in a new musical for Broadway, *Kelly*, which was about a rough Irish American who finally jumped off the Hudson Bridge.

We fixed up an apartment on 46th Street and paid six months' rent in advance as we took over after the run in Vegas. I was really cooking now. I looked at window-cleaners and thought myself very privileged to have such a great job.

Fiona located all the necessary food shops and we stocked up with the kinds of gourmet delights which had been outside our financial boundaries not so long before.

As we ate in style in our own apartment in the Big Apple, the phone rang. It was the advertising agency. They apologized but they had lost the contract with the brewery, and the commercial was scrapped. 'Sorry! Maybe we can work together again sometime. Have a nice day!'

Ah well! There is still the Broadway show! S'pose I'd better ring them about rehearsals.

'Oh! Didn't you know? The writers and director have had a blazing row and the whole thing has had to be shelved. Sorry. Maybe we'll be in touch later. Have a nice day!'

We hadn't even finished our first meal! We now had a New York apartment costing plenty and only one more *Garry Moore Show* – then nothing. Fortune and future had disappeared in two phone calls! What could be worse?

Do you really want to read on? Fiona had a miscarriage and had to be rushed into hospital. No national health here. She couldn't even be admitted until I had paid one hundred dollars and filled in a questionnaire. I saw her comfortable then returned to the apartment.

As I saw the same window-cleaners I was now envious of their steady life. I walked into our room and the phone was ringing. Maybe the show is on again! No, Fiona needed to eat and the hospital canteen was closed. Could I take a couple of sandwiches and a carton of milk?

Her treatment was successful and, although rather sad and left with a feeling of incompetence, Fiona soon began to feel better. I had a week to wait before doing the Moore show, so we set about trying to re-lease the apartment. One bright interlude was the arrival of Eric Morecambe. He and Ernie were guesting on the *Ed Sullivan Show*. We put him up in our flat and gave him scant privacy by tying string across the room and draping a sheet over it. We laughed a lot.

Eric got us a couple of tickets for the *Ed Sullivan Show*, where one of their gags was:

Ernie:	Eric! do you like English girls best or American girls?
Eric:	American girls.
Ernie:	Why?
Eric:	'Cos they're here!

That was the show on which Sullivan introduced them as

Morrycambee and White.

The *Garry Moore* team were very sad to know of our bad luck and managed to find someone to take on the apartment, so that little worry was sorted. After the show, we sorrowfully packed our bits and pieces and came home.

Sydney Grace jumped to it and got me a week's work in a grotty nightclub in Greasborough near Sheffield. It was a converted Nissen hut and looked like a giant woodlouse. The floors were hard and the table tops were hard; the audience, however, were surprisingly good, which cushioned the blow a little. The club owner was a chap named Les Booth and he confessed he wasn't a fan, but I did recoup for him the money he had lost on the previous show.

These last few weeks had made very little sense – praise from Frank Sinatra and castigation from Les Booth, owner of a gin palace. Thousands of dollars blown out of the window and a few hundred quid for a hard time. Greasborough was never quiet for the acts as it was a self-service room holding around six hundred to a thousand people. The cash tills were always ringing merrily away and overladen trays could easily spill and raise a cheer. The constant banter of the delivery volunteer, 'Whose is the velvet lady?' 'Two pints for t' lads an' a Mackeson for Alice.' The Master of Ceremonies sat in a little box to one side of the stage at floor level, with his own gavel. On one occasion he introduced: 'For your entertainment, Ladies and Gentlemen, a new group of singers called...' He looked down at his paper for assurance. 'The New Faces!' Mild applause for their entrance but the hubbub was still fairly loud. The trio started to sing 'Oh, Danny Boy, the pipes, the pipes are calling', the audience began to take interest. 'From glen to glen and o'er the mountain side.' Slowly the audience became quieter and quieter. By the time the New Faces were into the second chorus the place was transfixed. Everyone was listening intently. Even the tills stopped ringing, men were standing with trays of drinks, motionless. This had never happened before. It was almost at the stage where little tears were welling up in the eyes of the more sentimental. At this point, the MC climbed out of his box, padded up the few stairs on to the stage, pushed between the singers to the centre mike and threatened: 'And *keep* it like that!' He completely wrecked the atmosphere. I don't think he got the job of presenting *Blue Peter*.

The next time Fiona found she was pregnant, I was doing the *Birthday Show* at the New Theatre, Coventry. She began having trouble again so the doctor advised three months in bed. This seemed to do the trick and Daniel was born on 2 July 1965. It was very late at night when I drove Fiona to the hospital in Carshalton, Surrey, and we seemed to be the only ones there. She had attended all the Natural Birth classes and I had gone to the fathers' instruction evening. The deep breathing then low level panting had seemed silly as we practised, but proved invaluable on D-Day.

I did all the pacing up and down and thought of my Dad trotting back and forth to the phone box thirty-three years earlier.

Dr Peter Flinton popped his face round the door. 'It's all right! You've got a little boy.'

'*Wheeeeee* – how are they?'

'Both doing fine – would you like to see them?'

'No thanks!' (Never could resist a joke.)

I went in and there was Fiona looking radiant, clutching this piece of red and purple meat. My son! I looked at Fiona. 'You mean you've gone through all the agony and frustration for *this*?' She smiled and hugged him closer. We, by the grace of God, were parents.

My life suddenly had a whole new meaning. Instead of being involved in a hundred-yard career sprint on behalf of me, me and me, I was in a long-distance relay race. Someone to hand the baton to. The news was out and the photographers in. After a lot of deliberation, we settled on Daniel for a name. There were no other Daniels in either of our families, so that avoided favouring anyone in particular. He was going to be his own man.

I had been invited to go with Harry Secombe to the USA and appear as Sam Weller in *Pickwick*, but they graciously let me wait until Daniel's christening was completed. Eric Morecambe was his godfather and took on the onerous duties of overseeing and encouraging his Christian faith.

I joined the cast of *Pickwick* in Cleveland. They had started their tour in Los Angeles and were now covering a few more cities before opening on Broadway in November.

After a few rehearsals I took over from the young chap who had been holding the fort. I apologized for the fact that he had to move out before the show went to New York. He assured me everything was all right. 'I've got a part in a pilot for a new TV series. It's about a group or something.'

The 'group' turned out to be the Monkees, the young chap, David Jones. He shot to fame in a matter of weeks. I was delighted.

Fiona and Daniel joined me in Detroit, the hub of the American car industry. We were to play two weeks in the Fischer Theatre which was a fairly new establishment in the centre of a large shopping mall. All rather splendid, but we were rehearsing all day, every day, in this run-up to our Broadway opening. Trying new numbers, dropping them, trying something else. It was a real grind and I didn't get to see too much of Fiona and Daniel. Fortunately Harry's wife Myra and his manager's wife Beryl were around for company and advice.

Next stop Washington DC for two very successful weeks before the big move to New York.

Kevin Carlisle was the choreographer of the *Garry Moore*

Shows and had an apartment in New York which he loaned to us whilst he staged the Dean Martin TV series in LA, so we were very lucky on that count. Long walks alongside the Hudson river with Daniel in his pram.

Pickwick opened at the 46th Street Theatre during a newspaper strike, consequently our publicity was cramped to say the least and although the audiences were good and the show was going well, David Merrick the producer took the show off after nine weeks. I was so sad for the whole cast who had pinned their hopes on a long run. Harry's Rolls-Royce was halfway across the Atlantic and had to be sent straight back. However, Harry and I did get nominated for Tony Awards, which was some consolation.

A few funny things happened to us during our nine weeks on Broadway. Harry and I were invited to a Variety Club lunch just before we opened. Princess Margaret was guest of honour. Lots of big American stars were there, each with their own ring of admirers clamouring around them. Rather like a chrysanthemum. Each time the celebrity made a joke, the chrysanthemum would open up in gales of laughter, then close up until the next gem.

Harry and I were on our own, more like a pair of wallflowers. As waiters flitted by with trays full of aperitifs, we would just be about to take one but the tray went straight by us. After a few minutes of this, Harry looked at me, a wicked twinkle in his eye. He took a deep breath and, at the top of his voice, bellowed 'If I ruled the world.' Every chrysanthemum turned and stared at us ... for two seconds, then realized we were nobody and turned back again. The drinks waiters still flashed by us.

Anton Rodgers played the part of Jingle in the show – thin as a pipe-cleaner in those days but very accomplished and ambitious. He found out the address of the Herbert Berghoff acting studios and asked me if I would be interested in going for some experience. Berghoff and his actress wife Uta Hagen accepted us and we were regular pupils.

No reminiscences of New York are complete without taxi-driver anecdotes. One day Anton hailed a cab and asked, 'Could you take us to the Rockefeller Center, please,' in his perfect English. The cabbie looked at him and said, 'Huh?' Even better English: 'The Rockefeller Center, please.' The cab driver looked suspiciously at him and said, 'Hey! You English or are you affected?'

One day I was in a cab on my own; the driver seemed very happy and singing nothing in particular. 'Hoy-te-toy-te-toy-te-hoy.'

I said, 'You sound happy today.'

'Why not! It's my boifday. Hoy-te-toy-te.'

'You mean you work on your birthday?'

'Why not? It's a great day to woik on! Hoy-te-toy.'

I reached my destination, paid my fare, and gave him an extra dollar. 'Happy birthday.'

'Why, thank you. Have a nice day!'

It sounds far-fetched, but next day I hailed a cab and jumped in.

'Hoy-te-toy-te-toy-te-toy!'

'You sound happy again.'

'Why not? It's my boif...' he suddenly realized the impossible coincidence.

'My! You get plenty birthdays in a year!'

He drove me to my destination with his head hunched over the wheel and uttered not a word. He didn't offer me my birthday dollar back either!

Our nine weeks doing *Pickwick* in New York were very happy, although a longer run would have been preferable. Even so, we ran much longer than *Kelly*, which I heard was finally staged on Broadway and lasted only *one night*!

*

We returned home to Sutton and I detected an uneasiness in Mam and Dad which finally turned out to be an 'out of their depth' situation. As Sutton was a virtual dormitory for City workers, the village atmosphere was non-existent and Mam and Dad had very few friends. We discussed the problem and decided to look for a more suitable place for them. The ideal location turned out to be Birchington near Margate, and a pretty bungalow with a little white fence round the garden which was situated in a crescent close to the sea.

They settled very quickly and made friends in no time. Fiona, Daniel and I continued to live in Sutton – not too far away from them – enabling frequent visits either way.

Fiona became pregnant again and we began to realize that our house in Sutton was going to be a little cramped, so we made a few tentative enquiries at our local estate agents. There was no urgency, but we fancied somewhere a little more countryfied.

I was working constantly in clubs and on television, driving to and fro, providing for my 'family'. All very well, but gruelling. When a break turned up, we decided to make the best of it. We went for a few days' rest in the New Forest but the hotel didn't live up to the brochure. Daniel's cot wasn't damp, it was wet. Tents full of girl guides sang rousing songs under our window late into the night, and our quiet break broke down. We decided to abort and spent the rest of the weekend with Fiona's parents. We popped in to our house in Sutton for a few bits and pieces and found an order to view waiting amongst the mail. It was in Gerrards Cross, which was on our way to Speen.

I rang, made an appointment and we saw it that same afternoon. We were the first customers and liked it instantly. No alterations or extensions were necessary which was ideal, Fiona being so heavily pregnant. I did the deal there and then, although I thought I was biting off more than I could chew with the price – £22,500. At one time the house had earned more than I had. If the economy carries on in its downward spiral I shall be lucky to get my investment back!

This reminds me of the price my mother paid for our terraced house in Scholes around 1930: she bought it for £75. Last year, whilst visiting Huddersfield, I saw a pair of shoes priced £75. It brought a whole new meaning to 'There was an old woman who lived in a shoe'!

By this time, Mam and Dad were feeling remote and found the extra miles too much, so we sold the bungalow in Birchington and they came to live in a flat in Little Chalfont, just a few miles away. Regular visits were again resumed until Dad died in 1969. He had given up smoking after his heart attack in 1955, but started on those small cigars when 'someone' told him they were OK. They didn't tell him not to inhale them and his coughing sessions finally caused congestive cardiac failure, coronary thrombosis and cerebral infarction. He almost made his three score years and ten. We moved Mam to a flat in Gerrards Cross as she didn't drive.

Fiona and I had laboriously planned Daniel, and Julia who was born on 16 February 1967, and we were wondering if that should be it when Antonia bounced into our lives in June 1969. Then there were three.

They each had their own very different personalities and gave us many laughs. I took three-year-old Daniel and Fiona to Pinewood Studios during the filming of my one and only *Carry On* picture, *Carry On Up the Khyber*. We were wandering through the buildings on our way to the restaurant when, among the many bits of scenery and props, I spotted the elephant which had just been used to carry Sid James and Joan Sims whilst they delivered a few lines of dialogue. It wasn't a real live elephant, I hasten to add – in fact it was only the top half of a model as the lower half was not in shot. This top half was supported by scaffolding, which hadn't struck me as odd at the time. I wanted to show Daniel off to the others, so I said, 'Look, Daniel, what's that? You know what that is, don't you?'

He stared at it and said nothing.

'Come on, you know what it is ... ' Not a word as his expression told me he was bewildered. Time for a clue. 'It's an elly ... ' Nothing. 'An *elly* ...'

His eyes suddenly came to life as he got it. 'It's an 'ELLICOPTER!'

When Daniel was five and Julia three, we were walking through Gerrards Cross on a Sunday afternoon. There was very little activity, even the newsagent was closed. Daniel was running up and down the pavement and getting a little excited so I had to check him. 'Daniel! Be careful running around near the road, if you tripped and fell into the road and a car ran over you, we would never see you again and you would never see us.' Julia piped in with her own admonition. 'Yes! And you'll hurt your knees as well!'

At one of the many birthday parties, I overheard a rather obnoxious little boy bragging at the top of his lisp. 'Of courth, I'm the oldetht one here becauth I am thikth!' Three-year-old Antonia rose to the challenge and returned, 'Maybe! But Julia is VERRY five!'

At this time Anto was attending nursery school and her teacher said that the girls were allowed to take a favourite toy in their lunch boxes. Most little girls took a sandwich, biscuit and a favourite doll. Anto? .... a packet of crisps and a pair of boxing gloves. She is now 25 and a stage manager. Most daughters ask for clothes or perfume at Christmas. Anto? A tool box. (And she is quite a dish.) Julia, 27, is at present teaching English in Peru. Daniel is 29, and married to a beautiful Norwegian, Birthe, who is sharing his life as a missionary. Benjamin was born four years behind Antonia. He is now 21 and a professional musician playing mainly tenor sax.

I tell you this in order that you know all is well. All is very well and we are as close as any family could be. But – it certainly hasn't always been like this.

9

Near Breaks
and Record Breakers

When Benjamin was born in 1973, it seemed our team was complete. I attended the birth and he was delivered about 6.30 p.m. I phoned Granny and Grampa who were baby-sitting for us. Next day when Anto announced to her teacher that she now had a baby brother, the teacher asked 'When was he born?'

'In the middle of *Nationwide*,' replied Anto.

I was able to take bookings on cruise ships, performing whilst holidaying. The whole family were taken on board and our cruise was in lieu of wages. Benjamin at three years old had been told about our forthcoming holiday and looked slightly worried. We finally made the journey to Southampton and boarded the *Canberra*. As we walked around the huge deck, Benji asked us where the boat was. He must have thought a family holiday in a rowing boat was hardly something to relish.

Those trips, about three in all, were very happy. Children's fancy dress, crossing the Equator, seeing foreign countries and cultures. Buying local wares at the quayside. We found ourselves in the middle of a gunfight in Rio, standing stock still, huddled together whilst bandits stole the police car. We enjoyed the basket run in Madeira, the Tivoli Gardens in Denmark where the rule was 'If you get lost, stand still and we will come back and find you.' That works until everyone is lost – then we all stand still in different parts of the Tivoli Gardens.

We had some weird characters on some of those cruises. One lady was heard to ask, 'Does the crew sleep on board?' ('No, dear, they run around the edges.')

Halfway across the Atlantic, normally a five-day trip, a well-to-do lady asked the pharmacist, 'Do you have any talcum powder?'

'Sorry, madam, we are all sold out of talcum powder.'

'Will you have any tomorrow?' ('Sure, we'll have a shark drop some off.')

At the elevator between decks as the doors opened revealing the attendant in his boiled white jacket – 'Are you going up?'

'No, madam.'

'Well, where *are* you going?'

One lady insisted on seeing the captain. Nothing could dissuade her. When she finally got to see him, her request was 'In the event of the ship going down, I want a non-smoking lifeboat.'

I had worked in Bermuda on quite a few occasions, and this time we went as a family. Daniel swam his first length in a swimming pool there and won himself a jacket which allowed him to come and see my act in the nightclub. The only time he laughed was when I tripped.

There was no backstage in the club so I changed into my tuxedo in the bedroom and entered through the audience. One time, by way of a change, I swapped my tux for a smart red jacket. But only once! I must have looked like the hotel manager as an irate lady marched up to me and demanded: 'What are you gonna do about my daughter's suitcase?'

'Sorry?'

'My daughter's suitcase! Are you gonna find it or does she have to walk around naked?'

'Well, I er...'

'Come on! I want an answer!'

'Well, er ... I suppose she'll have to walk around naked.'

'Thanks! I got an answer!' She fumed off.

A big chap with a huge red wobbly face and deep gravelly voice asked me, 'What time's the fishing trip tomorrow?'

I said, 'Do you want to buy a red jacket?'

I had an Aussie heckler one night. He was crewing one of the Tall Ships which stopped off on their way to Florida. He had had more than his share of the amber nectar. He shouted: 'You pommies are full of SH★★!!'

I was lucky. 'That's because we have to stomach the likes of you!' End of conversation. I think the cheer and applause told him he came second. He crept out.

All these holiday highlights were wonderful and are still stand-out memories for us all, but the routine life back home was taking its toll. Slowly but insidiously our relationship lost its warm sparkle. I am sure this happens to nine-tenths of marriages. I was travelling up and down the motorway doing one-nighters, getting home around 3 a.m. stinking of smoke, often mingled with frying if we had to change by the kitchens. My idea of heaven was to stay at home. Fiona was feeding children, bathing them, putting them to bed, washing grubby clothes, feeding, bathing, changing, feeding... Her idea of heaven was getting away from it all. We loved our children dearly and we loved one another and we had everything any family could wish for, but Fiona felt trapped. A feeling she has shared with many young mothers as she has given talks around the country.

I was bewildered, for our love seemed to be there yet it wasn't. I felt that Fiona was looking for something we already had. She said she always looked forward to my coming home yet the moment I arrived she felt like saying, 'Guess what sort of a day *I've* had!' This attitude got worse and we would have cold wars and eventually forget what we were arguing about. People used to advise, 'Never go to sleep on an argument.' No chance. I sometimes used to wake up trying to remember if we were arguing or not. One look at Fiona and I knew – yes, we're arguing.

I didn't help matters by having a few drinks with the boys. I had a driver, so it didn't matter if I got a little 'bevvied'. Coming home drunk just fanned the flames of hatred and I began to think our marriage was going rotten. I would look at myself in the mirror and long for that naive, innocent, enthusiastic young chap I used to be. I know time lends enchantment, but I realized my present behaviour either had to stop or really topple into the dregs.

We put on a happy face for the *others* as we went to church on Sundays and lived a life of pretence. I was saddened as I felt our lives drowning. I didn't like myself one moment, then thought what the heck the next. The worst feeling of all was seemingly letting our children down. They were, I think, oblivious of our problems, apart from the odd slip, but I felt the tug-of-war was not far off.

Actually Fiona had been suffering from depression for quite some time now and although she knew she ought to be happy and thankful, that didn't help. She battled on as I bottled on and it seemed a split was inevitable. Nobody should have to live their lives in an unhappy state from choice.

One day, Fiona had been upstairs for a while. When she came down she announced she was 'Going out!' There was a determination about her demeanour which suggested 'And I'm not coming back!' My mind raced. Is this it? Has it finally happened to *me*? Oh hell! Everything I really cared about – shattered. What's going to happen now? Solicitors. Newspapers. Fights over the children. Who moves out?

I busied myself with Benjamin who was fourteen months old, talking complete nonsense to him. He didn't know what a significant moment this was. 'Mummmmeee?'

'She's just gone out.' I felt sick. How could we let such a precious situation just drift away? Had she driven off in a huff? Was she going to drive the car into a wall? My head swam. Would the phone ring with the bad news? Would a policeman knock on the door, 'You'd better sit down, sir?'

It could only have been an hour but it felt like a week when Fiona came back home and was warm and cheerful. She smiled at me – and meant it! Now I was really confused. She was transformed. Where had she been? What had she done? Our lives immediately returned to normal. Beautiful and normal. The folks who live on the hill! Love flooded the house again and all the metaphoric cobwebs were swept away and our home smelled of fresh paint and clean sheets.

I was waiting for this heavenly bubble to burst and said nothing. I dared not allow my emotions to be roused in a permanent fashion in case they were to be dashed again. For a whole month our relationship blossomed and it was as if we had never had any problems. Finally, Fiona picked her moment and almost shyly asked, 'Have you noticed anything different about me?'

I said 'No'. (Just for a laugh you understand.) I had an inkling as to what had happened but didn't dare to make a guess.

'You remember about a month ago when I left the house in a hurry?'

'Yes.'

'Well, that's when I became a real Christian.'

She had been at her wits' end, almost suicidal, and knelt down at her bedside and prayed 'God! If you really are God and you really are there, then you've got to do something and you've got to do it *now* because I've had it.'

The phone rang.

'Hi, Fiona,' it was Tamara, one of Fiona's friends.' I really don't know why I'm ringing you but I feel we ought to have a talk. I don't know what we would talk about, I just feel we should meet.'

Fiona put her off with a lame excuse, saying she would call her back later. Then realization hit her. *Wait a minute! I've just been praying for help. How stupid could I be?*

She eventually found Tamara's number in the directory and phoned back to see if she could pop round straight away.

'That's when I went out.'

'I really thought you had left me then.'

Tamara was a born-again Christian and had suffered from depression herself. They talked about life, especially family problems, and Fiona opened her heart. Eventually Tamara broached the subject of Faith. Fiona felt our faith was in order, we went to church whenever we could and *tried* to be good people.

'You say you're a Christian, but have you ever asked Jesus to take over your life?'

'Well ... er ... no.'

'Well, don't you think it's about time you did?'

'Well ... er ... yes.' She couldn't say no.

So! There and then Fiona became born again, and the result was astounding. No more did the problems of the whole month weigh heavily on her shoulders. No more did tiny niggling things get on her nerves. No more 'Guess what kind of day *I've* had!' She was Fiona again, *'and she's in love with you!'* Thanks, Eric.

Being 'born again' to high-fliers and cynics is made to sound insipid and pious. I'm not quite sure why because for me, it's just about the ultimate in New Year's Resolutions. I have met people who say, 'I've been too wicked, too stupid. God would never accept *me*.'

Wrong.

A genuine desire to turn away from evil and selfishness, and all the other garbage on offer, is accepted with open arms.

I don't think being born again would get you off a murder

charge or even a parking fine as that would be for the wrong
reason but sincere commitment to the future is accepted every
time.

Now we were back on track and harmony returned to our
family, I had to pull my socks up and get to grips with my
boozing habits. I refused to consider it as a problem, but
trying to kick it was much more difficult than I expected. I
had a private battle with it for quite some time and felt pretty
inadequate as I sneaked a wee one here and there when no one
was looking. I no longer needed comfort and relaxation from
elsewhere. My home life was super. So *why*? I could now
identify with all other people who found themselves
struggling with an addiction. The whole situation was
cock-eyed. I had no chance of getting away with it at home!
Fiona's sense of smell was so acute, she could tell if I'd 'had
one' as I drove in the garden gate (correction, was *driven* in the
garden gate).

Over all, it took a few years to get back to normal and I
sympathize with anyone going through the trauma of drying
out. I don't touch any alcohol now because of my condition,
but feel proud that I managed to beat it all by my little self.

Whilst all this was going on, my career was doing fine.
One-nighters, functions, radio series, and of course *Record
Breakers*. I'm often asked how that came about. Well, Alan
Russell was the producer of *Blue Peter* many years ago and
had asked me to pop along on occasions to demonstrate the
workings of bagpipes, alphorns, slate xylophones and the like.
I even gave a short recital on the spoons. During that
performance I claim to be the only person on a live show to
have been bitten by Shep. Either he took a dislike to my
playing or thought I had 'nicked' the spoons from the
canteen. Deputy Dawg!

When Alan Russell had the bright idea of using the *Guinness
Book of Records* as a magazine programme for Children's TV,

he needed a presenter who could turn a hand to most things and didn't mind looking a fool. Straight away, he thought of me!

I was invited to a meeting with him along with Ross and Norris McWhirter, identical twins who were the compilers and editors of the *Guinness Book*. It seemed a great idea and there was an abundance of material. Also, in those days before videos, the viewing clientele would change every five years or so. If it could run five years, it could run for ever. We were all happy with the prospects and, in 1972, recorded the first series. I was the main presenter and light relief, representing the viewers' inquisitive point of view. Ross and Norris were the authoritative part of the show. Our young studio audience could challenge them with questions and, between them, Norris and Ross would provide the answers and I promise you, this was totally unrehearsed. The twins knew nothing of the questions in advance. My first interviewee was Dr Roger Bannister, the first person to break the four-minute mile. Norris was the actual commentator on that historic occasion. When he announced the time, all anyone heard was 'Three minutes ... ' The rest was drowned in cheering. I was petrified at the thought of interviewing this great athlete but he was gracious and didn't patronize me. The interview satisfied my producer even though I finished by thanking Dr Bannister for talking to us about his four-minute meal!

Record Breakers was a marvellous show for me. The material was beautifully balanced between the acme of achievers, vital pieces of useless information, and complete cuckoos, but all completely factual.

I was fortunate in being able to travel to lots of foreign countries in search of records that gave the show that extra dimension. In Canada, I flew in a helicopter over Niagara Falls and rode with the Mounties (they gave me a retired horse). In Bermuda, I played underwater trumpet with Mark Gottlieb who had mastered the underwater violin as he

searched for a shark-repellent sound. I presented a few golf
records whilst hitting a shot or two. One of my approach shots
landed within one foot of the pin from 140 yards. My
producer wouldn't use it because 'They'll think we cheated.'

In New Zealand I boiled a can of beans in the hot springs of
Rotorua, known as Stink City because of the permanent
stench of sulphur. Some of the gurgling mud swamps
reminded me of those National Service breakfasts.

Holland provided cheese markets, the world's biggest
flower auctions, and Fierljeppen, the art of pole-vaulting over
dykes. I asked the champion what happened when people
tried it for the first time.

'Dey fall in de vorter!'

I did! And the dyke had a muddy bank.

Hawaii provided an opportunity to try surfing – which is
even more difficult than it looks. The toughest part is
paddling the surfboard out to sea against those mountainous
breakers. The expert had shoulders like Frank Bruno. I
should have used an outboard engine, it took me two tides to
get out there! Fell off twenty times trying to surf back to
shore. Eventually my surfboard returned without me. I
finished up on a baby raft as I delivered my lines.

Hawaii has one island completely devoted to growing
pineapples. Lanai is eighteen miles long and twelve miles
wide and produces in the region of eighty-three *million*
pineapples each year. The local planters and pickers live on
the island and 'off ' the island, so to speak.

The picking process is a combination of workers and a huge
machine with an extended arm supporting a conveyor belt.
The pickers place the pineapples on this belt which transports
the fruit to the main machine which separates the crown from
the pineapple.

I had to explain all this to camera whilst the workers carried
on with their jobs. It was a long piece and I had studied it for
quite some time the night before. Clouds were threatening

and it would be a good idea to do it a.s.a.p.

'Start the machine! Everybody ready? Remember not to look at the camera! Roy? Ready?'

Nod.

'OK. In your own time – good luck!'

Wait for camera to record a bit of the action then ...

'Well, here I am on pineapple island, Lanai is responsible for eighty-three million pineapples every year. It takes twenty-five thousand plants to fill an acre of land and every one is planted by hand. Some of the top planters handle up to fifteen thousand in a day. After about twenty months, the fruit is ready to be harvested, again by hand. For this, protective clothing must be worn as the spiky leaves are lethal. Heavy gauntlets, canvas sleeves, canvas overtrousers and gauze face-protectors. The pineapples are picked, then placed on this conveyor belt which carries them to the main machine which separates the fruit from the crown. The fruit is then shipped to the canning factory on the island of Oahu. The crowns are replanted and in another twenty months each one will produce another coconut! COCONUT???? Oh no.' It was starting to rain.

The workers all fell on the floor laughing. Alan Russell had a good laugh too, but graciously saved my reputation with a bit of skilful editing.

We found America bursting with eccentrics like Jerry Camerata who sang in a bath in Times Square for hours on end.

Ashrita Furman of New York negotiated the metal spiral-staircase fire escape of the Canadian National Tower – 553.33 metres, 1,967 steps in all – in 57 minutes 43 seconds – on a pogo stick! He balanced a milk bottle on his head whilst walking 70 miles (it was butter when he finished); he pogo'd for sixteen miles on Mount Fuji in Japan; he somersaulted for twelve miles and 380 yards; juggled continuously for six hours, seven minutes; juggled underwater; pogo'd under water ... had enough yet? Add yodelling for 27 hours in San Francisco and plenty more – oh yes, he carried a nine-pound brick for 64 miles. It took him a long time to build a house.

We covered the cherry pit spitting championship in Michigan Ohio. Talk about tongue in cheek! The big day was held in the middle of acres of cherry orchards and the tarmac pitch was marked out like a giant shove-ha'penny board. There was a windsock to register wind aid or resistance which might have a bearing on any records. A large mug was available for the safekeeping of dentures, and referees and timekeepers were in attendance. One contender had been practising whilst sea fishing and was responsible for the lumps on the heads of a few passing mackerel.

The rules stated that each contender was allowed one minute in which to chew the flesh away from the pit, 'You take a chance on the pit being round or oval, as the round pit tends to run further whereas the oval pit could take an awkward bounce'. The final measurement is taken from where the pit finishes.

If you spit out a half-chewed cherry pit, there's a likelihood that the remaining flesh on the pit will put the brakes on much quicker. The technique is a combination of nimble choppers and powerful lungs plus the ability to form one's tongue into a tube.

Naturally, I had to try it for our viewers' sake. I picked a particularly fleshy purple cherry and popped it into my mouth as the timers thumbed the stopwatches. The juice flowed around my teeth and gums as I sought the pit and proceeded to chisel all the soft bits away from what seemed to be a fairly round piece of ammunition.

'Thirty seconds.'

I was doing fine. A few more seconds to be sure the pit was clean and aerodynamic. Pump up the lungs with a few deep breaths, form the tongue into a 'toob'.

'Fifteen seconds.'

Time enough, repeat that last sequence to be sure I was prepared.

'Ten, nine, eight...'

Right! Tongue toobed, BIG breath.

'Three, two, one...'

I swallowed the pit!

The eventual winner cleared 92 feet (30 metres). It was the fisherman.

The following day we travelled to the 'cow-chip' tossing championships in the appropriately named small town of Clapham, Ohio.

There was a special breed of cattle which provided the ideal missiles used in what was proudly termed 'The Organic Olympics'. The cow 'chips' were allowed to sit in the fields in order to get sun hardened on one side. Then came the official 'turnover' day. Specially angled forks were slid under the crusted chips and they were levered over and left in the sun for a few more days, by which time I was assured the chips were 'odourless'.

On the morning of the big challenge, a large tractor-drawn cart was loaded with the ammunition and paraded around the town festooned with balloons and streamers. The cows were not included in the procession as their precious but prolific output was not confined to pastureland.

Crowds gathered on the green while bands played and the chips were inspected. There was a 'Go/No Go' gauge, a lavatory-seat lid with a six-inch (150 mm) hole cut out of the middle. 'If a cow chip passes through this hole, it is not eligible for the competition. Too small! Could be thrown like a baseball and that'd be cheat'n'!'

The reigning champion demonstrated the many techniques of this unique art of cow-chip tossing. 'First of all, you can use the discus type o' throw with a couple o' twirls then *fling the thing*! Another way is the frisbee style where ya sling it across yer body an' hope it'll ride the wind. O' course the choice of chip is critical for this one. M'self? I use the good ole shoulder-throw five paces to the line then *let it go*! With this technique, the chip slices through the air, and providing it doesn't break up, it has a good chance. Chip choosin' is crucial, I've seen some good throws disintegrate like a clay pigeon due to the chip bein' faulty.'

We filmed the competition and he won again with a toss of over 90 metres.

As we sat down with a cool drink after the presentation, our champ asked me how long I'd been in the States and what had I been 'doin' so far'. I told him about the cherry-pit spitting and explained the rules and special techniques. He looked at me with wide eyes and shook his head. 'Man! Some people sure do crazy things!'

Record Breakers had been running well for a few years and the viewing figures were healthy. Ross and Norris were a big hit with their off-the-cuff answers. I was enjoying the variety and wealth of material which didn't always have to get laughs. The only looming problem was my becoming typecast as a children's entertainer. I mulled the thought over and took the decision to stick with what I felt happy doing. Adult comedy was becoming more and more forthright and crude. To try the acting field would mean starting again and probably falling between two stools. I remembered the advice given to me by Arthur Askey, a man whom I admired as a professional and as a person. His advice was 'Don't wait around for the next James Bond part, you'll disappear from the scene. Take a look at the firm offers, choose the one that suits best then get on with it and enjoy it. When that's over, do the same again. When the offers aren't there, you've retired.'

Record Breakers was getting good reaction, I was enjoying it and, when I performed at company functions, the parents would say 'Our children are furious to think they can't be with us tonight' or 'Why don't you put the show on a little later so we can see it?'

I was happily mixing TV with one-nighters and family. Throw in a little gardening and life was trundling along very nicely thanks. It was whilst I was halfway up a tree that Fiona shouted 'Darling! Phone!'

'Oh no – can I ring back?'

'I don't think so – it seems urgent. It's Bill Cotton from the BBC.'

I climbed down and ran to the house kicking wellies off in all directions.

'Hello?'

'Hello, Roy. Bill Cotton here. I've checked with your agent and you're not working tonight.'

'That's right.'

'Bruce is ill and we need someone to host *The Generation Game*. Bring your best suit and get down here a.s.a.p.'

My heart was pounding as I drove to the Shepherd's Bush Theatre. I parked nearby and walked up the alleyway to the stage door where I was greeted with friendly gratitude and cushioned as well as possible whilst trying to absorb all the information for the show. It was a Thursday evening recording to be shown the following Saturday so editing, thank goodness, was possible.

It all went very well and producer Jimmy Moir was more than delighted. The celebration afterwards was another backslapping and twiglets experience, but I sensed a slight tenseness in the eyes of most of the production staff. I didn't stay too long as I had the drive home and I didn't want the adrenalin to subside too soon and leave me a bit sloppy.

The tension was soon explained as the stage doorkeeper said, 'Isn't that terrible news about Ross McWhirter?'

'What news?'

'Oh! Haven't you heard, the press have been trying to get hold of you all evening.'

'What's happened?'

'Well – er – he's been shot! They think it's the IRA.'

'Ross? Shot? Is he...?'

The doorman nodded. 'Died on his way to hospital.' Then he added, 'Apparently they were waiting in his garden and tried to abduct his wife as she drove in. He ran out when he heard the scuffle and they shot him. Got away in her car.'

Ross had headed a consortium of people who put up a reward of £50,000 for information leading to the capture of a gang who were terrorizing London restaurants with nail bombs. The gang had been hoping to kidnap Mrs McWhirter and demand the money as a ransom.

'Who's next' and all kinds of wild ideas were racing in my head as I left the stage door and made my way down the dark alleyway. I was almost at the end when, out of a doorway, I heard the words, 'Roy Castle?'

I froze. My temples pounded as I replied, 'Yes?'

It was a man. He stepped forward and thrust his hand into his overcoat pocket and pulled out ... an autograph book!

'Can I have your autograph?'

The blood rushed to my legs leaving my head empty. I was all set to go down fighting. I reflected later what a shame it would have been if I had laid into him and left him bruised and bleeding – *I only wanted your autograph.*

I believe the gang were eventually run to ground in the Balcombe Street siege but the experience was less than comfortable. As for Norris, we all wondered how the loss of his identical twin brother would affect him. The sadness went without saying, but losing a twin when they seemed inseparable could possibly reduce him to half a person. The opposite was the case and Norris took up the challenge. He continued editing and compiling the *Guinness Book* as well as appearing on *Record Breakers* and answering the wide variety of questions as he became 'Norris on the Spot'.

Record Breakers continued, private functions continued and our family was growing up. In 1980 I was offered a three-week season at the Gaiety Theatre in the Isle of Man. As it was during the school holidays, it seemed a good idea. Daniel was now 15, Julia 13, Anto 11 and Benji 7. We all stayed at the Sefton Hotel which was next door to the theatre. The promenade was good for a pre-breakfast jog and we set out to explore a different part of the picturesque island each day. No matter what the weather.

Mornings were devoted to practising in the theatre, bringing back memories of my own youth. Daniel and Anto were on trumpet, Julia wasn't quite as keen but played a little classical guitar and danced very well. Benji knocked seven bells out of the drums as we worked towards toppling the Osmonds and the Jacksons within the three weeks.

We were invited to inspect the local ice-cream factory which proved more popular than climbing to the top of Snae Fell in a gale-force wind.

One Saturday afternoon, 23 August, we were invited to open a day of Celtic games including a hill run and all the fun of the fair. We turned up as a family and did the honours, leaving six-year-old Benji the last word 'OPEN!' The hill race started simultaneously and all the other games were under way. Our gang were given some money each to spend on whatever they wished, as Fiona and I were introduced to the stall holders. About 25 minutes into the proceedings I noticed a gate was being opened to let in a pony and trap. The intention was to give rides and make a little more money for the charity. As the erstwhile placid animal arrived in the field full of excited people cheering on young athletes, it panicked and set off into the crowd, running amok with the trailer bounding along behind. People were being trampled and bumped as the pony galloped aimlessly amongst the screaming islanders. It was resembling a battlefield with bleeding bodies lying all around and men trying to halt the charging animal. Fiona and I suddenly thought about our four and waded anxiously through the crowds in search of them.

Eventually, after a few minutes of seering apprehension, we found them a little shaken but unhurt. Then, and only then, did we try and help the unlucky ones. It appeared that only one was seriously hurt but many were in a state of shock. The games continued and we said farewell and resumed our exploration of a part of the island named Glen Maye. As we drove there, Fiona and I were explaining to our children how disasters can happen at any time, to anybody. The important thing to remember is 'don't panic' and try to keep a clear head. Advice we could well have heeded just half an hour later.

We arrived at Glen Maye and parked the car as it was about a half-mile walk down a riverside path to the little sandy cove. We spotted the dark shadows of trout darting to safety as again I was transported to my own childhood. The river finally ran out into the sunlit beach and joined the Irish Sea.

There was quite a high grassy bank overlooking weather-worn rocks and Daniel was making his way along the top. It didn't look alarmingly dangerous. Fiona had taken Anto off in search of pebbles and shells. Julia was poodling around on her own at the bottom of this small cliff as Daniel had made his way down on to a ledge and was throwing small pebbles in her vicinity. I had taken Benji to the edge of the water and we were throwing pebbles at the lively waves telling them to 'get back!'

There were plenty of noises going on from other families so the thud didn't arouse any anxiety. That is, until Anto screamed, 'Daniel's fallen!' I looked up at the bank and there was no one there. I have no recollection of running back to the rocks but remember seeing Daniel in a position that can only be described as halfway through a forward roll. I knew he shouldn't be moved but, in that position, he would suffocate. He was obviously unconscious as I very carefully moved him enabling him to breathe. Fiona arrived in a state of high-pitched anxiety. 'Is he dead?'

'No, he's still breathing.' I checked his pulse, but was alarmed at a trickle of blood coming from his nose and mouth.

He groaned quietly but was not coming round. A chap we didn't know came to help and another ran up the path to try and phone for an ambulance. I have to admit to being in a bit of a state as I kept on talking to my son, whether he could hear me or not. We were given towels and clothes to keep him warm. Fiona was praying and our other children were crying as they cuddled up to her. I felt totally helpless and inadequate as I kept on talking to him. The chap who had joined us was trying to keep me calm. A policeman arrived to help but his walkie-talkie wouldn't work amongst the rocks so he had to go back up the path. The ambulance couldn't get down the pathway as there had been subsidence. The helicopter couldn't get in with any degree of certainty and was already out picking up some bits of a motor cyclist who had been practising for the TT races. Our only chance was the coastguard who had to sail round from Peel then take him back, transfer him into the ambulance then drive him across the island to Nobles Hospital in Douglas.

I must have repeated 'Come on, Daniel – stick with it' ten million times. In fact, the dinghy arrived fairly quickly for such a choppy sea. They gently but expertly moved Daniel on to a sort of wrap-around stretcher and carried him to the dinghy. I went with them while Fiona drove the rest of our family back to the hospital.

The journey back around Peel point was agonizingly slow but had to be, because of the lively sea. During this return trip, the coastguard held a finger on Daniel's neck, checking his pulse. His expression was pretty grim as my boy's face seemed to be getting greyer and more transparent. It felt like a whole cruise before we arrived at Peel harbour where an inquisitive crowd had gathered to see what the ambulance was waiting for.

The transfer was extremely efficient and we were on our way across the island. I had always had a dread of being in an ambulance and not hearing the siren drop a half-tone as it went by. This was it. The siren stayed constant but Daniel, now wrapped in foil, was getting pinker again and the coastguard looked a little less agitated.

As we reached the Nobles Hospital, extreme professionalism again took over and Daniel was whisked into the emergency intake. I was given a cup of tea and settled in a waiting room, where I was asked to fill in a form, very shakily!

Fiona arrived with the children, all composed but still in shock.

The doctor responsible for the inspection finally came in to tell us his findings. 'He's badly concussed and is likely to remain so for quite some time. He may regain consciousness, he may not. He may have permanent brain damage or he may not. In any event, don't expect too much.'

He was preparing us for the worst which, in retrospect, was best although it seemed harsh at the time. We were allowed to see Daniel in the intensive treatment room. He was lying there with wires and tubes attached to most parts of his body. He had an oxygen mask over his face and screens behind him relating his pulse in bleeps on a green line.

In the next bed was an old lady who had been hit by the runaway pony and trap. She had an extremely black eye and crushed ribs but was expected to pull through.

There was also a tiny baby in an incubator who was fighting for his life twenty weeks early. The IT room was full of competence mixed with caring love and gentle humour.

We were met by another doctor who had obviously given Daniel a thorough examination and told us he didn't expect any improvement for quite some time and, apart from just sitting and looking at him, there was nothing we could do. I was meant to do a show that night and asked his opinion. 'You would be better occupied doing it,' he replied matter-of-factly. So, we returned to the hotel, I went to the theatre as Fiona put our three little sad ones to bed, arranged for a babysitter, then drove back to the hospital to sit in vigil at Daniel's bedside.

At the theatre, the audience were completely unaware of the drama, and I decided it would be best to leave it that way. Had I explained the situation it would have put the damper on the whole show and we may as well have cancelled it. Laugh, clown, laugh, even though your heart is breaking. This was the classic test for a performer. All the way through my act visions of Daniel lying at the bottom of the cliff merging with visions of him lying in bed all wired up were flashing across my mind. I was managing reasonably well until I came to the part in my act where I ask for requests on my trumpet. The usual response is 'Far Away', 'The Flight of the Bumblebee' or 'T' Post Horn Gallop'. Not this night. As the town had many Irish people filling the hotels and boarding houses, one clear voice rang out with 'Play "Danny Boy"'. I graciously accepted, then it hit me. *Danny Boy*. We never called him Danny but many of his friends did. I looked at my musicians who looked back with sympathetic apprehension. I launched into it as if I were playing for his life. I would be interested to hear it back to see if the same emotion came out as I put in, but it was not recorded. I got through my act without further dramatics and drove off to the hospital. During the journey there I was bellowing at God: 'Why? Why? Why?'

In my mind I went through all the possible outcomes. 'Either give him back whole or take him! Don't make him suffer!' Over and over again I thought I should have stopped him wandering up there. But it didn't seem dangerous and you can't keep a 15-year-old boy in a glass case. 'Why? Why? Why?'

I was calm as I reached the hospital but when I walked through the main doors, that special clinical smell filled me with apprehension. I prepared for the worst as I approached the IT room. 'You can go in,' said the nurse clutching a clipboard. I looked at her enquiringly. 'No change,' she smiled a mixture of sadness and understanding.

Fiona was sitting there holding his lifeless hand and

stroking his forehead. All the machinery was still pinging and bubbling away.

'How is he?'

'Same.'

'No change?'

'He's groaned a couple of times but nothing special. We *were* told not to expect anything. How was the show?'

'Fine … someone requested "Danny Boy".'

It took a while for it to register with Fiona too. 'Oh, darling, how did you manage?'

'Very well, I think.'

I stayed about an hour then Fiona suggested I go back to the hotel and check the children. She stayed on at the hospital and promised to ring me immediately anything happened, good or bad.

I peeped into the room and the 'winkies' were all fast asleep. They'd had a tiring and frightening day. I was pleased they had managed to settle down and went to bed realizing they would be up early and full of questions.

The phone didn't ring during a fitful night of animated dreams and anxious wakeful imaginings. I was up first and phoned the hospital. It was a bleary-voiced Fiona who reported no change. 'How are the children?'

'They were asleep when I got back and I haven't heard from them yet.'

'Better check they are all right.'

'OK. See you after breakfast.'

I went into the children's room and they were awake but not up. Julia was first to ask, 'How's Daniel?'

I sat down amongst them and we discussed the possibilities of the future from dying, remaining unconscious for a long time, having brain damage and being very different from the brother they knew, to the possibility of his total recovery. 'We just have to trust in God and the doctors and nurses.'

The press got wind of our plight, and a young lady

journalist was assigned to stay around us until something positive happened. She was most discreet and compassionate, but there were also gruesome connotations.

Daniel remained unconscious throughout Sunday as Fiona and I swapped duties between bedside watch and family entertainer.

Monday saw the national headlines 'Roy Castle's son in Cliff Fall! RC's Nightmare Vigil', etc etc. It was even emblazoned on billboards outside newsagents.

Out of the blue we received a message from two elders of our Church. They were on their way to pray for Daniel and if they weren't allowed in to see him, then they would pray outside the IT room.

Happily, they were allowed in and were able to pray over him whilst anointing his forehead with oil. We all stood around his bed as we concentrated on the proceedings. At the end of the prayer, Daniel said 'Amen!' I am sure you can imagine how we felt at that moment. There wasn't a hair on my neck that wasn't standing straight out rigid! Then a flush of warmth flowed through every vein and artery. My temples throbbed as I looked at Fiona, who was crying.

Daniel said no more at this stage but began to regain consciousness throughout the day. He didn't remember anything about his fall, which was a blessing really, but he remembered us and the earlier happenings that day. The dear old lady with the black eye was so pleased to see his improvement and we introduced them to each other. Our Elders flew back right away to spread the good news to all our friends back at Gold Hill.

That night, the theatre was packed. Not an empty seat. I got a huge cheer and thunderous applause as I made my entrance. Then the audience went deathly quiet as they waited for news of Daniel.

'It's all right. He's on the mend.'

The place erupted, people were cheering and dancing in the

aisles. It was like the last night of the Proms. Flowers were thrown on the stage and the whole evening was a celebration. I hardly got into my act.

Next day, Daniel was sitting up in bed and looking much better. He still had all his tubes and wires but was speaking almost normally. I told him about the previous night in the theatre and the fact that it was a packed house and the booking office was doing a big trade. 'So, if I do a summer season again next year, how do you feel about a repeat performance?' He cottoned on and replied, 'Couldn't Julia do it next time?'

The specialist came and sat on Daniel's bed and told him how well he was doing, then went on to explain what the wires and tubes were all about. 'We'll start at the top, shall we? First of all you have a fractured skull which explains the lost two days. We are very pleased you joined us again so quickly and so efficiently. You broke your collar bone which possibly saved your skull from more serious damage. You broke a rib which punctured your lung. That's why this tube travels from it to that bottle under your bed. As soon as that stops bubbling, your lung will have healed and we can take the tube away. You won't be riding horses for a while because you have broken your pelvis, and it's just as well you don't have to write home as you have broken your wrist.' The specialist gave Daniel an old-fashioned look containing the faintest suggestion of a twinkle and said, 'In fact, you could say you've got a full house!' Daniel attempted a laugh but the pain checked it. It was a good day. The dear old lady had taken her black eye and cracked ribs home and our incubator baby was kicking happily away.

Next day, we were asked to stay in the waiting room. As we wondered what might have happened, the door was flung open, the nurses shouted, 'TARRAAA!' and in came Daniel with a walking stick! The newspaper lady got some photographs and that concluded her story. Daniel was moved out of the IT room and into a small ward which he shared with three other males. He was a bit miffed when he found out the ailments of his co-patients. 'The one beside me is an appendicitis, opposite left is a broken leg and the one opposite is gall stones! And here's me! A *sky diver!*' He was definitely getting better.

When the three weeks were up, I flew back with our other three children whilst Fiona waited a few days and brought Daniel back by boat and train. He received a hero's welcome when he came home. We all donned bandages and walking sticks to make him feel easy.

The following Sunday, as he walked down the aisle of our church unaided to thank everyone for their prayers, it was the last night of the Proms all over again.

We learned that, over the weekend, a huge Christian gathering under the collective name of 'Greenbelt' had prayed for Daniel. Sixteen thousand of them, and the locals in the Isle of Man couldn't have been more concerned and loving. I never *did* get the chance to thank the chap who raised the alarm, or the one who stayed with me on those rocks, but I hope they knew how much I appreciated their action and concern.

10

Biting the Bullet

Apart from pantomimes and summer season at the Palladium my West End appearances were non-existent until 1969 when Michael Codron asked me to take over from Eric Sykes in *Big Bad Mouse* at the Shaftesbury Theatre. Jimmy Edwards was staying on and, although I was a little nervous of following Eric, the prospect was exciting. This was my introduction to farce – albeit well sprinkled with ad libs. Apparently the play had toured the provinces with a view to coming into the West End but, whilst in Manchester, Michael Codron had decided it wasn't successful enough. The notice went up on the Thursday night informing everyone of the termination of the run. Now, with nothing to lose, Eric and Jimmy ran riot with the script and had the audience in hysterics.

They repeated this formula on the Friday with the same result. Michael Codron was alerted, travelled up to see for himself and decided to bring it into the West End after all.

Following six successful months Eric decided to leave but the bookings were still good hence the invitation to me to take over. It was a great privilege to inherit all the ad libs that Eric had created over the six months and it was a great relief for me when the audience reaction was favourable. We ran for another year as I wallowed in the luxury of full houses in hysterics.

In the mid-seventies, I was asked to take over the lead in *Billy* at Theatre Royal Drury Lane. Michael Crawford was leaving after two years of capacity audiences. Again, a magnificent show but a real work-out. I rehearsed for five gruelling weeks before taking over and felt I had done the show quite well but unfortunately I didn't have the drawing power of Michael Crawford and the business was only mediocre. We lasted nine weeks before we were bundled out by *Chorus Line*.

I was feeling pretty bruised after this until I was approached by Lord Willis to star in a new musical called *Mr Polly*.

The original production was to open the new Churchill Theatre in Bromley in 1977. This then could be the big one. I had no idea how to assess a new production but felt it was building nicely. Comments from casual onlookers were favourable and our hopes for a success were quite high. The opening night was a big affair attended by Prince Charles and all the local dignitaries plus, unfortunately, all the main critics. We got a pasting. I was warned not to read some of the reviews. Back to the bottom of Grandma's cellar steps. The new theatre received good write-ups but the readers were advised to wait for the next production. In retrospect I fear they were right but it was difficult to take at the time.

You can imagine my dilemma then, when, in 1983, Tommy Steele asked me to join him in a new musical at the Palladium. I was going to turn him down flat until he told me confidently: 'It's *Singin' in the Rain*' and did I 'fancy the Donald O'Connor part?'

This had been my favourite film of all time and, when on tour in the provinces many years ago, I had watched it dozens of afternoons and slowly learned a lot of the routines. I really

wanted to play the part of Cosmo Brown but, at the age of 51,
I wondered if I would be up to the furious knockabout *Make
'em Laugh* routine.

This incorporated running up a wall and performing a back
somersault – twice – at the end of an exhausting routine. I had
to prove to Tom that I could do it before we went into serious
rehearsal. I got close and he gave me the benefit of the doubt.

On opening night, I went for my customary warm-up
attended by two of our stunt men 'in case'. Maybe I was a
little more wound-up for the big occasion but I ran up the
wall, pushed off and overshot the two helpers *and* the landing
mat. The result was a severely sprained right foot and two
cracked ribs. We could hear the first-nighters taking their
seats as I hobbled back to the dressing room, and we sat and
watched my foot turning purple and blue. We were applying
an ice pack as Tommy came into the room. His emotions were
a mixture of sympathy and obvious concern for the show. I
didn't have an understudy at this stage and to have to cancel
would be a major disaster – on the other hand, to have a
limpalong wrecking the routines would be equally bad. I tried
to answer his unasked question. 'I'll be OK.'

'Are you sure?'

'It's not broken, so I'll get through.'

There was great relief in his face though it didn't lose
concern. 'Bite the bullet.' (Later on he presented me with the
bitten bullet mounted on a blue ribbon.)

We got through the show which eventually ran for two
years and three months at the Palladium.

I'm often asked whether it gets boring repeating the same
thing over and over again. Not at all! It's like a steady job
really, with plenty of spare time and lots of fun back stage.

One evening I noticed a lady in the audience about four
rows back and she was wearing the biggest Afro hairstyle I've
ever seen. Right behind her, there was what must have been a
man but he had no chance of seeing the show. He had a bald

head and was resigned to the fact that for him, the show would continue in sound only. I know I shouldn't have mentioned it but I told Tommy to look four rows back at about the ten o'clock angle. 'There's an ostrich's nest.' Nobody dared look in that direction for the rest of the show.

Tommy was a hard disciplinarian but also had a warm friendly side to him. Just before we broke up for the Christmas weekend, he threw a party between the matinee and evening performances. We all assembled in the specially prepared room and found our place names. The big surprise was ... oysters!

Tom gave us a demonstration on how it's done, adding a squeeze of lemon, a dash of Tabasco then 'straight from the shell in one'. A sip of champagne to follow then on to the next one. I dared not even consider sliding *one* down let alone half a dozen so my close neighbours helped me out.

On Boxing Day, many green-faced actors and dancers dragged themselves through the stage door. Most of them had experienced an explosive Christmas but felt they had to turn up for the show as their illness may have been interpreted as having had too much rum sauce and brandy butter!

Once they met at the theatre they realized that a lot of them had suffered in the same way. This time I took great pleasure in talking about greasy pork chops and cold thick-seam tripe and kippers.

Once *Singin' in the Rain* ended at the Palladium after 896 performances I was back into the hotch-potch existence of motorways and one-nighters and, of course, *Record Breakers* filming. As I was as fit as I had ever been due to the regular exercise over the last two and a half years, we decided to try for a physical type of record. Tap-dancing was fairly obvious – but what tack? One idea was the first to accomplish one million taps. That suggestion lasted only until we realized that Fred Astaire, Gene Kelly and Donald O'Connor and many others would already have passed this mark years ago. 'How about the *fastest* to a million?'

This seemed a feasible proposition so we all agreed. I had made a quick guess in my mind and assumed it would take around five hours. The BBC special effects department were alerted and started work on an electronic mechanism which would count and display the number of taps as they were performed. Four charities became involved and my neck was on the block. When I eventually calculated the challenge ahead, I needed to average 11 beats per second for 24 hours non-stop! At first, I didn't believe it but the ominous truth gradually dawned. Now I had really bitten off more than I could chew. This was almost like stringing eight marathons together. How stupid of me not to have done an official calculation before diving in with both ageing feet.

I recorded some special music and, providing I could keep up with it, I should get the required amount in the required time.

It was long and boring but with a quarter of an hour to spare, Frank Bruno and Gloria Hunniford jumped in with me for the millionth tap. I doubt if anyone would ever want to break that record.

One-nighters were plentiful as we strung Yarmouth, Cannes and Ilkley into the same week. Private cabarets on the *Silver Barracuda* as it sailed up and down the Thames. As we got closer to Christmas the shows became almost every night. Hilton, Savoy, Grosvenor House, Heathrow Hotel, all grouted with charity raffle draws, and scanner appeals all over the place. I had stopped doing pantomimes just after Benjamin was born as I found I was entertaining everybody's children except my own! In the old days panto and summer season were the bedrock of our year. In between these two foundation stones, show business could be a bit thin on the ground. Now, with functions and television work, panto and summer season were not as absolutely necessary. I certainly enjoyed *doing* pantomime but it was extremely demanding and when Christmas Day came along, all I could do was sleep. I was a non-contributor for my own family. So I stopped it.

Just before Benji was born, I had finished payments on our house in Gerrards Cross and was feeling very proud of myself. You can imagine my surprise when my accountant said, 'It's no use to you any more from a tax position. Either re-mortgage it or buy another place.' I was thoroughly confused but other opinions confirmed this course of action to be favourable. Having done a summer season with Tom Jones at the Winter Gardens, Bournemouth, in 1971, I was invited back to play in a nightclub the following summer. We had rented a house for around £100 per week in 1971 and it seemed common sense to start buying a place down there with a view to keeping it as a holiday home. Ten weeks' rent money would take us a thousand smackers nearer the final payment. We looked at many. Some were beautifully appointed but not 'free' enough. Others were nicely situated but not 'cheap' enough! Eventually, I was told about a house which was new on the market but was in fairly poor condition and reasonably priced. I went to see it: and 'fairly poor' should have read 'tumbledown and rat-infested'. The dear old lady owner had lost her husband and had turned the place into flats with coin-operated meters, night storage-heaters, and everything higgledy-piggledy. The place had a dilapidated smell about it. However (you sensed this coming, didn't you!) it was beautifully situated amongst Scots pines and had a short walk to the beach. Perfectly secluded but not remote – and cheap! I shook hands on it and warned Fiona not to be shocked by the first impression. She was shocked, but trusted my vision for the place. My builder friends Peter Brown, Ralph, Cliff and Co. knocked lumps out of the ramshackle residence. Apparently, the first cold chisel had rats running everywhere but, as the story goes, disturbed rats don't return. So far, the story is true. We did that summer season sitting on the proverbial orange boxes and going to bed by ladder. The builders lived down there whilst knocking two rooms into one, fitting central heating, rewiring and plastering. We even managed an outdoor swimming pool and that's why I stopped doing summer seasons. We have had wonderful Christmases and summers together and I have always been glad we took that decision. Maybe not as rich in the bank but certainly rich in memories and love.

I suppose it all depends on personal priorities. Holiday villas abroad are all well and good but the fuss and bother of getting there would have been irksome and wouldn't work if we suddenly got the urge on a particularly nice day. With Bournemouth, we could, the instant we decided to go, pile in the car and be there in under two hours. It was also easy for mates to come along. I spent my summers being a lifeguard and pool attendant as there were sometimes as many as thirty youngsters thrashing about in the water. In the evenings they would all pile in for hot chocolate and demolish a whole tin of broken biscuits then scamper up to their sleeping bags and giggle for hours. Great days. Pool barbecues, beach barbecues, oh yes, I don't regret one minute.

Mam was beginning to fail a little and wasn't quite responsible enough to handle the flat, so we found a cosy rest home for her in Southbourne, near to our place in Bournemouth. She was well cared for and had no responsibilities. The sea was very handy, as were the local shops and it was simple to pick her up for the day. Our conversations were always the same and I felt really sad that this vital and energetic woman was now becoming a confused old lady. I realized how much she had done for me and, although I had tried to repay her and take care of her, I still felt I should have done more. After a massive stroke in 1975 she passed away.

Once or twice I would be asked to do some filming for *Record Breakers* during the summer as a lot of attempts were made then, what with better weather and holiday times – for instance, hot air ballooning, for which conditions have to be perfect. Many charity fêtes would attempt a record as the drawing card. We attended quite a few 'longest conga lines'; 'unsupported circles', where everyone sits on the knees of the person behind them. Biggest musical chairs. Largest orchestra. Largest number of people skipping over one rope. The list is endless.

When my producer asked me if I felt up to trying the 'wing walking' record, I couldn't refuse and still keep my street cred! You will notice he said 'Do you feel up to', as if I might be getting past it!

I had a practice for about ten minutes with the aerobatic team who were based in Cheltenham. They provided me with a zip-up leather suit, helmet and goggles. There was a wooden post sticking out through the top of the bi-plane's upper wing to which I was strapped. My feet slotted into loops similar to water skis, and that was it. I was warned not to stick my arms out sideways once we were travelling at a speed of 80 to 100 kph or there could be a nasty dislocation. The practice went fine and I almost enjoyed it. The rain stung my face once we got up speed but I kept my arms well tucked in.

The record we were trying for was duration, not distance, and stood at three hours and eight minutes. Our plan was to leave Gatwick sometime in August and fly a circuitous route to Le Bourget just outside Paris. There were two static cameras fixed to the Boeing Steerman, one directly in front of me and one on our starboard wing giving a profile view of me. I had headphones and a face mask containing a microphone similar to ones pilots wear in those war films. Goggles kept flies from hitting me in the eyes and a life jacket was fitted in case we dumped in the English Channel. I thought it strange not to be provided with a parachute but was told 'If it opened accidentally, we would be in all kinds of bother.'

There was another plane, a Cessna, carrying the film crew and producer, who would be taking shots along the way.

Sitting in the queue for take-off amongst the 707s and
Jumbos was like David sitting among Goliaths and must have
looked pretty odd to any plane spotters. We taxied behind
these huge lumps of roaring metal and got closer and closer to
the start of the runway. I checked the safety belt a few times
as it was my only means of being secured. I daren't think
about that too much. The pilot, Brendan O'Brien, asked me if
I felt OK and I replied 'Roger'. He asked me again and I said
'Fine'. He then asked, 'Can you hear me?'

'Yes.'

'I can't hear you. If you can hear me, give a thumbs-up.'

I did.

'Oh no! Your mike isn't working! Right – er – now – if you
are feeling all right, don't make any big gestures but if you
want to abort, give me a pronounced thumbs-down and I'll be
able to land within ten minutes, OK?'

Thumbs-up.

'OK. Sorry about this!'

There was only one pilot although there were two seats.
The front seat had been fitted with an extra petrol tank in
order to keep us flying for the necessary three hours eight
minutes plus.

The 707 in front of us roared into life as the heat haze
distorted its wings and it slowly gathered momentum as it
trundled down the runway. It finally nosed into the air and
was on its way to destinations unknown.

'OK, Roy?'

Thumbs-up.

'Good luck.'

Full throttle and we were off. We had hardly reached the
first white markings and we were airborne. A slight wobble to
begin with and then we started to climb. Our camera crew were
next on the runway. Apparently, as they started to gather
speed, their undercarriage did the splits and they were left
stranded in the middle of the runway. Gatwick Airport was

brought to a shuddering halt for, according to which newspaper you read, one to five hours.

We were on our way and there was a big debate going on as to whether we should abort the attempt or not. The eventual decision was to carry on and try to establish the fact that I was really *doing* it and not using a stunt man.

It was a lovely day and I was amazed at how much open countryside and farming land there is between Gatwick and Dover. Haymaking was in progress and huge bales of rolled-up hay littered every other field. From some two thousand feet, everything appeared so neat and tidy, with toy tractors driven by toy farmers. It was all so interesting as I became used to the thermals lifting us over light-coloured patches then dropping as we flew over dark forests. The pilot was constantly speaking with different air traffic controllers as we passed into fresh areas – all rather piercing on the ears. I couldn't ease the helmet into a different place as it would have more than likely blown away taking my goggles with it. It was something I was just going to have to endure.

After about twenty minutes I realized I should have had a head rest. The post to which I was fastened stopped about the top of my spine, consequently I had to support my own head against a continuous wind of 80 to 100 kph – *for three hours!* This was a serious mistake and I felt that it could easily be a reason for failure. I tried all kinds of ways to ease the pressure but nothing worked. Something else I was going to have to live with. After a while, my heels began to get hot as I stood stock still in the foot loops and the only way I could ease them was to lift the heels up and take the weight on my toes. This made my knees bend slightly and the wind caught the relaxed part of the leather trousers behind my knees and made them flap so the back of my legs got a fair old spanking. Back on my heels, sharpish.

The view was splendid as we flew along the white cliffs of Dover and the starboard-wing camera produced some good shots of my profile against those magnificent chalk elevations.

There was an eerie sea mist on the Channel and we flew quite low for reasons best known to the pilot. Possibly to let the camera establish we were in fact crossing the Channel. As he spotted a small ship, he banked round it to let our starboard camera get a shot. We did the same with a small fishing boat. One chap was standing up wielding a rod, so I gave him a careful wave and he waved back and returned nonchalantly back to his rod as if I *always* passed by at that time of day whilst standing on top of a plane!

It was much cooler over the sea, in fact it was getting chilly so France was a welcome sight. At least I assumed it to be France as the countryside was much the same as Sussex. My confirmation was the air traffic controller gabbling away *très fort*! I could hear the garlic as my ears winced with the reverberations. The pilot was also getting messages from base with plan 'B'. The film crew were chartering a larger, faster plane and should catch us up around the outskirts of Paris.

After two hours up there, I was beginning to wonder what on earth possessed me to accept this stupid challenge! My neck ached, my legs were sore, my heels were boiling and I had to keep throwing out those niggling thoughts about the plane being held together with a few nuts and bolts. 'I'm only strapped to a piece of wood! What if it broke! What if the buckle came loose? What if the pilot had a heart attack? What if? What if? What if!! Think about something else! Oh look! There's a church. It must be a French church … what if we came down on a spire?' A new traffic controller rattled my skull thereby taking my mind off crashing.

The pilot talked to me. 'Three hours, Roy – how are you feeling?'

Thumbs-up, doggedly.

'You're doing great. We'll soon have the record.'

Our 'other' plane caught up and got some film of us as my pilot gave them a few puffs from our exhaust to add a little animation. We were now approaching Paris but were not allowed near the Eiffel Tower – for safety reasons, I assumed.

'Three hours eight minutes. You've DONE IT!' The pilot was as pleased as I was although we were airborne for another twelve minutes before I spotted a small runway in the distance. As we landed I whipped the helmet off and my ears heaved a sigh of relief. The controller was jabbering instructions to my pilot as I held the helmet at arm's length. His faint ramblings were akin to putting sugar on an extracted tooth and watching it throb!

I was welcomed by my producer, Greg Childs, whose first words were 'Don't talk to the press!'

The phones had been buzzing regarding the hold-up at Gatwick and, although my assessment of undercarriages wouldn't be acceptable to any airport authority, I got the blame! One of my 'pranks' had held up holidaymakers by the thousand! I felt Thursday to be an odd day for multitudes to travel on holiday, but I'm no authority on package deals either. I am pleased I actually did achieve the wing-walk record, but if asked again, I would have an extremely convincing excuse ready. I'm just very thankful my pilot didn't loop the loop as a gesture of success.

My next spot of recklessness was in Blackpool, a town which has played a significant part in my life, and nowhere more so than the Tower, now celebrating 100 years of great entertainment.

When I was a kid, as we rattled along in our Jowett through all the towns now by-passed by motorways, Dad would offer sixpence to the first person who spotted the pride of the Fylde coast. I always won, being an only child, but that first sighting set the heart pounding. This was it, we were almost there and all the recollections of our last visit would jockey for pride of place in my young anticipation. The huge beach where I could bury Dad in sand again. The Golden Mile with lettered rock, pink candyfloss, ice-cream cones, funny hats and jokey side-shows. Last year it cost tuppence to see the largest water otter in captivity. It turned out to be a massive kettle. The laugh was worth tuppence but we wouldn't be caught by *that* one again. The Tower Circus was a must with the new clown prince, Charlie Cairoli, wowing Blackpool with his famous slapstick and multi-instrumental expertise. The famous deposed King of the Tower, Doodles, was an old man by this time and just made a token appearance. We still bought a 'Doodles' badge as we 'didn't know if there'll ever be another! This might be worth a fortune one day!' Boarding houses were funny in retrospect as Mam and Dad became different people in the company of strangers. A pseudo posh accent confused this little seven-year-old. The beds were first of all checked for damp before the cases were unpacked. If Mam's make-up mirror didn't cloud over, a rheumatic week was avoided and we could concentrate on impressing the other guests by changing into our holiday togs. New socks, still held together with sticky backed plastic which, when peeled away, managed to stick to various parts of the body as the efforts to flick it into the wastepaper bin became more and more aggressive. Short-sleeved shirt tucked into belted trousers and the new socks amply visible through open sandals. Mam didn't wear sandals because her feet were not a pretty sight as she sported two large bunions due to ''aving to wear 'and-me-downs'. I would be warned to behave and 'not to ask for any more toast! We don't want to look like gluttons on t' first day!' As an afterthought: 'If anything falls from another table you can get it but be discreet!' This was the Dad I knew, but not the one who faced the other visitors at high tea. 'Good afternooonah. It lewks like beingng a nice deay.' He would nod to others. He nodded with a Yorkshire accent! ... he still had his cap on. Mam would eye up the guests then discreetly whisper to Dad, 'I don't think we should bother with them at the window table!'

'Why not?'

'I've just seen 'im lickin' 'is knife.'

Dad would wait a diplomatic second then casually glance over, and quickly look back – trying to look nonchalant by crossing his legs revealing the sandals and the new socks with their insteps instructing the whole boarding house to 'wash in lukewarm water'!

The trip to the top of the Tower was a must but, naturally, needed a good-visibility day. On these occasions, the queues were long but good for candyfloss and ice-cream sales. The tingling in my knees as, once at the top, we looked through the huge safety bars at the ant-like people way below on the promenade and beach, is still with me today as I reminisce. Little did I know I would be standing *outside* those safety bars over fifty years later.

It was another 'I don't suppose you feel up to ...' challenges from the producer of *Record Breakers* which, when six months away, was relatively easy to accept. As the day grew nearer, the Blackpool Tower death-slide took on bum-tightening proportions. The specially made rope – assembled by the Royal Marines to begin at the top of the Tower, some five hundred feet above the promenade and stretch out at an angle of approximately 45 degrees to a landing pad on the promenade – had to be over one-third of a mile long to allow for wrap-arounds at the wynch and landing area either end. No knots, of course, for obvious reasons.

We all travelled up to the resort on the day before the drop. Blackpool Tower appeared to be much, much bigger than I had ever remembered. My co-host on the show, Cheryl Baker, was going to whizz down the rope too, and we were to follow a Marine who had done this kind of thing many times. He was very relaxed and chatty the night before which was more than could be said for either Cheryl or me. I have to record that Greg Childs, our producer, assured us that if, at any time, we had second thoughts, we were to be honest and 'no one would mind'. I didn't eat much that night! (Didn't want to put too much pressure on the rope ...) Sleep did not come easily as my mind ran riot. Would the rope have a loop trajectory allowing us to hurtle down the first few hundred yards then gradually slow us up as we got about halfway? Then, would the strain on our arms be fierce? I had to shut out any thoughts of the rope breaking. What about the wind factor? It could be *very* gusty around that famous Woolworth's corner!

Next morning was calm and fairly cloudless. *Drat*! We ate a tentative breakfast and accepted the fact that the 'Rope Slide' (as we preferred to call it) was on. 'Are you sure you are happy to go ahead with it?' With the Marines all around us, we would have to have been braver to chicken out than to go through with it.

The journey up in the lift was scary enough. Plenty of rattles and jolts had us looking at each other with wide-eyed, inverted smiles. Our hearts were certainly working overtime as we reached the top and strode over the small gap which gave us a glimpse of the Tower base five hundred feet below. That set the knees tingling again. There were quite a few people busying themselves around the rather cramped area on this upper deck. We were shown the launching platform which had been specially erected *outside* the safety barriers. Scaffolding had been fixed in place and supported three short planks. Our come-uppance was now getting dangerously close as we were talked through the journey once again. We were given our specially made figure-of-eight ropes which had been double wrapped with strong hessian and soaked all night in order to prevent it burning through halfway down. Our hands just fitted through the two loops as it was passed over the main rope. We were reminded to keep our arms straight otherwise our figure-of-eight might slip causing the knuckles of one hand to touch the main rope and become severely burnt. Wide-eyed, upturned smiles were exchanged once more.

The lift arrived again with the local press and TV. 'Could we have interviews first, please?' Suddenly it felt extremely ominous ... 'and his last words were ...'. One question was 'What makes you want to go from the top of Blackpool Tower by rope?'

''Cos I don't trust that lift!'

One thing I *did* notice. The Marine was rather quiet and just a little transparent. I didn't know whether to be pleased or worried about this!

Crash helmets were donned and safety harnesses buckled up. 'These will just about save your life but it will not be a pretty sight,' confided the gravel-voiced sergeant in charge. The frighteningly thin black nylon safety line was all we had to rely on should we slip out of our figure-eight.

The actual record breaker was a weighted bag which was pushed off from the launching platform. We watched it hurtle down the surprisingly straight rope as it appeared to get smaller and smaller and almost disappeared before it arrived at the big air bag, specially placed to cushion the landing should it be a little too speedy. It was! The tension was slightly adjusted for our first live attempt. The Marine climbed out on to the scaffolding platform with, apparently, no qualms.

'Cameras ready.'

'All set?'

'OK.'

'Go!'

Off he went with our eyes glued on him as his trousers flapped in the self-perpetrated breeze. He obviously arrived safely as the walkie-talkies exchanged the news. All was well and ready for my turn.

'Are you sure?'

'Yep.'

'Good luck.'

I did my piece to camera and stepped gingerly out on to the

platform. There was nothing to stop me falling all the way
down as I passed my figure-eight rope over the main line. It
was a real tingler as the sergeant grabbed the back of my coat
and someone else fixed my flimsy safety rope to the main one.
'You'll be all right,' assured the gravel-voiced Marine. 'Enjoy
it!' My knees were jelly as I saw all the seagulls flying way
beneath me. Even a helicopter was hovering below. 'Hope
he's seen the rope!' crossed my mind. We had to get a move
on as all the promenade traffic was halted until the manoeuvre
was completed.

'Roight?'

'Yep.'

'Go!'

I launched into space and don't remember much about it
until the sergeant bellowed, 'STRAIGHTEN THOSE ARMS!'
I reacted accordingly and realized I was on my way.
Surprisingly, the ride was very smooth and after halfway I
began to enjoy it. The whole journey took about half a minute
which meant I was travelling at around 30 mph. There was
quite a crowd at the bottom and, as my momentum wasn't
quite sufficient to carry me as far as the air bag, I had to be
pulled to the landing stage. The exhilaration was tremendous
as I waved to the admiring crowd.

'Come on! Get down! Cheryl's on her way.'

'Ooops.' I was unhooked and lowered on to the most
welcome promenade as the crowd applauded Cheryl's arrival.
We celebrated by cutting a special cake and guzzling 'prop'
champagne. One more Marine came down the rope with a
camera fixed to his helmet in order to give shots of the actual
feel of the death-slide, but he didn't keep his arms straight
and one of them covered the lens. Shame!

Trams and cars were waved into action again and we went off
to finish our most welcome breakfast. I'm just dreading the
telephone call: 'I don't suppose you feel up to the Eiffel
Tower? ...' (*Merci* – '*non!*')

*

Tingling and even jellified knees were one thing – they recovered quickly – but all my dancing and acrobatics were beginning to tell. A twinge developed in my left hip, which over the years grew more and more painful. Remembering Tommy Steele's words and presentation, I bit the bullet for as long as I could but towards the end of 1990, it was becoming extremely troublesome.

I had been receiving physiotherapy for a few years but the decision had to be finally made in favour of a replacement. I thought this would be the end of my tap-dancing but, if it eased the pain, there was no contest. My surgeon also tended many members of the Royal Ballet Company so I felt I was in safe hands.

Six weeks after the operation I performed my first gentle tap-dance, and I have had no trouble whatsoever from the replacement. The relief from constant pain was heaven and it was not long before I had forgotten about it altogether. I wasn't in line for the Olympic Games – but what 58-year-old is?

When we toured Australia in search of record breakers, I was most impressed by the country, weather and attitude. We featured the Sydney Bridge and Opera House, and Ayers Rock where our cameraman was also our pilot. He positioned his plane in a gentle anti-clockwise bank, locked off, then abandoned his controls to take up his camera. He filmed as I read out the information for our eventual viewers. The unwritten, but well-understood law regarding the filming of Ayers Rock from the air was the obvious one that all planes must circle in an anti-clockwise direction. It was quite alarming when we encountered a newcomer. Filming stopped immediately, and our pilot started barking down his radio! (I was relieved I wasn't wing-walking at the time!) Within seconds the newcomer had banked off in a puff of embarrassment.

We visited Alice Springs, interviewed flying doctors, explored 'Schools-on-the-air' where children 'went' to a school many miles away by tuning in on their two-way radio. The night before we covered this, I broke one of my gastronomic rules and ordered half a dozen oysters. The seafood was reckoned to be the best in the world and there wasn't an R in the month. However, there *was* an R in the *year*! I spent that night emitting from both ends with absolutely no control. Sitting on the loo with plastic bag in hand was not the ideal way for the host of *Record Breakers* to spend the night before a day's filming. As everyone else was bright and breezy next morning, tucking into their bacon, eggs and fried bread, I decided it was a personal thing between me and oysters. They considered me an undesirable résidence. I survived next day on a diet of the Oz equivalent of Rennies.

Koalas, kangaroos, emus and possums hovered in background introductions and 'Waltzing Matilda', billabongs and didgeridoos were featured along with Aboriginal demonstrations in lighting dry grass with the stick friction technique. However, the *pièce de résistance* was yet to come. We flew over the rain forests up the east coast and put down in Brisbane, Queensland.

This was paradise, albeit brief, as we helicoptered out to Heron Island, a small coral deposit topped with mainly palm trees surrounded by pink crushed coral sand. The island got its name from the hundreds of white herons nestling in the trees and hovering the well stocked waters. We managed one walk around the island which took us all of twenty minutes, before we filmed many of the 365 different types of coral to be found in such a confined space.

Sunset was finer than Disney's best. Almost unreal silhouettes of trees and herons against a red, orange, yellow and sepia sunset. Gentle waves lapping the coral beach and reflecting the mellow yet vivid evening. Every step was another photograph worthy of any competition. My own amateurish efforts give me great pleasure whenever I delve into my collection. The following day was to add even more unbelievable excitement. I was transformed into a six-year-old on a Christmas morning as we dinghied out to the edge of the reef and back-rolled overboard wearing snorkel and flippers. I still hadn't seen below the water as I delivered my piece to camera, then submerged. I almost swallowed my snorkel! I had seen so many Jacques Cousteau-type TV shows and they were so very beautiful, but *this*! It was a massive kaleidoscope of all the prettiest imaginable colours darting to and fro, sometimes collectively in shoals, sometimes singly and haphazard, but the sea was *full*! Those herons needed no technique at all, it was just a lucky dip for them. This experience topped the lot. I wondered how many of my mates from Scholes had seen this. (Probably plenty!) Our stay was far too brief as the budget for Children's TV didn't allow 'swanning' time, but fleeting as it was, my visit to Oz impressed me greatly. I really wanted Fiona to experience this continent, but naturally we would have to wait until our children were independent and we could be away without her feeling she was shirking her duties and being unable to 'relax', which was the key word. *Relax*!

Our first real opportunity came after Christmas 1991. Benji was 18, Anto 22 and they were almost glad to get rid of us for three weeks. We pointed out where the vacuum cleaner was, where the washing-up liquid was, and took them on a quick exploration of the fuse box.

Our plan was to fly to Brisbane, hire a car and just drive around as the mood took us. No rigid plans or schedules. I had talked to Pat Cash during a record-breaking speed-serving tennis item in the studios and he had recommended Cairns as a must, so this was high on our list. He also recommended a Hotel and Country Club which, although truly magnificent, would have blown our budget in two days.

Our outward journey was long but comfortable (we were up-graded!) and, as we perused the brochures, our anticipation grew into something that was going to take more than three weeks. Oops! We were already breaking the rules. *No* definite plans!

It was late evening as we landed in Brisbane and the car hire companies had sold out. There were plenty of hotels on freephone and transport was inclusive. Almost a one-man band, the proprietor of one of these picked us up and carried our bags to our room, then explained the workings of the adequate double room. We were tired enough to have slept on corrugated hedgehogs.

Next day we reversed the procedure, flew straight to Cairns, and phoned an 'affordable' hotel in order to settle, explore and think. The weather was idyllic and my white knees got an airing as we wandered around the medium-sized town. New shopping precincts hatched in the middle of older surroundings. An ancient railway chugged up through the mountains to a small village of local entertainment and Aboriginal culture. It was known as the Kuranda Railway. A market sold corked hats and painted silk scarves, pottery and carvings, but the bungee jumping ... I didn't 'feel up to'!

Our affordable hotel boasted a pool which, on close inspection, resembled more a concrete hole – three people filled it. This was a disappointment as we felt we would like to stay at least a few days whilst the weather lasted. A cyclone was hovering out at sea and it could decide to visit fairly soon. As we sauntered along the promenade checking the boat trips to the local islands incorporating snorkelling, swimming, fishing, glass-bottomed boats and all other reef pursuits, we also wandered through the Hilton Hotel. A huge building slightly curved with many floors. A jazz pianist was entertaining the residents who were contemplating in the main lounge, moving out, moving in, or waiting for their trip to an island or the rain forests. As we walked through this high-ceilinged, tree-dotted five-star jungle with tropical birds flitting about, we encountered a huge blue swimming pool which was the length of the hotel and curved in a corresponding arc. It was all of one hundred metres long and probably more. We 'oohed' and 'aahed' and thought of our salt-water hip-bath back at the other hotel, and trotted out the old adage, 'We might never get the chance to come here again!' The cyclone didn't seem to be advancing, so I asked the price of a double room. I was genuinely surprised when the answer didn't make credit card tremble. This was our best break so far and we booked in – for a couple of nights at least.

The cyclone stayed way out at sea and we had constant sunshine whilst the weather forecasts for the rest of the country were not encouraging. Trips by boat to different islands, visits to the rain forests, river-boat explorations in search of crocodiles (we never saw one!), Dinkie-toy hire-car to chance a coastal drive. We had to be careful if we wanted to swim in the sea as box jellyfish had invaded the shallow waters. The name 'box' comes from the fact that should one of them sting you, that's what you ended up in. Some of the vast beaches were covered in tiny balls of sand surrounding one small hole. Stand still long enough and the tiniest of crabs would burst out and deposit another mini-boulder in formation, then scurry back. This was obviously an excavation exercise and not a sandstone factory. Raising your gaze from this one tiny hole surrounded by sand balls, the mile-long beach revealed millions of the same. A whole world of non-stop action as the next tide would wash away the boulders and fill in the cavities ready for another display. Further up the beach and they'd only have to do it for 'streemly high tides. Still, if it keeps them happy! At least they don't have to commute (or eat oysters).

Walking along the grassy, tree-lined path from the town centre one evening, I noticed what appeared to be Dracula hovering above, looking for business. A sharp intake of breath brought Fiona's attention to this likely cause of someone's anaemia. 'Oh yes! Now where did I read about them? They're fruit bats, known as flying foxes.' They certainly looked like winged foxes! Very scary. I was glad I wasn't a rabbit. We got quite used to them as they gathered in a huge tree near our hotel screeching and fighting over the fruit, I suppose. We slept with our windows closed!

We stayed in Cairns, at the Hilton, until we had to return home. It was exactly what we had wanted and we congratulated ourselves on having gone there first – had we chosen Sydney, we might have braved it through dismal weather and just arrived at Cairns for the last couple of days. As it was, we just wallowed in the pool and gorged ourselves on the splendid array of tropical fruits and wide range of cereals including a type of muesli which had been steeped in some concoction overnight. Not appetizing to the eye, but when topped with mango yogurt, it was a nutritious gastronomic powerhouse. Newly baked wholemeal rolls, freshly squeezed orange juice and large, sun-ripened bananas set us up for the rest of the day. Two and a half weeks of paradise, including a warm, short-sleeved New Year's Eve followed by a fax from Julia to Mum which luckily reminded me of Fiona's birthday! That might have brought the cyclone ashore! Saved by the belle.

We returned home via Singapore, where we had a short stroll around the beautifully appointed airport interior. Oooohed 'n' aaaahed, but didn't buy!

Heathrow was the unsugared pill of reality. As we descended through the January clouds, the rain streaked across our windows giving distorted views of our grey-green land as it lay there slashed by shining motorways with little beetles spraying the headlights and windscreens behind.

'Welcome home, darling.'

'Umph!'

Part II

The gang who endured my practice sessions of 'Flight of the Bumble Bee' in *Humpty Dumpty*. *Back row, left to right*: Gary Miller, David Davenport, Paddy O'Neill, Harry Secombe; *front*: Stephanie Voss, Svetlova, Alfred Marks.

Good times on the *Garry Moore Show* in America. *Left*, with Carol Burnett and Julie Andrews; *right*, with Mel Tormé singing 'Let's Call the Whole Thing Off'.

Oh Happy Day! 29 July 1963, St James's Church, Gerrards Cross. *Above*, Harry Secombe was the *best* best man a man could have. *Below left*, the smile on my face says it all. *Below right*, a honeymoon adventure in Bermuda.

Publicizing the 'pleasures' of parachuting with Eric and Ernie in Coventry. *Right*, Eric stayed with us in our 'luxury' flat in New York … the toes in the foreground are *not* mine!

With Sid James and Dick Van Dyke (who had dropped in for a visit) during the filming of my one and only *Carry On*.

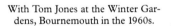

With Tom Jones at the Winter Gardens, Bournemouth in the 1960s.

Three generations of the Castles: proud parents and grandparents pose
with Daniel flat out in the pram!

That wasn't the only time Daniel was flat out ... this photo was taken –
much to our relief – after his accident in 1980. *Left to right*: Julia,
me, Anto, Fiona and Benji, with the patient in the middle.
(*Manchester Daily Mail*)

Record Breakers! (*Clockwise from above left*): pineapples in Hawaii; cow chips in Clapham (Ohio); a million taps; the world's tallest man; and parascending on the Thames.

I *wish* I could remember what I said … but it was lovely to see Her Majesty laugh. (*Doug McKenzie*)

A great night in May 1992 when Bruce Forsyth invited Benji on to his show for a chat and a duet – and I tagged along!

Doctor Foster went to … The Duke of Gloucester was very kind when I admitted a case of 'mistaken identity' at the ASH and British Heart Foundation Awards in 1992.

Going … Going … Gone! When the chemotherapy started to take effect I eventually decided to shave off the few wisps of hair left.

The radiation unit. The 'business end' (above me in the photo) swings round on the large disc in the wall, zapping at different angles.

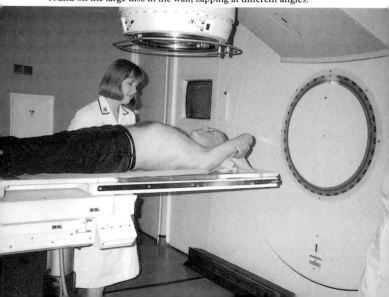

Above: my favourite family photograph, taken the day after my sixtieth birthday. *Below:* thirty-one years and still going strong – a kiss from my Fiona. (*Daily Mail*)

Wednesday 15 January 1992

We arrived home armed with presents for the children and a few friends. We'd taken an extra empty fold-up bag especially for this purpose.

16 January heralded an amazing lack of mangoes, pawpaws and sun-ripened bananas. The grey morning wasn't pool-enticing and snorkelling down our local muddy river had no takers. Our videos proved to be quite interesting ... to me and Fiona at least.

Over the next couple of days I caught up with some of the mail mountain and phone calls, and checked with Anglia Television that all was going ahead with a planned trip to America, starting the first programme in New Orleans. I had been asked by Anglia Television to do a short series based on the story of the Salvation Army. This was to replace Harry Secombe's *Highway* programme during his summer break.

I had always had a healthy respect for the Salvation Army and their genuine love for all the destitute and needy, but this series made me realize what life was all about. They are certainly not rich in a materialistic sense but I have never met happier people. Great musicians too.

The late-night soup run was quite scary as we knocked on cardboard boxes and enquired 'Soup?' A grimy hand would venture out of the flap and wait for the paper cup to be placed in it. The cup would be retracted and the hand re-emerge for the customary lump of bread. The whole Salvation Army experience was very important to me.

The following summer there was a short series based on the

Hymn Writers, then a series – *Castle's in Europe, Castle's Abroad* and *Castle's USA* – was to be next. I was to play my trumpet with some of the old-timers in Conservation Hall and tap-dance with the street buskers. One of my ambitions was to be realized. All was set and I was due to fly out in ten weeks' time.

I went along to the official receiving of the new ambulance for our local Cheshire Home and tried to be the life and soul of the celebration. Press pictures and an attempt at a speech that was less than radiant. I thought my jet lag was taking longer than usual to right itself. I was not feeling well and my friends noticed it.

Sunday 19 January 4 a.m.

I was awakened by a headache the like of which I had never experienced. When I was in my teens and early twenties I had suffered bouts of migraine, but the very worst ones didn't go halfway to this one. I felt my head was about to explode and truly thought this was *it*! I woke Fiona and actually made my peace with her, confessing my love and making sure our children would know how sorry I was to do this to them all. She immediately phoned our on-duty GP, a lady doctor, who arrived in minutes. She performed the necessary tests and phoned an ambulance right away. All the signs were pointing to a possible heart attack. I was expertly stretchered into the ambulance (*déjà vu?*), only this time the alarm bell wasn't needed, we had just about beaten rush hour!

High Wycombe Hospital had me wired up in seconds and it was my turn to 'bleep'. Overnight observation revealed nothing alarming from a cardiac point of view so I was sent home with instructions to 'get back in touch if you're worried'.

I now assumed it was a massive migraine attack which would gradually subside. I was wrong.

For two days, whilst the headache fluctuated between acceptable and excruciating, I noticed a developing fidgety, claustrophobic feeling. I felt as if an invisible boa constrictor was slowly tightening its grip and trying to suffocate me. Every few seconds I had to jump up and free myself of this enclosed feeling. Going to bed was like sliding into a torture chamber. Within twenty seconds I was having to jump out and pace the floor in order to avoid suffocating. This was *very* strange. I just paced up and down all night, mainly downstairs from room to room. The following day my GP gave me an injection to relax me. It lasted four glorious hours, then the condition returned. There was obviously something seriously wrong and I was becoming extremely tired but unable to rest.

Wednesday 22 January

My doctor fixed me an appointment with our local neurologist who took time to see me as an emergency. After a few questions he put me straight into hospital for a series of tests. I stayed in for six days during which time I was X-rayed, given a series of blood tests and administered various pills. The brain scan was extremely distressing as my head was inserted into a closely fitting tube which aggravated my acute claustrophobic state. It was a relief to be told that this was a fairly normal reaction and an injection helped me to relax during the 40-minute scan. This test revealed nothing alarming – in fact, all the tests, which included ultrasound on my stomach and liver areas, proved at this stage to be negative. My eyesight was playing tricks and I was unable to focus on either books or TV, so I found my mind wandering back to that superb holiday in Oz which made me realize how doubly important it was to have built up all those happy and loving memories.

New Orleans on the horizon raised my pulse rate until the 'ifs' began to materialize. If my eyesight didn't improve, it would be a struggle to learn my lines and deliver to camera. If the claustrophobia and headaches continued, how would I cope with the flight? Forget it! Think of Oz instead.

Friday 24 January

The neurologist finally discovered a discrepancy in my blood. The sodium level was almost nil and I had double the amount of the normal water content – hence the violent headaches. I was put on a low-liquid diet – one litre per day, total! This included milk, soup, tea and even water with pills. The equivalent of 6½ cups of liquid per day. I drew up a chart and crossed 'em off as they went down (rather like hedgehogs on the side of a Reliant Robin).

Saturday 25 January

Had to phone Cheryl Baker from the hospital and apologize for being unable to go to her wedding with Steve. That was a disappointment but nothing could be done. They were sad for me but, of course, fully understood. At this stage I still felt as if my problem was a sustained migraine attack.

Tuesday 28 January

I was allowed home but had to keep to my low-liquid diet and take things easy. As my condition eased a little I felt rather optimistic: maybe it was a virus and all would soon be back to normal.

Friday 31 January

Another blood test was good news indeed: my sodium level was almost normal and the water had receded. I was told to 'Stick with diet but go back to work.'

In February I began to feel that everything was returning to normal. A blood test on 7 February proved very satisfactory and I was told to return to my normal liquid intake, with the proviso 'you won't go mad though, will you?'.

I was able to work normally over the next three weeks – including taking part in the recording of the BBC Radio 2 *Big Band Shows*, plus an introduction to the first part of this six-week series, which I had missed during my stay in hospital. This was a great personal thrill for me.

I performed at Grosvenor House for a private function, giving a short act, drawing the raffle and, later on in the evening, joined Kenny Ball and his Jazzmen for an ad lib session. That was a *great* feeling.

Towards the end of the month I played four 'Family Nights' at Butlins in Minehead, which proved to be hard but rewarding. I didn't feel too well at the end of this stint, but it wasn't a worry. I was also able to turn up at Cliff Richard's launch of his tennis trail in search of young talent, but wasn't feeling good and my voice was cracking up. Barry Cryer's thirtieth wedding anniversary in early March was a great night, but I was working hard to be bright and breezy. A show in Bristol with the Royal Marines and Squadronnaires was a better night as my voice was coming back.

Tuesday 10 March

A blood test on this day was disappointing and arrangements were made for me to visit St Mary's Hospital, Paddington. A tap was inserted into my vein and used to fill up about ten different small bottles of samples to be checked in all departments. It reminded me of the Tony Hancock classic 'That's an *armful!*' After a cup of tea, I was taken in for another chest X-ray.

Wednesday 11 March

An early morning phone call came from the Professor at St Mary's.

'You'll be pleased to know that your blood tests are perfect.'

'Great.'

'However...'

'Er – yes?'

'We would like another X-ray if you could get back down here.'

'Er, when?'

'Now?'

'Yes.'

I had started yodelling again.

Many of you reading this bit will have had previous experience of X-rays. A cubicle is assigned to you in which to undress, in my case down to the waist only. A boiled-white coat is provided but the tapes must be fastened at the back. Almost impossible when you are anxious!

A smiling nurse ushered me back into the X-ray department with the danger warning on the door. Chest bared against the cold plate and arms to the side with backs of hands firmly placed on buttocks. She went behind the screen and shouted:

'Deep breath!'

I did as I was told.

'Hold it!'

Click.

'OK. Relax. Take a seat, won't be long.'

Another lady radiologist joined her as they looked at my X-rays and mumbled to each other, just out of earshot, pointing to a certain area of the developed plate. They kept glancing at me without giving me any idea of what was going on. Much worse than an audition.

Eventually, after leaving me alone for 'Won't be a minute', the second radiologist came to me and confided, 'We'd like to see you in the scanner if you wouldn't mind. We could do you in a few minutes if that's OK?'

'Certainly,' I replied. What else could I say?

I remembered what seemed to be hundreds of concerts, raffle draws, fun runs, personal appearances, football matches, cricket matches and bed races to raise money for scanner appeals all over the UK and now I was to be introduced to one for the very first time. Maybe it was one I helped to buy!

The room resembled the inside of a sci-fi set with Dr Spock at the controls. The stretcher-type bed was able to pass through a large circular hole which could accommodate persons of greater bulk than me, so there was no claustrophobic tension. All well so far! I was positioned on the bed and asked to keep still. Everybody disappeared after warning me that 'the next part will continue automatically', and to just do as I was told. After a short pause, a Dalek said, 'Take a deep breath, hold your breath'. The machine contained in the hoop encircling me whizzed around once then the bed moved up about half an inch.

'Deep breath – hold', etc for around twenty shots. There was then quite a perusal pause, whilst I lay there, head swimming with every doubt imaginable.

I was suddenly aware of a doctor type chap who said, 'We'd like a more intensive look, if you don't mind. This inspection will help us to get a better idea.' It was, I think, an iodine job and would 'make your mouth feel a bit warmer but don't worry about it, it's perfectly all right. You'll just feel a little scratch.'

Internal yodelling as I tried to remain macho about the 'little scratch'. My mouth began to get warm so he must have been a good shot. The Dalek instructions ran through again for what seemed an eternity. Pause. Boss radiologist came and helped me out of my scanner and made pleasant conversation for a short time. Then his tone changed as he asked me seriously, 'Are you a smoker?'

'No.'

'Have you ever smoked?'

'No.'

'Never?'

'No, never.'

He looked puzzled.

'Mind you, I've worked in a lot of smoky atmospheres. A lot!'

'Hmmm.' Then he half muttered, 'Big in America now ... passive smoking.'

He said no more about it and I left with serious doubts for the first time. When I told Fiona, she tried to make light of it but we both knew the ominous implications of the situation.

Thursday 12 March

Turned up at the Savoy Hotel on the Strand to take part in some publicity stunt for the shoe trade, with a bunch of other celebs. A lot of frivolity and fun for the cluster of cameras, followed by catching up with long-established but seldom met-up-with-lately mates.

As I was presented with my pair of shoes in the traditional box, the Jimmy James days flashed across my mind and brought a nostalgic smile. It was amazing how memories were suddenly becoming important to me. A few weeks before and the same recollection would have just been 'Oh yes, great days!' Now it was a more precious part of what might turn out to be a pruned version of my ambitious contribution.

Friday 13 March

Outside the Oxfam shop in Beaconsfield, I met up with a

brave chap who was about to walk around Britain and visit
every Oxfam venue, dressed in top hat and tails. That put
my own selfish priorities in order. We posed for pictures and I
wished him well before travelling back to see my specialist
neurologist who had seen my scan plates and the radiologist's
report.

I could read nothing in his immediate facial expression as
he welcomed me into his consulting room. There was another
gentleman sitting in a corner to whom I was introduced. He
was tall, rather gaunt and serious as he asked me a few
questions about my previous health and habits. He was, in
retrospect, being very careful not to alarm me unnecessarily.

He suggested a bronchoscopy, which would entail the
insertion of a flexible, manoeuvrable tube up my nose, down
my windpipe and into the suspect area of my lung. 'There is a
small camera at the end of the probe and I can also take
samples of tissue for inspection in the labs.'

I attempted a grin which was not convincing.

'Don't worry, you will be lightly sedated and will feel
nothing, and afterwards you will probably not remember
anything about it. It's quite friendly really. But it will give us
as much information as we shall need to determine what the
problem is. At this stage, it could be quite innocuous and
cleared by a few pills, but I'd like to be sure and I'm certain
you would too.'

'Fine. Let's get on with it.'

We set the date for 15 March, at 3.30.

Saturday 14 March

Went to the Science Museum to present prizes to young
scientists for achievements during the past year. How I
wished one of them had invented a cure for my condition. It
was another uplifting day to see all these keen-eyed
youngsters and wonder what their lives and ambitions would

provide over the ensuing years. We finished the afternoon trying to create the biggest bubble, which provided lots of hysteria but, alas, not a world record. I travelled home with mixed feelings about their future and my own.

Sunday 15 March

Fiona's big brother Tony and his wife Anne came to visit and stayed for lunch – a 'slap-up' mingled with giggles, family news and, eventually, the probabilities of my imminent bronchoscopy. I wasn't allowed food. Suddenly it was time for me to leave. I tried to appear nonchalant and left with a gritty smile, which I am told looked more like Daniel's first attempt at a smile as we left him at the prep school gate. Fiona dropped me off at the hospital.

Back into the boiled-white-back-tied gown, white socks and paper cap. On to the stretcher and wheeled into the operating theatre, watching ceilings pass by and masked faces hover over me.

My bronchoscopist was waiting for me and explained the strategy more thoroughly so as to leave me in no doubt concerning the next few minutes or so. 'You'll just feel a little scratch.' The needle provided me with a relaxant but apparently didn't put me out. My nose was greased and the probe expertly inserted and guided around the tubes into the suspected area. Chat was constant, I believe, and according to my chimney sweep there were some good funnies flying around.

'We've got good pictures of the area!'

'What's on the other side?'

'*Coronation Street.*'

'Can you get *Through the Keyhole*?'

Maybe it's just as well I remember nothing of it!

Fiona picked me up and wobbled me into bed.

Monday 16 March

The long wait! Plenty of discussions at home. What if …?'
Steady on, this could still be something simple and easily
disposed of. The trip to America was just one week away and
could be hanging on a rather slender thread. On the other
hand … Oh forget it!

Tuesday 17 March

I phoned in to the hospital about 10 a.m. but the results were
not through. I would be 'notified as soon as we have them to
hand'. This was like waiting for my school exam results. No –
it was worse. Relaxation was as easy as roller-skating up
Everest.

At 4 p.m. the phone rang. I didn't give it a chance to get in
the second beep. 'Yes?'

'Ah! Is that you, Roy?' It was the doctor.

'Yes!'

'Well – er – the results are with me.'

'And?'

'I'd rather not talk on the phone. Could you possibly come
in and see me?'

'Yes.' I yodelled again.

'Say this evening, around seven?'

'OK. Oh – er, what about my trip to America?'

A long pause…

'Er,' he cleared his throat. 'I – er – don't think you'll be
going to America.'

My heart sank into my left kneecap. This was the prelude
to the news we were secretly dreading. Fiona, although visibly
shaken, was glowingly supportive and gave me a tremendous
feeling of togetherness through thick and thin. 'In sickness
and in health'.

I had to telephone Malcolm Allsop at Anglia TV and

apologize for being unable to fulfil my commitment and having to drop them in it at such short notice. He was very gracious although it must have presented him with enormous problems as the production team headed by Eddie Anderson was already out there. Even so, his disappointment was not as great as mine. I snatched at the hopeless possibility of still being able to fit it in, but thought they should be alerted as soon as possible. A substitute would have to be found. Au revoir New Orleans, the Conservation Hall and the street buskers.

I entered the consulting room, a room I shall *never* forget. My bronchoscopist had invited another doctor along and they welcomed me with guarded smiles and asked me to sit down. I took off my navy-blue 'skipper' cap and laid it on the desk whilst my sentence was administered. I asked for the absolute truth with no cushions, which I feel they understood and were about to give me anyway. There was concern in his face as my bronchoscopist prefaced the vital information with 'We are both devastated, Roy. This shouldn't happen to you of all people.' I had done lots of work for this very hospital, including their carol concerts in the main hall.

'You've led a reasonably healthy life and we are extremely sad but mostly confused by your diagnosis.' He paused. Here it comes. 'The tests have revealed a small cell cancer known as "oat cell" and it is extremely virulent. What is perplexing to us is the fact that this particular illness is known as the regular smoker's cancer – yet I believe you don't smoke.'

'No.'

'You've *never* smoked?'

'I tried half a Woodbine when I was eight, my Dad found out, introduced me to a clay pipe and that was the end of that!'

'Did your father smoke?'

'Yes.'

'In the house?'

'And in the car.'

'Hmmm.' Pause … 'And your work?'

'Well, I've worked a lot in smoky nightclubs and hotel dinner dances, dressing rooms…'

'Hmmm, it's very likely an accumulation of all these things which have contributed to your inhalation of other people's smoke which is a classic example of what's becoming known as passive smoking.'

'So what's next?'

'The prognosis is not pleasant. Without treatment, we could only guess at about three months of gradually deteriorating health. If you went to America, you would become seriously ill and may be unable to make the journey back. We think you would be ill advised to go.'

'So what do you suggest?'

The second doctor took over. He was the area expert in the treatment of cancer, particularly my type. He explained, 'After consultation with the surgeon, it has been decided that the cancer is inoperable. It is lodged rather delicately where the windpipe joins the lung behind the breastbone. An operation could be highly dangerous.'

I looked at his concerned eyes and tried not to drop my stare as I fingered the rim of my cap. He continued:

'The only option I can suggest is a course of chemotherapy, which has a slightly better chance.'

The chance was revealed to be a five to ten per cent possibility of recovery according to past statistics. This was the best prospect they could offer me. A mixture of hopelessness and desperate heroics permeated the consulting room.

'Well,' I cleared my throat, 'it's fairly obvious, isn't it!'

'Would you like a second opinion?'

'What do you think?'

'You will probably get the same advice, but it's your choice.'

'Let's go for the treatment.'

They were both immediately spurred into action. The decision was made and I was to turn up for my first treatment two days later on Thursday. I shook hands, donned my skipper cap at a jaunty angle and walked out into the night.

That five miles' drive home was the loneliest time I have ever experienced. I was numb and had to concentrate very deliberately on my driving. Humming, clattering wheels were ringing inside my head as past memories and future doubts thundered and flashed. Preparations for Fiona and our children. How much time before I started to deteriorate?

Arriving home, the strange car in our drive reminded me of my promise to Dave Foster of a voice-over for his video appeal in aid of Albania. He is a great friend and works incessantly for Eurovangelism. In a sense, it was a diversion for me as I had to pull myself together and get on with it. Naturally, he was aware of the situation, so I told him the truth as matter-of-factly as possible. Fiona's eyes welled but she didn't blurb as she made a cuppa, and let us get on with it. Here we go again. 'Laugh clown laugh.' We got through it surprisingly well, considering.

Dave went off as diplomatically as possible leaving me alone with Fiona.

Nothing was said. We just embraced and sobbed. The sluice gates were opened and we just held on to each other with all the love and tenderness we had built up over our thirty years together. Fiona was first to speak. Again, she was strong with definite commitment to the task ahead. We are both strong Christians with a total trust in God, but this was stretching our faith somewhat! Fiona told me that whilst I was doing the voice-over she was praying and asking delicately 'What's happening, Lord?' She became aware of the message, 'Just stand back and see what I am going to do through this.' She was very convinced and I promise you Fiona is not a person to clutch at straws or hallucinate.

We had to break the news to Benjamin as he returned home

with a face full of questions. The answers took time to sink in as he turned seriously transparent, unable to evaluate the implications of a life-threatening illness. Fiona eased his dilemma by drawing him into a threesome hug whilst we all sobbed again.

Antonia came home from her stage manager's job at the Orange Tree, Richmond and we all blurbed again. Anto was cross at the seemingly unfair dismissal of her Dad in his prime. That meant a lot to me. A bit of defiance was what I needed.

I got no sleep that night. My heart pounded as I stared at the ceiling, planning the truncated future and wondering what death was really going to be. From a distance, these thoughts are easily contemplated, but once you are really on the high diving board the pool seems a daunting venture. I remembered the words of Diana Dors in the same circumstances: 'It wasn't supposed to end like this!'

Wednesday 18 March

No need to awake. I was numb yet excited with lots of preparations queuing in my mind. First on the difficulty list was letting Daniel know. He was based in Norway with a Christian group named 'Youth With A Mission' shortened to YWAM (Whywam), sometimes referred to as Young Women After Men, or Youth Without Any Money.

I dialled and waited, as I tried to plan a way of easing the news gently.

'Ya?'

'Oh, er, do you speak English?'

'Ya, a leedle.'

'Could I speak to Daniel Castle, please.'

'Daniel? – Oh, *Daniel*.'

'Yes, it's his father speaking from England.'

'OK. I be as kvick as poshible.'

Long wait – then, 'Hi, Dad!'

I couldn't speak, my throat stalled as I pictured my first-born. He sounded so bright and cheerful and, obviously, totally unaware of the distressing news. Fiona realized I was incapable of speech and took the phone. As she explained the situation in what could only be described as the gentlest of ways, I tried to pull myself together for a final word. I couldn't. My emotions took a firm grasp of my vocal chords and strangled everything that was desperately trying to pour out. When he said, 'I love you, Dad', I burst. That was the most difficult phone call I shall ever have to make – and I said nothing.

Around mid-afternoon my GP arrived to explain what would very likely happen over the next period. It sounded pretty gruesome. Later that evening, our Pastor, Jim Graham, arrived with Peter Falconer, an Elder from our church, to pray for me and claim healing according to James, Chapter 5 in the Bible, whilst anointing my forehead with oil. A peace flowed through me as I was now committed to the expertise of the doctors, nursing staff and faith.

Thursday 19 March

I was booked to do a charity request for LBC Radio asking people to 'skip lunch' and put the money towards aid for the children in Africa, so I arranged to call in on Julia at her shared flat in Wimpole Street prior to my session. We found a quiet corner and I stumbled through the story. I think she half expected it. As I related the grim possibilities we sobbed quietly, but had to pull ourselves together in case anyone bobbed in. Julia was remarkably strong and resilient as she encouraged me to battle through. I hardly remember the recording session at LBC, but it seems that the producer was satisfied as they thanked me and wished me luck, not knowing how much I was going to need.

That evening, Fiona drove me to the Nuffield at Wexham,

near Slough and I was admitted for my first chemotherapy treatment. Documents had to be perused and signed before I was settled into my ultra-clean room with private loo and shower. And TV with remote controls.

Once I was in my pyjamas and sitting up in bed, the sister came and took the token pulse, blood pressure and temperature.

'Oh, and there's a phial in the loo for a sample whenever you feel ready.'

'No problem.'

The session would last for 24 hours. A tube would be inserted into my vein, through which the drugs would be administered. That made the cheeks tighten a little. The tube from my arm would be attached to a plastic bag which hung from a high transportable stand rather like a hat rack on wheels, as seen millions of times on TV hospital soaps. The bags would be replaced when empty by various solutions, some sympathetic, some harsh. I found out later that the severe ones were covered with an outer dark blue bag to shield the contents from excessive light. Curious that this threat to the mighty oat-cell cancer was afraid of the light! Shine, Jesus, shine!

At 9.30 p.m. the ball game got under way as my specialist inserted the tube into my left wrist and the drip was adjusted to speed. Saline just to clear the tubes for a few minutes, followed by a new anti-nausea drug to ease the awful sickness which by all accounts is the worst of all the possible side-effects. I slept on and off as my left arm had to be kept fairly still to avoid a disconnection, which would administer the treatment to my mattress!

Friday 20 March

The tube dripped on with various fluids through the day. No effects so far, but it was early days yet.

Fiona visited and we phoned Daniel again. This time I was

much more together as I chatted easily and apologized for breaking down before. He then told me how he couldn't have wished for a better Dad and 'did' me again. That was the *best* phone call I have ever made. He had talked it all through with his girlfriend and she had shared his grief which was a great consolation to him as he felt so helpless out there. I glowed as I remembered his emotional words of comfort. Then I thought, 'Wait a minute! That was almost an obituary preparation. Steady on!'

At 9.30 p.m. the tube was slowly taken out by my specialist who also prescribed some pills to counteract at least some of the effects caused by the chemo treatment. Not much of a problem yet, but I knew that after about the third visit my hair would start to fall out. There were to be twelve chemos altogether, then the situation would be re-assessed.

Fiona took me home, snuggled me into bed and I tried to sleep. Now my arm was free of the apparatus, I could turn sideways and thrash about if I wished. The first uncomfortable side-effect was a strange type of indigestion. I suppose it could be a suppressed version of the violent sickness experienced by the less sophisticated treatment endured by earlier sufferers. This must be pleasant by comparison.

Saturday 21 March

After a fitful night, I felt tired and my energy was very low. Had to cancel a presentation ceremony for a local youth football team which was a big disappointment, but I was in no condition to do the honours. Indigestion worsened and 'over-the-counter' remedies didn't help. It was a floppy type of day.

Sunday 22 March

The day I should have flown to New Orleans! Two things to feel bad about. I heard that Anne Gregg had volunteered to take over the series, which was very brave as most of the situations were aimed at a trumpet-playing, tap-dancing, jazz enthusiast. She did a great job at such short notice whilst working out eleventh-hour rewrites.

Tuesday 24 March

Following a Monday, which came, throbbed and went, Fiona drove me to the hospital for a blood test and X-ray prior to my next 'hook-up'. This time the chemotherapy was to last just twelve hours as it was a different cocktail. My specialist breezed in after a long day tending many patients over a large area. He was satisfied with my blood count. The white cells had been replaced sufficiently to withstand another onslaught of the chemo. The whole conception of the treatment, in lay terms, is to retard the cancer cells from developing and eventually shrink them. Unfortunately, this concoction has the same effect on the white cells, which make up an important part of the immune system. I gathered that the white cells recover slightly faster than the cancer cells, so the next 'bash' should have the cancer ones on the run – providing the whites have regrouped. My GP explained, 'So, no matter how bad you are feeling, the cancer is feeling *worse*!' That was a sort of comfort when one is clutching at straws.

The specialist was also satisfied with the X-ray. 'It certainly hasn't developed any more. That's an encouraging sign, but don't start waving the flags yet.' A quiet morale boost.

The tube was inserted again. 'Good man.' Drip-drip-drip. Here we go again. Incidentally, for the uninitiated, the fluid didn't flow into the actual body tissue and bloat me into a Sumo wrestler! The fluid that was not absorbed by the body followed the usual route and ended up in a handy bottle, the contents of which were measured and compared with all liquid intake.

Sleep was difficult again, but not too necessary as the World Cup cricket final was on the radio at 4.30 a.m. You may remember that in the 1992 tour our hopes were raised by a Pakistan slow start. Then Imran Khan unleashed himself and piled 'em on. We lost! I'd have gladly given him my next chemo session!

Wednesday 25 March

9.30 a.m. Fiona picked me up and drove me back home to hear the final stages of the match. I lost my will to live! I had nothing to contribute to the rest of the day. Floundered around a bit then gave in.

Friday 27 March

Anglia TV had to announce the fact that I would not be presenting the forthcoming series so, for the first time, the news was out in the open and mentioned on TVam. That lit the blue touch-paper and the phone rang incessantly through what was going to be a long hard day. It seemed the whole of the media had parachuted in. Press cars queued along our street as trench-coated reporters and well-equipped photographers made their way up our path. We had to make a quick decision between sending them away and trying to keep a low profile, or throwing open our doors and owning up. Get it all over with at one go and eliminate speculation, which could become an eventual noose as rumours may have to be refuted. Let's get on with it!

The procession lasted well into the afternoon and included virtually all the national newspapers and TV stations. I repeated my story many times while Fiona kept coffee flowing and folks were shuttled in and out. We were a transit lounge. I posed for all kinds of pictures, mainly with my trumpet and some with my son Ben. I felt two emotions which mingled bravado with desperate tiredness. Everyone from the media was genuinely concerned and nobody came to look for an 'angle'. The next day proved their genuine compassion as hardly any misquotes appeared (apart from the estimated value of our house! Had some of them been correct, I would have sold on the spot.)

Saturday 28 March

Reading the newspapers took up most of the morning which took the edge off the expected drowsiness and gave us a boost of relief at the lack of melodramatics or sob stuff. Naturally, the reaction from my friends was instant and warmly encouraging in very different ways.

Cliff Richard and Harry Secombe were first to telephone, followed closely by Bernard Cribbins, another friend of long standing. The chemo together with steroids had affected my voice and pitched it much higher. When I answered the phone Bernard said, 'Could I speak to your father, please?'

'It's *me*, Bernie, the treatment's got to my voice.'

'What are they giving you? Helium?'

The Water Rats have been extremely attentive and caring and someone from the Grand Order contacts me regularly. Percy Edwards phoned many times, as did Norman Wisdom, who always hid his identity and had me baffled for ages. Roy Hudd was a regular mate and wrote frequently, and Barry Cryer wrote lots of nonsense letters paying no attention to my illness whatsoever. All these laughs were a real tonic.

Michael Bentine phoned and we had a hilarious conversation until he had a coughing fit and had to ring off. I found out through subsequent calls that he has been a lifelong asthmatic and was struggling with his own cancer. And *he* was encouraging *me*!

The love was overwhelming, notes were dropped in the letterbox and flowers started arriving. It was extremely therapeutic and I considered myself strangely blessed to have this healing reassurance.

Sunday 29 March

Mustered up the energy to go to church with Fiona. We both received massive encouragement and were assured of prayer support from just everyone. We also attended the evening service which set us up spiritually for the week ahead.

Monday 30 March

If the weekend's attention seemed overwhelming, this morning was staggering. Literally. Our postman had to abandon his bicycle and use a van. The mail was enormous, delivered in a sack. The contents buried our kitchen table, and flowers kept on arriving every few minutes. The second post was the same. It took the rest of the day to open half of them. Obviously, if we were to acknowledge this show of affection and encouragement, some form of duplicated letter would be necessary. We drafted a couple ready for the task ahead and put the letters in a box designated the In Tray.

Tuesday 31 March

Chemo number three! Fiona drove me in for my X-ray and blood test in preparation for the 9.30 p.m. twenty-four hour dribble. My specialist was again happy with my blood count and, after a long study of my X-ray compared with the previous one, paced around my room with his finger on his chin, looking at various parts of the ceiling and mused 'Hmmm, I think we're in with a fight!' There was guarded excitement in his voice as he made the statement to no one in particular. I felt the glow of a five-to-ten-per-cent chance being a possibility. The tube was inserted into my left wrist again. 'Good man!'

I accepted the treatment with more confidence, feeling we were 'in with a fight'.

My twenty-four hours were slightly easier but chemo-bag changing and bottle swapping had to be carried out just, it seemed, as I was sliding off into oblivion. Never mind, round three was well under way.

Wednesday 1 April

No April Fool jokes like 'Ooops! we gave you the wrong cocktail! Could we suck it all back?'

I decided not to fill my mouth with shaving foam and ring the emergency bell. The joke was on me, had I been in the USA filming this would have been a day off and I was to have met up with the BBC Big Band who were touring American venues with George Shearing. I remembered the time I proposed to Fiona. We were playing his Velvet Carpet LP; 'Dancing on the Ceiling' did the trick. That album is well worn and precious, as you can imagine. I felt warm again.

Thursday 2 April

Stayed in bed most of my day at home. I couldn't face the mail yet. Lazily opened a few and dropped off to sleep with them all over the bed.

My mouth was becoming a little tender, but not enough to alarm – yet.

Friday 3 April

An approach was made from BBC TV regarding a series they were filming entitled *Fighting Back*. 'Would it be possible to come and chat about the possibility of covering your particular battle?'

This meant filming an interview at home, then coming along at regular intervals to register my progress or problems. It was the only one in the series which was 'live', so to speak, as the others were stories of past battles. Here was a chance to be in on a current one.

I agreed on the understanding that, should the last shot be the heat-haze shimmering above the crematorium chimney, it had to be the truth. Warts an' all!

'Well...'

'Otherwise, I'd rather not bother!'

They agreed and a provisional meeting was set up.

I felt that other cancer sufferers who were fearful of what it all entailed could at least share my experience and maybe not feel so desolate and helplessly lonely. I had received lots of letters from folks who had gone through the treatment and informed me of all the side-effects I could expect. I was warned of wanting to give in at times, urged to keep battling on with faith and patience. Many letters ended with the comforting news: 'That was eight years ago and I'm still here!'

If, in any way, I could pass on this kind of encouragement, at least some good would come out of it all.

That was looking on the brighter side! On the other hand – if it all went down the tube? Fiona did have one letter which informed her of the writer knowing of many cases such as mine. Relatives and close friends, 'but they've all died'! She added a PS: 'I don't know if you should tell Roy this.'

There's always something to set the cat among the pigeons, but once you are started on the Cresta Run it's best to keep your head down and leave it to the driver.

Monday 6 April

Picked up at 5.30 a.m. to appear on TVam with Mike Morris and Lorraine Kelly to discuss my problem, prognosis and the whole passive smoking time bomb. Dr Hilary Jones was well versed on the subject so I wasn't made to look a whinger with a 'poor me' complex. Jimmy Greaves piped in with one of his ricochet thought-flashes and suggested, 'Maybe it's because you are too fit. I know when racehorses are too finely tuned they catch everything there is going!'

It took me the whole journey home to think of a reply. 'But maybe the finely tuned horse notices something amiss long before the sloth and the early treatment could give it a better chance of success?' He would have thought of some answer to that. Anyway, I admire his attitude and, of course, his own successful battle with life's problems.

Back home to a *stack* of letters: we estimated around eight hundred. The phone rang constantly and more flowers poured in. I had absolutely no idea how many people cared. My career, as I saw it, was gently phasing out and I was content to slow down; I'd do a bit more gardening and a bit less motorways and airports; I'd have time to stand and stare. Not on your life. This situation had bumped me right back into the spotlight like a Bingo ball being blown up the tube to be shouted out to the whole place.

Gloria Hunniford rang to offer a phoned chat on her Radio 2 programme. 'Tell us how you are and perhaps thank everyone for their good wishes and alleviate some of the pressure of the mail.' Gloria has been a staunch friend throughout the whole saga. It worked well ... but stimulated more mail.

The back door bell rang. More mail? No. The builders had arrived to start some repair work on our drains which had been damaged due to settlement caused by two dry summers.

'And we shall have to do some extensive drilling.'

'How long? Any idea?'

'Oh, couple of days, no more!'

I just remembered the TV crew were coming next day for an establishing interview. Can't put the builders off – we'd waited over a year. The house might fall down! We'll just have to work it out.

Tuesday 7 April

Pouring down! Builders arrived with the kind of machinery you only see on motorways after three miles of cones. I didn't realize our drains were part of the Piccadilly Line! Fiona felt we should 'put the TV off '.

'They'll be here in a minute.'

'It'll be *bedlam*! And think of the *mess*!'

I was on a short fuse and couldn't handle the problems of a summit meeting with builders and TV projects and muddy carpets *and* chemo. I regret snarling at my wife who was only thinking of me and trying to shield me from all the hassle. I couldn't see a clear way out apart from getting on with it. It was horrendous!

In between showers – 'Could we get a couple of shots of you wandering arm-in-arm through the garden? Hold it! Builders in the background!'

Halfway through a poignant part of the interview: *BRRRRRRR*! – a drill.

'Cut! Could someone ask the builders to give us another ten minutes?'

Builders' accommodating smiles gradually turning into threatening looks of frustration and disbelief that a 'bit of filmin' ' could take so long. 'It'll only be two minutes when you see it!' I considered explaining to them that filming is a 'belt and braces' business – you must be doubly sure that you don't drop your trousers in public. Hence the trouble taken to cover every possible aspect of the action, from two or three different angles in order to have plenty to choose from in the editing suite. Keep all options open. But five huge sweaty builders waiting to scrum down is an awesome sight. They finished around 5.30 leaving the heavy goods ready for tomorrow. 'Don't worry, we'll catch up … *if we can get on with it.*'

As it was my fourth week of treatment, we all had to convoy to the hospital for the cameras which meant plenty of stops and starts and swapping crews from car to car in order to show different points of view. (Only one camera!)

Then interviews with both specialists. Close-ups of X-ray perusals. The blood test – that was fun as our poor nurse was so nervous, it took three or four stabs before she hit a vein.

We filmed my hospital table smothered in mail then panned over to my drip, from three different angles. Progress chats with my doctors who needed to get on with other duties but, I suspect, quite enjoyed the change of routine in this case.

The crew eventually shuffled off at about 10 p.m. and I settled down to what now seemed to be a peaceful night. Just me and my chemo.

Wednesday 8 April

I was picked up at 9.30 a.m. after the twelve-hour drip. Strangely, the shorter treatment seemed to have a harsher effect. The mouth ulcers were becoming more painful and spreading to my tongue. This was my worst reaction to the treatment so far.

Another mail mountain had arrived. I was receiving so many different 'cures' from people, all totally convinced they had the answer. Videos, books, cassettes, copper wire, instructions to phone certain numbers, advice on which direction my bed should face. Masses of info on diet but many conflicting views. All of these were sent with genuine love and concern. Had I taken notice of every recommendation, I would have been stirring, brewing and standing on my head in crystal whilst sleeping in wellington boots with a pocket full of prunes wrapped in fig leaves. Even if cured, I wouldn't know which one had done it. I decided to have full faith in my specialists and God. If I'm wrong, so be it! He will prepare a place for me. I just didn't have the energy for effort of that kind, and to add to it all, my nose was becoming raw.

Workmen battled on in the rain as I laid on lavish apologies about the previous day and 'You know what it's like when you have to film...' They understood (without stopping).

Thursday 9 April

Mouth *rotten*. Throb-throb. Throat aches and dull insidious indigestion is relentless. *Is it worth it?* A few strands of hair on my pillow. Here we go! I wonder what I will look like? Noticed sensation in area of cancer which felt like a local battle was taking place. 'Come on you Whi-ites!'

Rev Bob Allen came and prayed, and we giggled (noticed *he's* rather bald!).

Wrote letters until shattered. I added a personal PS for each individual and folded the paper whilst Fiona addressed the envelopes. We discussed getting a secretary but felt we could lose the real feeling of gratitude. Each letter felt like a personal friend. The real heartbreakers were masses of drawings sent from whole schools of *Record Breakers* fans. Drawings of trumpets, TV screens and broken records (mainly 78s!). When a seven-year-old writes, 'I like watching you on *Record Breakers*. PLEASE DON'T DIE,' it leaves you a bit dewy-eyed. A matter-of-fact reply to this was just not right. We plodded on. Well, there wasn't much else to do. I couldn't play the trumpet because of the ulcers, and tap-dancing was disappearing into the sunset.

The next few days saw the mouth ulcers spread and my hair fall out as we tried to continue with interviews, mainly for magazines now, photo sessions and, of course, dribbling away at the continual mail influx.

As my hair became really straggly, I decided to tidy it up and shaved it off very carefully with my safety razor. I was amazed how it changed my appearance from sadly pathetic to fiercely threatening. Each time I caught myself in a mirror or shop window, it startled me. My relations all remarked how much I now resembled my father. He had lost his hair in his late twenties. He lost his brown teeth quite early too. Apparently they were reasonably healthy but the Woodbines had left a layer of tarmac and in warm weather they almost welded together and set overnight. His dentist felt that dynamite would be more effective than a pneumatic drill so, to the relief of Mam, out they came! His 'new' smile was extraordinarily white and pink but, for quite some time, rather uncomfortable as he jockeyed them around intrusive seeds and gritty bits hitherto refused entry. This had a muffled castanet sound which would have gone well with his attempts on the harmonica. They finally settled down and slept well in the bubbling tumbler beside his bed. I was rather pleased that the side-effects of my treatment didn't include the choppers falling out as well.

It was in this stark bald state that I tried one of my rare visits up to the village as my energy level seemed sufficient. The reactions of friends, acquaintances and shopkeepers were vastly different. Some would see me, blush and hurry past as if they didn't know what to say. I identify with this sudden feeling of 'Oh dear, it's him! What can I say?' What *can* you suddenly say to someone who is probably going to die soon? 'Chin up, you can beat it!' is really a false bolster yet morbidity sounds like the Last Post! When I met Bernie Winters during his illness, I had *no idea* what to say. Same with Stanley Baker. I went over and over what I *should* have said afterwards, but that was a little late. 'How's your golf?' rings around in my stupid head to this day. So I understand the embarrassed avoidance issue.

As I entered the newsagents to check on an interview included in a magazine, I had the full range of reactions as I selected my purchase and went to join the queue of four people. The person in front of me, a young lad, was smoking and was holding the, by now, red rag to *this* bull, behind him. I stood far enough away in order to avoid sharing his momentary pleasure. Up comes another customer who turns out to be a Jack the Lad and enquires of me, 'Is there a queue here then, son?'

'Yes.'

'Well, shall we move up a bit then?'

'I'd rather not join in with his fag, if you don't mind.'

'Well, it may 'ave escaped your notice, but this 'ere establishment *is* a tobacconist's!'

Eyeball to eyeball. 'Yes, they also sell magazines on KARATE!'

His cocky stare slowly wilted as it dawned who I was and he slunk away for a further perusal of the stationery department. It was a hollow victory, had we been in Boots 'condoms' would have been a better put-down.

The next days went by almost routinely. Mail, phone calls, rest, pills to try to replenish my immune system, different applications in my mouth to try and ease the, by now, excruciating pain of the ulcers. They were everywhere and even drinking was a chore. However, I had received letters from other sufferers warning me of this and urging me to have patience. 'It *will* go away.' It wasn't easy to believe this as I felt my gums eating themselves away and every tentative exploration with my ravaged tongue seemed to discover more bomb craters queuing up to get in there. It felt as though *nothing* could heal it.

Tuesday 14 April

My next treatment was due, and blood together with X-ray were dutifully endured with a closed smile. My specialist was away on this occasion but 'Dr Bronchoscopy' was reassuringly there to perform the link-up. He was pleased with my blood and X-ray. 'There seems to be almost nothing there.' This was a magnificent boost to my battle as I remembered his

original prognosis administered in such grave terms. He also
prescribed some Fungilin lozenges to try and help the mouth
ulcers but also to help prevent thrush joining the foe. The
nurses seemed a little more relaxed this time. "Cos we don't
have to be on TV this week.'

'Didn't realize how nerve-racking it is!'

'The amount of time it takes.'

'People don't understand what goes on, do they?'

'Time and time again. I don't know how you put up with
it!'

17–20 April, Easter

LETTERS, LETTERS AND EXPLODING GUMS!

On Good Friday, as I lay in bed and watched *King of Kings*
on TV, I felt just the slightest affinity with Him, which also
made me feel so very inadequate for whingeing about a few
mouth ulcers and headaches. I read the whole story in my
Bible – twice!

Julia was home for Easter and we were almost a full family
again. She looked so beautiful and I was so proud to think
there was even a tiny suggestion that I was part of this
creation. We laughed and giggled as her photographs from
Peru were handed around, laughed in spite of the
unbelievable stories of poverty and hardship. Squalor
surrounding these defiantly happy little faces. How she was
invited out to dinner by one family who proudly lived under a
corrugated lean-to. The reverse culture shock was impossible
for her to accept and it was obvious she had left a large part of
her heart out there.

On Easter Saturday, I slept in and tried to lay some white
cells! No luck. Someone had recommended Difflam Rinse, a
sort of anaesthetic that lasted around 1½ to 2 hours. Mustn't
use it for more than a week. *Or what*? My gums drop off? My

tongue comes down my nose and my ears start applauding? Must make a note for next week. This could be good for the *Fighting Back* programme.

A new gum treatment was prescribed by my GP. It was a kind of gunge putty which had to be spread over the ulcers and left to do its work. The painful part of this exercise was the attempt to dry the raw meat before administering this grouting, or it would probably all slip down the throat at the first swallow. Three years of constipation could ensue. Once applied, talking was out. Pointing to my tightly shut mouth meant I was now incommunicado until the gums needed repointing. As I was only sleeping for two hours at a time, this ritual could be performed through the night whilst everyone slept. It didn't seem to be doing much good but I persisted.

I had just finished one redecorating session at around 4 a.m. when Antonia wandered in unable to sleep, so we chatted – well, *she* chatted while I just nodded or shook my head as appropriate – joined by a slowly awakening Fiona. As we 'discussed' the problems of insomnia, we became aware of a neighbour's alarm ringing away. Fiona peeped through the curtains and ascertained it to be 'Almost opposite, on the other side of our road'.

I was still gunged up so Fiona phoned our local constabulary in true Neighbourhood-Watch style. Naturally, she gave our name as proof that it wasn't a hoax. She kept sentry at our bedroom window for interest's sake rather than flying rugby tackles, I suspect. Before very long we heard a car arrive and doors slam.

'Oh no!' Fiona looked at me. 'They're coming here!'

Torches in hand, two policemen were wending their way up to our house.

'What shall we do?'

I was gunged up!

Fiona hurriedly put on her dressing-gown and went downstairs. I felt I should follow and give her my macho support. As Fiona opened our back door, the two sleuths were just appearing around the corner, ready for confrontation.

'Can I help you?'

Fiona was barefooted, so was I, but I had managed to grab my cap which I hastily flopped on my barren bit.

The first constable looked at us without registering any emotion so far.

'We understand you reported a burglary, madam.'

'Well, it's not us ...'

His glance fixed on me and he stared enquiringly. My mouth was newly gunged up and I didn't want to spoil my handiwork. He seemed transfixed and continued to look at me for an explanation. I tried my best!

'NGOO! ITCH THE WONN ACWOSH THE WOAAD!'

His eyes widened as he wondered about my nationality, then he was suddenly jerked into motion.

'Sorry to bother you, sir, we'll go and investigate.' A touch of the hat and they almost bumped into each other as they clumped off.

As we returned to bed, we collapsed in hysterical laughter as we thought, 'What MUST we have looked like!' On top of it all, it seemed to have been a false alarm (they arrested two mice for gnawing the cable).

Easter Sunday was a tremendous day, as the celebration bristled with hope and joy. Julia made lunch and I was determined to take part and join everyone at the table. Carrot and ginger soup with sour cream and walnut topping was an experience only a Dad could fully appreciate. The walnuts were finely crushed for me and I managed to get them past the craters with only a modicum of discomfort. Chicken marinated in honey overnight and delicately curried was really a no-no under normal circs but these were not normal circs! Mashed potatoes and chopped broccoli were not too difficult to swallow and the mango sorbet was like a cold plunge after a sauna.

We listened to tape recordings I had made of them when the children were very young and we were hysterical. For me, it was a very emotional time, remembering those delicate and fragile little ones, now grown-up, with their own lives and worldly experience. I was really proud that they were here, happy and well adjusted in a confusing and tempting world. Dads do get a bit soppy at times. I remain unapologetic.

An afternoon 'zizz' was unavoidable and, as the young folks went off to the evening service, Fiona and I settled down to more mail.

Easter Monday dribbled in after a few spasmodic bouts of sleep mingled with gunge treatment to my mouth. Some of it slipped down the gullet and formed a kind of carpet – weird! I was aware of the soles of my feet becoming rather tender as I walked around our bedroom. The skin wasn't being replaced as normal and the new sensation was strange. I also noticed my fingernails were becoming dull and the half-moons were disappearing.

In spite of my tender feet, I joined the others on a morning walk – about five miles, stopping to play Pooh Sticks under the bridge of our local river. I was surprised my energy didn't collapse on me as I was dreading the possibility of being helped home.

Nutritional porridge slipped down reasonably painlessly, followed by carrot and apple juice. Half-slept whilst watching TV sport: Man United lost. Leeds had an evening game. Attempted more mail at 5 p.m. Felt a bit faint at 8 p.m. Series of back spasms. Took two painkillers as mouth pains became intense. WORST YET! Slightly worried about tomorrow's chemo. Tried to learn script for Anglia TV regarding a charity home to be filmed tomorrow.

Tuesday 21 April

Reasonable night – amazingly! 6 a.m. news, Benny Hill found dead. Shortly after Frankie Howerd. Shock waves throughout the country. Dozed until 9 a.m. then had a bath and dressed in readiness for TV crew arrival. Comforting to see they were mates from past series and we got through easily by noon.

Turned up at hospital for blood test and X-ray. My blood was very shy this time and didn't want to play. Like Tom Mennard's gag:

'Is your name Stone?'

'No. Why?'

'I can't get any blood out of you!'

It finally worked and we came home. My mouth was really raging now and I *had* to apply the gunge as my tongue was becoming a disaster area. In spite of this, I was in good enough condition to tackle another dose of chemo. 'Once more unto the breach.' 'Bite the bullet.' Just remember how many more folks are going through the same and get on with it!

The drip finished at 7.15 a.m., a bit early, but I stayed on and had a little liquid breakfast. Fiona picked me up at 9.30 a.m. and got me home where I just flopped around dozing fitfully. This could have been due to a new attempt to quell the ulcers with a different drug. During my sleepy bits, I dreamt my tongue and gums were cured. I really felt *terribly* let down when I awoke to find the ulcers were still there!

Watched sport on TV as Frank Bruno scored with a haymaker to stop Jose Ribalta in the second round. I wondered if he would come around and put me out of my misery for a while. Man United lost to West Ham. What right have I to feel sorry for myself?

Thursday 23 April

Mouth very bad and I'm getting seriously fed up with it now –
'Come *on*!' I felt I was getting nowhere with anything.

Rolf Harris called to check how things were, which jolted
me into life again. He was 'just poppin' over to Oz for a couple
of months'. I was crazy with jealousy as the holiday memories
flooded back. 'Good on yer, Rolf,' I gritted. I was genuinely
lifted by his real concern when he was probably in an
embarkation froth.

I attempted some soft cod roes for tea *hurt or not*! I was now
declaring war on my mouth. 'See how you like *this*, pal!'
Together with mashed potatoes and bananas and custard, the
exercise was almost successful. I enjoyed it and felt less
subservient to the dominating issue. So a headache took over
and I had to succumb to a couple of painkillers. It *was* a fairly
naughty one.

Fitful night.

The next couple of days shunted through attempts at
interviews for mags and TV. My finger ends were becoming
slightly numb and the fingerprints were disappearing – now's
the time to do the big robbery! But I felt faint about 4 p.m.
and had to go to bed. A boisterously warming phone call from
Harry Secombe was my oasis for that evening as I lay down
with the TV on stand-by and my script for *Record Breakers*
tomorrow. We were covering the first Aerobathon at Earl's
Court in aid of the Royal Marsden Hospital. This was also
going to be covered by the *Fighting Back* documentary team.
I hoped the energy level would be up to it!

Sunday 26 April

After a reasonable night, I ate a hearty breakfast of porridge,
yogurt, and pills for the immune system. My legs were a bit

weak but not seriously – so far.

The car arrived at 10.45 a.m. and we high-tailed it down the surprisingly jam-free A40. It's almost worth travelling down it into London on a Sunday for the experience of gliding through all those usual snarl-ups where you have time to see those rotating billboards run through their range.

As we arrived at Earl's Court, the documentary team were waiting to 'cover' my day. Here we go! Emerge from car three or four times (remember belt and braces – 'There was a fool waving to his Granny behind you. One more time, please! *Sorray!*').

Up the staircase and into the celebrity room. Many well-known names had given up their day for the occasion in order to mingle and be introduced to our, hopefully, thousands of gyrating participants, all sponsored to the hilt. Our 'green' room overlooked the vast main hall. There didn't seem to be too many aerobicists at this time but, we were assured, 'They'll be here! Don't worry.'

Greg Childs, my producer for *Record Breakers*, arrived at noon and we went outside again to set up the opening piece for *our* show. Crowds were now beginning to emerge from the underground station and long-distance coaches were pulling up. Two or three 'takes' whilst jostling with well-wishers and we were back inside.

More celebs had turned up and the green room was gathering decibelic momentum. Through the bubbling throng, the documentary producer edged towards me with a young boy. He was about nine or ten years old with a roundish face, big warm eyes and – no hair. He was also a cancer victim. We chatted, loudly, for ourselves first, then 'Once more for the cameras, please.' He was such a pleasant young lad and took his illness so bravely that I felt a complete wimp beside him. We posed for the photographers as his mother stood by dewy-eyed, yet proud and hopeful. It was an absolute delight when, a few months later, he was a surprise guest in the *Record Breakers*' studio. His hair was now well grown and wavy, crowning a very handsome young chap with a radiant grin. A great thrill – here was the very reason for that fund-raiser at Earls Court. To give back life and dignity to young people is worth more than fancy cars and lifestyles. Try it.

There was still concern regarding the numbers of participants. We were hoping to beat the world's largest Aerobathon, the record currently held by Czechoslovakia, which stood at 13,824. *But* this was an outdoor record. Even so, Earl's Court could easily accommodate this number – if they came.

'OK, everybody! Would the celebrities make their way outside for the press photographers?'

We all trundled out for the group photo followed by selective group and solo shots according to the requirements of the different newspapers. This was the most gruelling part so far. Permanent grins for half an hour or so left the mouth in spasm. I was, however, surrounded by beautiful young ladies a couple of times which eased the pain a little.

Back in the green room to 'relax'. They had set a small room aside for me in the event of my needing to flop, which I made grateful use of for a short time. Norris McWhirter came in for a chat and with the news that approximately 8,000 had turned up so far and 'They are still arriving'. It seemed disappointing as we were getting close to the off. As long as the numbers grew throughout the four sessions, the final count would be official.

Clayton Marshall choreographed and led the whole work-out from the huge stage whilst local instructors were dotted around the hall on tables. It was getting busier. I now had to wander through the participants and interview a few for *Record Breakers*. It was a very happy little tour but the music was rather loud and the voice was given a fair testing. Backstage now to introduce some more celebrities including 'Norris McWhirter who has our final figures to hand'.

'And the final number for our Aerobathon is a World *indoor* record standing at … Thirteen Thousand Two Hundred and Twenty-Two.' The cheers were unbelievable. 'We are only six hundred and three people short of the World *OUTDOOR* record and there are two thousand tickets bought by people who didn't get here. So! Maybe next time?'

Massive whoops and screams of enthusiasm. As I thanked everyone for their tremendous support, they started into 'Dedication', followed by 'For He's a Jolly Good Fellow', and I can tell you, thirteen thousand people in full voice on my account was a boost the like of which I had never ever experienced before. As I made my exit through the crowd to the back of the hall, the love that flowed was very precious.

It was necessary to do some voice-overs for *Record Breakers* in the relative quiet of the foyer, then a quick résumé for the documentary before I gratefully stumbled back into the car. I don't remember my journey home.

Leeds United had beaten Sheffield United and Liverpool were beating Man United 1–0. Eventually Man United lost and Leeds were league champs. I was sad for Manchester but, naturally, being a Yorkshireman, happy for Leeds.

I ate three Weetabix (very soggy ones), yogurt and build-up pills and slowly lapsed into a smiling sleep with memories of the Aerobathon coming in and out of focus. I felt very warm and blessed. Apparently, on my back, I snored like a train but, lying on my side, Fiona thought I had died.

Monday 27 April

A floppo day which included a local interview regarding yesterday. Media coverage was good. A consignment of Biotta arrived for me. It is a skilful blend of organically grown roots, main flavour being beetroot. Quite a pleasant taste and can do no damage.

Mouth a little easier but around the wisdom teeth is still very angry and the original ulcer under my tongue is still trying

to distribute. Finger ends becoming a little more numb.
   Patchy night.

Tuesday 28 April

Seventh chemo treatment due. Went in for X-ray and blood
test. We had great difficulty with the blood again as one vein
gave a little then switched off. The findings showed a poor
white-cell count and I was unable to handle more chemo at this
stage. My specialist advised a week's rest in order to build up
my resistance again. I phoned Fiona who wasn't expecting this
change of plan and was out, so I stayed on for a while and
accepted lunch. Why not! Minestrone, cheese omelette and
mash, ice-cream with strawberry sauce. Hold on to *that*,
gummy! Fiona came for me around 1 p.m. and we attended to
our mail for the rest of the day. I can't say I wasn't worried
about the blood count but the only answer was to get on with
the build-up.

Daniel was due to come home from Norway, with his
girlfriend, on 1 May. We were really looking forward to this
event and busied ourselves preparing for their long-awaited
arrival. 'Welcome' signs all over the place. We had not met
Birthe or even had the slightest suspicion that Daniel had
finally become serious about a young lady. My first inkling
came to me hearing Fiona on the phone to him. The usual
Mum's question is 'Anything on the horizon?' followed by,
'Never mind. One of these days!' This time the answer caused
a flush to Mum's cheeks and 'Really? What's she like? How
long have you known?' He had been aware of this young lady
for quite some time but fraternization was not allowed within
the organization, so long-distance eye contact had been the
best on offer. They were coming by car via Newcastle and
phoned to say they had arrived safely on the ferry and were
well on their way. We were now a blur of activity as helium
balloons were assembled and welcome banners tied into place.

We had no idea what Birthe was going to be like. 'As long as Daniel loves her, I'm sure we will.'

'They're here!'

The car pulled up and they got out all red-faced. She was – and is – absolutely beautiful. Big welcoming hugs all round as my heart soared. I can't say it was with relief. I just had not dared hope for someone so special. I think she was slightly overcome (not knowing we were more nervous than she). Eventually we settled down a little and showed her to her bedecked room, then felt it time to allow a little peace. Fiona and I went up to the village absolutely glowing with excitement. 'I daren't even hope she would be this good.' 'Steady, they're not married yet!' 'I know, but it looks like it!'

We had really taken her to our hearts. The welcome burst into life again as the rest of our family arrived in dribs and drabs from work. A very happy Dad slid into bed at 2 a.m., the first to leave the gabbling throng.

Next day was a comparatively early start for me as I tackled more mail until the young folks gradually filtered downstairs and ate a walkabout breakfast.

Harry and Myra Secombe came over for a visit in the afternoon laden with books and gifts. An hour and a half of hysterical recollections had Birthe somewhat bemused, but she smiled a lot. I felt very special even though my finger ends had started splitting as much as my sides.

Gloria Hunniford rang to pledge her support for a Jazz Evening to be held at the Barbican in aid of Turning Point, a charitable organization helping mainly those with drug- and alcohol-addiction and those with mental-health problems and learning difficulties. I don't know how she gets through all the work but she certainly is a big-hearted lady.

Cheryl Baker rang to see how things were and told me, 'I'm just off to Australia for a bit of filming.'

'Can't you get out of it?'

Unfortunately they didn't get the same weather as we had

had. Pity.

The next crunch was nearing, as the days slipped from the calendar, but I was feeling much better for the chemo rest together with the buoyant atmosphere at home. Finger ends were worse and I had to wear protective gloves to handle the mail. The ulcers were still there in my mouth but with a definite sign of improvement. I longed to be able to clean my teeth but that was not possible. It would be like drawing barbed wire across my gums. Have patience. Many of those who wrote me letters of encouragement had been through it and promised that 'It *will* eventually clear up.'

Tuesday 5 May

Blood test! I felt good but not confident as the nurse approached me with the needle which took on missile proportions. I looked away in cowardly style as the probe searched my arm for a gusher.

'Ah!' said everything. What a relief as the phial filled up quickly. I even chanced a look at the dark red container as it was being labelled ready for inspection. I wondered how many white cells were in there – the colour gave nothing away!

My blood count had recovered and was eligible for another cocktail hook-up. There were ten different applications involved in this particular session scheduled for 24 hours:

1.	Saline: for a flush of the tubes	–	10 mins
2.	Kytril: anti-nausea	–	10 mins
3.	Etoposide: Chemo! (paint stripper)	–	30 mins
4.	Saline: restful flush	–	1 hour
5.	Cisplatin: Chemo again	–	4 hours
6.	Saline and potassium: (Big bag)	–	8 hours
7.	Litre 5% Dextrose: sugar energy	–	10 hours
8.	Kytril: anti-nausea	–	10 mins

| 9. Etoposide: Chemo | – 30 mins |
| 10. Saline flush | – 10 mins |

END

Bring me sunshine!

It goes without saying that, with all this liquid being administered through my body, sleep was interrupted frequently to release the pressure on the waterworks. At least we were into the second leg of the treatment. My vein clogged up towards the end of the session and the needle had to be transferred to the other wrist which wasn't too happy about it. Tough!

Thursday 7 May

A great day as I ventured a tentative brush of my teeth. What a sensation! I never imagined a simple pleasure could be such an important part of life. I smiled a lot. It compensated for my loss of voice. I tried to shout 'Eureka!' but nothing happened. Hit me again. I ran my tongue around my clean choppers and wallowed in luxury.

Our minister, Jim Graham, popped in on one of his regular visits and we had a good laugh about my breakthrough with the sparkling teeth. His constant encouragement and prayers have been a great comfort throughout the whole business. When my faith sagged, he was there to give me a boost and, I'm sure, always will be. Many of our Elders dropped by to assure me of their care and love during the treatment. I was almost embarrassed to be taking so long to feel better. Was *my* faith strong enough? I really did feel a closeness to God in my simple way, but, as a theologian, I was nowhere. All I could do was trust Him along with the expertise of my doctors and nurses. Miracles were bandied about on occasions by well-meaning friends but I felt it to be a bit selfish to expect one. Get on with it. I mowed the lawn and showed Daniel and

Birthe around the garden. Birthe seemed quite keen to have a 'go' at the weeds, so we discussed which were, and which were not, in case Norwegian weeds were different. Pulling out the chrysanths in favour of ground elder would have been difficult to pass off as 'Oh, that's fine!' She did a great job and I went back to bed with supreme confidence. I then started to think about my 28-year battle with that cussed ground elder. No matter how meticulously I ferreted out every last millimetre of this virulent squatter, within a couple of weeks, there it was again – Na-na-n'-na-na! It was annoying to think that it would have a field day once I had popped my clogs. Then I thought how ironic it would be if ground elder eventually proved to be the main ingredient in the cure for lung cancer!

I suppose all this seems quite boring to the normal person but, when brushing your teeth is a highlight of your week, these insignificant happenings are all you have to look forward to as you struggle on with, at times, a seemingly hopeless tussle. Bruce Forsyth was marvellous in so much as he invited my son Benjamin to appear on his show, have a chat and play a duet. This was a lovely gesture and Ben was really excited about it. He had done tiny bits of TV with the family but nothing as high-powered as this! He went in for a rehearsal and came back glowing with anticipation.

'They say if you feel well enough you could join in a second piece, but there's no pressure.'

I hadn't 'blown' for a long time and wondered if I could still get a note out of the trumpet. My lip was as soft as tripe and my breathing was rather limited, but I really wanted to have a try. The show was recorded so any total disaster could be patched up well before air-time. I didn't want to steal Ben's limelight but thought a possible surprise entrance halfway through would be quite emotional.

On the day, I was reasonably well and decided at least to turn up and see how I felt. We had a rough rehearsal which was from my part adequate, so we opted to take a chance.

Bruce was very generous and encouraged Ben all the way. They played 'Blue Moon' beautifully together while I stayed hidden away at the back of the set. My surprise entrance brought a wave of affection, applause and cheering and I launched into 'How High the Moon' alongside the pair of them, backed by the orchestra. I was really scared of letting them down as a mistake on the trumpet seems to be picked up by the clothest ears and is the only bit anyone ever remembers.

I got by and we all finished together as the audience roared. WHEEE! Another tremendous moment for me. Ben's eyes were shining as we returned to the dressing room. He wasn't so much nervous of facing the cameras, 'but knowing I was playing in front of all those first-class musicians in the orchestra!'. Some of his idols were there 'and I was out front, I wonder what they thought.'

'They were applauding.'

He smiled.

When the show was due to be aired, Ben popped up to the newsagent's to see if he was mentioned but, alas, not this time. Probably to keep the surprise element. 'Don't expect *too* much at this stage.' He understood. I remembered my own enthusiasm at his age and felt disappointment for him as this was his big moment. 'There will be plenty more' was rather empty consolation. Come to think of it, when I was his age, I was just starting my National Service. 'Nice to see you, to see you?' AH*TennnnSHUN*!'

Saturday 9 May

Watched the Cup Final between Liverpool and Sunderland as I dealt with my post, wearing my protective gloves. Kept looking up as the commentators got excited. The two Liverpool goals came in the second half so I got through quite a bit of mail. Ireland won the Eurovision Song Contest and the UK came second. Can't remember the song. Can't

remember who scored for Liverpool either. 'Blame the
chemo!' It has its good side now and then. I needed to get
some good rest in preparation for a Cancer Research
Campaign event in Birmingham the following day.

Monday 11 May

Fairly restless night as my nose was playing up a bit and
causing a headache. All I needed! I suppose I slept some of the
time as I had to be awakened at 7 a.m. for breakfast. Susan
Osborne and a TV crew from Pebble Mill picked me up at
8.45 a.m. and we scorched away up the M40 where there was
a notorious sign telling us of 'Emergency Toilets – 20 miles'!
Just to *see* that message makes you check the pressure – and
laughing doesn't help.

As we arrived in Birmingham and made our way to the
square outside the marvellous Symphony Hall, there was a
huge gathering of hundreds of schoolchildren waving balloons
and cheering. Out of the crowd stepped Jasper Carrot, who
welcomed me to his beloved home town. Laughs were in
abundance as we compared our relative baldness. He did it
with*out* chemotherapy. I checked his gums for side-effects.
Plenty of picture opportunities for the media. Another great
thrill was being introduced to a massive card at least fifty
metres long and ten metres high, supported by scaffolding. It
was covered with Get Well messages in an attempt to create
the Biggest Get Well Card in the World.

I was introduced to a young girl who was also struggling
with cancer. She was *so* pretty and her hair was just beginning
to grow again. She was engagingly shy about her appearance
but felt a little happier to have someone else sharing her
strange world.

Don McLean was there, and we renewed a friendship of
many years; and there was a kindly gent who *insisted* on taking
me into a caravan and praying for me. He was extremely

forceful in his enthusiastic expertise and I appreciated his concern but, as he gathered momentum, I wondered if he knew I was due at Pebble Mill for lunchtime TV. LIVE! I had to butt in as diplomatically as possible and we piled out of the caravan to join a rather anxious Susan and crew. Hasty farewell to Jasper who bade me a confused 'See you, mate.'

The programme was already under way as we jockeyed our way to the studios and we arrived as Angela Christian was singing, accompanied by Brian Dee on piano. Two of my favourites.

'You're next, Roy.'

A standing make-up was administered in the 'wings' and I was on.

A rather relieved Judy Spiers chatted about my Brummie welcome and the charity which led us to an amazing link-up with a team of climbers on Everest. We talked to each other through the multi screens and publicized a charity drive named 'Climb Your Own Mountain'. It has always bothered me that people have to rally to the call in order to provide these essential services for the good of our nation, but that is well-trodden ground on twisted priorities and if *some*body doesn't do it, who suffers?

The journey back was a sleepy one. I even missed out on the Emergency Toilets sign and had to be roused when we reached home. I stayed awake long enough to be ushered into bed in order to rest up for the chemo session number eight tomorrow.

Tuesday 12 May

I suppose being rather shattered gave me a good early part to my night and, apart from a couple of hours wrestling with the crossword book bought for me by Daniel, I managed through to 6.30 a.m. when a headache decided to have a throb. Nose was still rather sore.

We had a morning start at the hospital and arrived to find the *Fighting Back* TV crew awaiting us. I had forgotten they were coming but it was no problem as I had no script to learn. They covered my turning up at reception, being given the blood test (but not the X-ray!) then establishing me in my room. Blood pressure, pulse, temperature and weight. Once my blood had been analysed, my specialist came in to explain the situation so far. 'Your blood count is good and the X-ray is almost clear.' He was looking very happy as he inserted the needle, closely perused by the camera.

'Right, everybody. That's lunch. Back here at 2 p.m. OK?'

The crew scuttled out for a local pub lunch whilst my specialist stayed back a few seconds to reassure me he wasn't overacting for the camera and the results so far were very encouraging. I had a good lunch.

The afternoon session was fairly easy as we chatted about the prospects while my X-rays were perused and by 3 p.m. they were done. Chemo finished at 8.30 p.m. and Fiona drove me home. We had a nostalgic look at our Aussie video and drooled over the tropical fruit, large pool, coral islands and rain forests as we sat together in our cosy little snug. Video travel! The cheapest holiday in the world! No jet lag. No delayed flights. No hotel mix-ups. No charge. Sounds good to a little Yorkshireman.

The following week staggered through as the chemo did its duty. My attitude was a little more confident as I remembered the hospital prognosis.

Bruce's show was aired on the Friday and the reception for Ben was very warm. He looked and played so well and didn't seem at all nervous. The trio was very emotional and the reaction of the audience was most gratifying. I realize the amount of sympathy there was driving it along but make no apologies.

Next day, Harry Secombe sent his driver to collect us and

we enjoyed a great day with him and his brood. It was a beautiful May day and the sprawling lawns were so peaceful, with unspoilt views almost to the Sussex coast. I tried to play cricket with Harry's grandchildren which made me realize how totally out of shape I was. It was very funny as I bent down to 'snatch' a ball which had passed me ten seconds ago.

We wandered around the big garden and budding fruit trees as more memories flooded back. Harry told me of the possibility of resurrecting *Pickwick* sometime in the future. I had been his Sam Weller on Broadway 28 years ago. More precious memories. I dared not even consider that I would be a small part of it at this time – so I didn't!

After being fed luxuriously – twice – we piled back into his limo and were smoothed home. We were in a happy, dreamy state of euphoria – until we discovered our oil-fired boiler had burst and water was trickling gaily down the path!

Emergency services came to shut it down and all the fuss and bother of a replacement loomed ominous. 'Hurray! Hit me again!'

Sunday 17 May

Pooped! Stayed in bed until 4 p.m. but was determined to get to church that evening as Ben was being baptized. Anto played the piano, Daniel trombone and I took my trumpet in the hope that I might join in with his choice of hymn, 'Teach Me Your Ways'. The lip lasted sufficiently well not to spoil the occasion and we were complete as a family in our celebration. I remembered the little boy as I saw the man emerge. I'm getting soppy again.

Monday 18 May

Had a good night and a 7.30 breakfast followed by a refreshing bath. No need for a shave as my beard had gone so wispy that the sight of a razor gave it withdrawal symptoms! I could have shaved with a tissue.

A car arrived to take me to a small TV studio in Bushey where I recorded five stories for children. I wore a cap to avoid looking too menacing. Kojak telling children's stories could be counter-productive. I was through much quicker than anticipated and home by mid-afternoon.

Our boiler-house door had to be knocked down and widened to get the dead boiler *out*. Could it have grown? Check your boilers, folks, they also suffer from inflation.

Tuesday 19 May

Chemo number nine! Daniel drove me to hospital for the usual tests. White cells slightly low again so, rather than miss another week, treatment was reduced to match and started at 11.30 a.m. This was the twenty-four hour stint to which I was well resigned by now. A swab was taken from my nose for analysis. The day drudged by followed by reasonable naps between bottles! The chemo overran through lunchtime next day and Fiona picked me up at 2.30 p.m. Straight back to bed – whacked. Nose was throbbing inside and out reminding me of Jimmy Wheeler's routine, 'If you're gonna have a boil – HAVE A BIG 'UN!' It made my head bang – along with the boiler-house demolition squad. It was kind of them really to start the work so quickly in order to prevent our house assuming igloo conditions. I had to take a couple of painkillers reluctantly as the head and nose were pretty bad – *and* I was becoming constipated! Hit me again! No energy whatsoever. 'Just a little miracle. Please!'

Thursday 21 May

Lolled around. Boiler was being exchanged as my own boil was ravaging my nose. Could Cliff and his team replace *this* one whilst they were at it?

Next day they were finished and the new recruit was up and running. Great.

Nose and head still clanging away and I couldn't wear my specs so I got a very short-sighted view of England beating Pakistan in the one day test.

Painkillers again. It was a beautiful day – apparently. Norman Wisdom phoned and we had a good laugh at my voice doing somersaults whilst the whitlow on my left-hand index finger took on lollipop proportions.

I hope, dear reader, that you are not by now totally sick of my problems but, I promise you, I am not overdramatizing the situation. It is factual and true. It amazes me, when I see folks happily smoking away, that they are volunteering for *this*! I am, at present, doing better than most so what they are experiencing is beyond anyone's imagination.

Tuesday 26 May

Prior to treatment number ten, it was discovered that I was anaemic and would need a blood transfusion before a three-quarters cocktail. Liquid intake cut to 1½ litres per day and my nose had an infection to be treated by antibiotics. Hurray!

This turned my treatment into the twenty-four-hour job instead of the twelve. Hurray!

All went well as the three pints of blood took twelve hours to move in. My temperature and pulse were taken every half-hour and blood pressure every hour. I was weighed every three hours. No problems.

During the next week I gradually improved and felt quite well as we sailed into the post bag again.

Tuesday 2 June

Session number eleven and *pen-ultimate*!! Not long now. Another month and then 'We'll see.'

In the middle of the night the drip slowed up and finally stopped. It was aching and swelling. I prayed it wouldn't have to be shifted to the other wrist, 'Pleeeeese.' The pretty young Asian nurse gently twisted and squeezed it and finally got it to flow again. Oh! the relief. 'Thank you' was totally inadequate. The final chemo bag hadn't been delivered so the flow was kept open by a stand-in saline solution until it arrived. Here comes the Foreign Legion in the nick of time. I expected Gary Cooper to stagger in covered in blood. Tarra! My vein was still working. ONE MORE SESSION. Home by 1 p.m. with renewed determination and imagined vigour.

As I walked around the garden, picking out a weed here and there, the smell of freshly baked bread had me drooling as, with nose in the air, I was roped into the kitchen to sample Birthe's Norwegian bread. *Douze points*! I could hardly wait for it to cool.

The week staggered by pretty much as usual. Interviews on passive smoking. I felt quite inadequate in this area as I could only echo what the ...edical profession had diagnosed. I had no chance of catching up on all the involved research over many years and was merely a pawn in the issue. I was desperate to be instrumental in helping unsuspecting potential victims to avoid the slightest possibility of having to go through all this. As time has gone by, I'm shattered to see the volume of young folks happily dragging their health away. Like driving 100 mph in fog. You can't see ahead but hope there's nothing in your way. OOOPS! Too late! Then we trot out the 'If onlys' and 'Why *me*s'.

My nose showed slight improvement but I was still whistling in my sleep. Poor old Fiona.

We pounded away at the mail and on Sunday walked to the

church and back. The service was a rousing occasion and the whole place fairly rocked along. Love and concern was piled on in abundance and we virtually floated home.

Next day I attended a charity lunch and presented a bravery medal along with many other personalities which included members of the Grand Order of Water Rats. They also had been particularly active in phoning me throughout the rough times, and it was a good opportunity to say 'Thanks' publicly. Naturally, it was important to make light of the situation with 'How marvellous it is to have friends. Only three days after my illness broke in the media – the bills came flooding in!' A frivolous remark which was, unfortunately, taken seriously by just one journalist who pestered me as to who the bills were from. I *knew* I shouldn't have said 'The tax man.'

'How much?'

I now realized he saw a story looming: 'Tax Man Hits Dying Man!'

I explained it was just a joke but, next day, there it was! Not a headline I hasten to say, but sensationalism of the miniest kind. My accountant paled at the news and barricaded himself in. Apparently there were a few rumblings but I wasn't marched off to the Tower.

Tuesday 9 June 1992

THE LAST SESSION.

This was my lap of honour. We went to the hospital armed with modest presents for the nurses and staff, together with an embroidered 'Thank You' made by Fiona. The atmosphere was rather heady as the tests proved me to be ready for the off.

As the different cocktails were administered it was almost like a football team being well in front and passing the ball to one another as the crowd shouted *Olé* for each move.

Kytril:	– 10 mins 'Olé'
Doxorubicin:	– 10 mins 'Olé'
Mesna:	– 15 mins 'Olé'
Ifosphamide:	– 1 hour 'Olé'
Mesna:	– 8 hours 'Olé'
Saline flush:	– 3 mins 'Olé'

FINISH!

WE ARE THE CHAMPIONS!

9.30 p.m. and the last needle was finally withdrawn and that was *it*. I had no idea how much I had been steeling myself against these insertions over the past three months until that final dreaded tube was taken out of my wrist. The relief just cascaded all over me. The biggest carbuncle in the universe had burst and I was FREE! Our farewells were happy-cum-sad with smiling 'We don't want ever to see you again' wishes.

Back home and into bed. *Aaaaaah*! Smile, smile.

In my eagerness to have finished with the treatment, I forgot the fact that the last session still had to do its duty and I was shattered when the mouth ulcers wanted a lap of honour too. I also noticed my eyelashes had disappeared apart from just one in the centre of each top and bottom lid. I blinked quickly, trying to crack them to no avail.

My next check-up proved to be encouraging and the specialist assured me 'If the scan is as good, we could allow a little dancing in the streets.' He also warned me that tumour cells could, on occasions, make their way to the brain as the chemo treatment is not as effective up there. 'Don't be alarmed, but you should know.' We also chatted about a cancer counselling unit to be established at Mount Vernon hospital. A truly necessary addition to cancer care: the initial shock of diagnosed cancer is a shattering blow, and the doctor, with a queue of patients, has little time to explain all the implications of the months ahead. I'm happy to say the Lynda Jackson

Macmillan Centre is now up and running (charity funded!).

I was furious with my mouth for erupting again, for I longed to feel normal. I felt I had earned it but had to face reality and put the brakes on my eagerness. Ah well – 'to sleep, perchance to dream'!

The media was, again, interested in my improvement and it was difficult to dissuade them from claiming a 'cure'. This set off the mail avalanche again and the congrats flooded in. There were just a couple of 'nasties' from bereaved ladies who told me to 'belt up' and stop crowing. 'My husband was also a fighter and battled all the way.' These letters really hurt and I needed some help in coming to terms with understanding their hate. On the other hand, I was receiving so many 'thanks for the encouragement' letters, it was obvious that my way ahead had to be as honest as possible, no matter which way the whole thing unravelled. I still wish those two unhappy ladies had given me an address for a reply.

Letters kept on pouring in as we shambled on, taking each day as it came. Small TV spots. One highlight was an interview with Tom Jones for *Record Breakers*. We had worked together at the Winter Gardens, Bournemouth, in the late sixties. He held the record for 'The highest paid British artist for a series of TV shows to be seen in the UK and America'. £9 million for just over one hundred programmes in 1968. Some arithmetical genius worked out that 'with inflation, that would be worth £75.6 million today!' But it didn't alter Tom's lifestyle.

He was very gracious and spent time with us in the middle of his rehearsals. We did the interview on the set of a series he was filming for Central TV in Nottingham, then he went back to rehearse whilst I topped and tailed the piece. 'Thomas Woodward! – Who is he?' etc. I wore my cap.

We had been contacted by a representative from Spring Harvest, the annual celebration held at Easter, when thousands of Christians gather at various Butlin's Centres for fellowship, praise and family fun, who said that a rather large Get Well card had been signed for me and when would it be convenient to deliver? Fiona and I had guested at a similar occasion and participated in an interview with Dave Foster (our Eurovangelist friend who was at our home when I arrived with the news of my prognosis).

The 'card' eventually arrived in a station-wagon and was set up on our lawn in a 50-metre-long zig-zag. It was over a metre high and contained 15,000 signatures and get-well messages coming from Ayr, Minehead, Skegness and Pwllheli. One was from an American family: 'We don't know who you are but GOD BLESS YA!'

My mouth was still bad and making me a bit tetchy. Finger- and toe-nails had stopped growing at the base and were beginning to show a gap as the jettisoned leftovers made their laborious journey to oblivion. 'Don't worry, they'll grow again.' As time went by, they kept catching on everything, especially shoelaces. My mouth started to improve again and I was actually beginning to feel better. Sometimes almost normal. The *Fighting Back* team came along for an update of my progress and took a few shots of photographs from yesteryear 'to add a little colour'.

Friday 26 June

I was booked in for another scan which proved to be satisfactory and my specialist rang me in buoyant mood. All was set now for the radiotherapy follow-up treatment – 'To try and *zap* the thing altogether.'

I played trumpet in our church band on the Sunday and my lip was surprisingly steady for the first time in a long while. That felt good.

The Monday morning started with a trip to LBC News Talk in London for an interview with Michael Parkinson regarding the situation so far, and I met scientist James Burke 'backstage' who discussed the powers of the brain in the healing process. 'We're only scratching the surface so far,' he told me.

'Well, let's get the JCBs in!'

I got home in time to catch a little bit of Wimbledon as Jeremy Bates was showing good form but had to leave him to it as I drove myself (it was good to be allowed to drive again) to Mount Vernon for the first of my 25 radiotherapy sessions over the next five weeks.

First of all, the high precision measuring and planning of the combat area. Meticulous care was taken by my specialist and local radiologists. I took off my shirt and was 'marked up' and given a few tiny indelible pin-prick tattoos for future reference (all this was covered by the documentary TV crew) before being taken into the actual treatment room. More sci-fi atmosphere, with an adjustable bed above which was a long, thick protrusion fixed to a huge, seven-foot-diameter (2-metre) disc housed in the wall. At the end of this arm was the radiation unit which resembled a small TV set. The apparatus was fully adjustable at the push of a button which responded with a hum. Red laser beams flashed across my face as I lay in position. 'Hands behind your head and don't move.' Otherwise the rays would cure a place that didn't need it. Now, everybody left and I was on my own. A series of strange short noises were the prelude to the actual whine of the radiation unit which lasted, on average, about seventeen seconds then stopped.

A few seconds later the radiologists padded back in and readjusted the set. There were five different angles in all. Two fairly close together on the front chest, one each side and finally the bed was 'hummed' up a couple of feet to allow the arm to swing underneath and fire upwards through a window in the bed. Nobody escapes out the back door! They play comforting background music throughout this fairly short experience but, on this, my first visit, the string orchestra was a quarter-tone flat with the zap machine and I couldn't squirm! As the final position was set up, they launched into a can-can.

Next day's session had Barry Manilow singing at the Copacabana.

The atmosphere over the five weeks was a very happy one as the gang of victims in the waiting room got to know each other and bolster up the fearful. The actual treatment gave no sensation whatsoever and didn't seem to make me as tired as I had been expecting. Great! I was feeling pretty good.

As I was able to get it over with fairly early each morning, the rest of the day was available for whatever turned up and, providing I could handle it, for me to get some work done.

Mail, publicity stunts for cancer research and the anti-smoking lobby ASH (Action on Smoking and Health). One radio phone-in from Leeds gave me a fair old shock. I was interviewed about my condition and thoughts on passive smoking, then a chap came on, representing a bunch of people who demanded the right to smoke wherever and whenever they liked under the banner of human rights – thereby trampling into the ground anyone else's human rights to breathe unpolluted air. However, he was very clever and well genned-up with his facts and figures. It was like walking into a threshing machine.

I was pathetically incompetent and really needed another lawyer type to match this pompous prig. The majority of people that phoned in were on my side but I felt pretty bad about my efforts on that occasion.

On a happier note, a few awards started coming my way, something of a rare happening for me. The first being from ASH and the British Heart Foundation for my 'Outstanding achievement in the Campaign against Smoking', to be presented at the London Hilton. At the reception, I thought I spotted a doctor I had met in Birmingham at the CRAB appeal (Cancer Research at Birmingham), so made my way over. 'Hi, how are you? Nice to see you again.' He seemed bemused as he gave me a guarded but polite 'I'm very well.' He was trying to place me. We sat together at lunch and I slowly realized he was the Duke of Gloucester who was presenting the awards. I apologized for my familiarity earlier on, but he was generously 'quite flattered to be mistaken for a doctor'.

I was particularly proud of my Red Nose Award voted by viewers of *Going Live* and *Comic Relief*. The other contestants were Lenny Henry, Sir Ranulph Fiennes and Linford Christie. I secretly felt to be rather lucky as the other three really *meant* to do what they did.

BBC Radio One voted me Man of the Year as I pipped Nigel Mansell to the chequered flag. It was all very heady stuff. I was awarded my own special 'Otter' by the Young Environmentalists 'For Valour'. I had been a supporter of the organization for a few years along with many other showbiz personalities. The presentation by a sweet young environmentalist bowled me over.

I received a huge Waterford Crystal Trophy from the Institute of Entertainment and Arts Management for Outstanding Service to the Entertainment Industry. Any more and I would have to buy a cabinet. Evian Health included me as did the British Safety Council at a rather splendid evening at the Grosvenor House in Park Lane. I was beginning to enjoy this award lark and if a week went by without one, I had withdrawal symptoms. I realized my illness and the publicity it had generated put my name back in the limelight but, after those few months of anxiety and fear that it was all over, this was dreamland.

One of the greatest nights was again at the Grosvenor House when I was made 'Rat of the Year'. This seemingly derogatory accolade was, I hasten to add, awarded by the Grand Order of Water Rats. King Rat, Bert Weedon, was retiring after his year of office and was obviously instrumental in my being chosen. This was one of the grandest gatherings in the show-business year and the Great Room was packed. Famous faces everywhere from television, films, radio, theatre, sport, even a couple of critics which was pretty daring! Sitting next to TV Doctor Hilary Jones, I felt safe.

After the dinner and a couple of hilarious speeches, King Bert bounded up on stage and introduced his choice of Rat of the Year. As I walked from my table and through the applauding and cheering guests it was like a 1950s film, 'The hero returns from the jaws of Hell'. We just stood there together as the welcome went on and on. My opening remark went well: 'I've died here many times!' I managed to stagger through a bit of a tap-dance and we walked back past the same standing applauding tables. The Cup I received was massive and solid gold and stayed on our table for the rest of the magical evening. Fiona was worried we might have to take it home. I'm not sure how much it was worth, but we would have had to mortgage the house to insure it! It was later picked up by two security men who had been hovering around all evening. Phew!

As climax to the evening, Bert had invited every famous guitar player one could imagine, many of them first influenced by the Bert Weedon Guitar Books, and joined in a mass guitar 'jam' session which, I'm sure, will never be repeated. Joe Brown, Lonnie Donnegan, the Bachelors, Brian May, George Harrison, Bruce Welch. The room went wild and it seemed *everyone* had brought a camera. This really was bonus time.

Throughout my radiotherapy sessions I battled on with grumbling gums, a weird metallic taste in my mouth and aggravatingly catchy fingernails which developed a velcro technique on all clothing, soft furnishing and the like. I was pleased I didn't have to wear tights. Eventually the day arrived when my last treatment was due. Hooray! We certainly couldn't let this pass without some sort of celebration, or perhaps a giggle with my radiologist ladies. I fished out one of the many silly 'props' I had acquired over the years, popped it in an M & S bag and took it in with me and left it, with my shirt, on the chair in the treatment room. I had worked out that, after the final zap with the bed in the raised position, it took them around nine seconds to come back in. I could easily jump down from this height, so as the zap stopped I vaulted from the bed, nipped over to the bag, took out this skull and put it on the bed and hid in the blind corner. The nurse came around from the safety zone and was launching into her automatic instructions: 'You can relax your –' she suddenly spotted the skull and babbled on – 'ARMS NOW BUT DON'T GET …!' She realized the prank and saw me in hiding. 'YOU-YOU-YOU!' then collapsed into laughter. I only wish I could have got the skull to say 'I think you've overdone it this time.'

Now my treatment was over we were able to relax and see what happens so, naturally, we decided to go down to our house in Bournemouth and swan it. All the signs were good and my hair had started to grow. White bum-fluff at first, then, as it started to thicken, the colour came back and I looked rather trendy. I had received letters from people whose hair had returned with a totally different colour and texture. Curls where there had been none. Red hair instead of black. One chap's hair had returned to its youthful shiny black from being grey. He kept writing to say 'It's still black'. Mine more or less returned to normal apart from a few extra grey ones. A bit disappointing really.

Whilst down in Bournemouth, the *Fighting Back* crew came along to wrap up the whole sequence and we were interviewed by the hostess of the series, Lynn Redgrave. Covering shots of Fiona and me walking arm in arm by the pool were, I'm told, very moving. Our local butcher came out of his shop after it was shown and said, 'Don't do any more programmes like that! We ran out of tissues!'

Now the mail *really* flooded in but was taking a different slant. Many people with friends suffering from cancer asked if I would write or phone with some encouragement. This again took up a lot of time but was well worth it. A mental boost can sometimes tip the scales, and from the follow-ups I received, it worked. There were some sad ones, of course. 'Thanks for your concern and encouragement. You really made my husband's day. Your letter was framed and by his bedside. He unfortunately slipped away shortly afterwards, but we shall never forget your kindness.' Some were about young children, and were particularly heart-breaking.

During that precious summer, my health and strength gradually improved and I could have my check-ups whilst on holiday. *Bliss*!

My sixtieth birthday was a triumphant celebration bearing in mind that numbing prognosis seven months earlier. We had a big party for many of my close friends in and out of showbiz, plus my doctors and their wives and families. Benjamin set up his group and played live music. I had a short blow with them and the atmosphere took off. The following day, we had the best-ever family picture taken by a newspaper photographer. Very seldom can you get six people to smile naturally at the same time. We never could. It was a sunny day and we were outside on the patio sitting around my other cake. I had to try and hide my grotty finger-nails but that picture has pride of place in our house. It embraces our lives together so beautifully, for me especially.

At the end of that glorious summer, now back home, it was considered provident to have another exploratory broncho-scopy purely as a safety measure (belt and braces!) and so we went through the giggles once more. The result was 'A few cells still there but we can't tell if they are active or dead.'

'They might lie dormant or even disappear.'

The samples were sent to a top specialist at University College Hospital in Gower Street, London, for scrutiny. The results were encouraging and it was felt that regular check-ups were all that was necessary for the time being.

Hooray! *Record Breakers* here I come.

I wallowed in feeling normal as I interviewed Nigel Mansell when he posed by his waxwork likeness in Madame Tussaud's. Fiona and I were invited guests for Bruce Forsyth's 'Fifty Years in Showbusiness Party' at the Dorchester. Played squash and swam in our local Leisure Centre at the Bell House. We had a marvellous trip to the States to meet up with our relations and friends of the 'Birthday Club' (another promise we had made rather hollowly months before). Maine was magnificent as the autumn colours were blazing.

I did a private function for the local hospital who had administered my treatment not so long ago. Gave them all a bit of stick, especially my bronchoscopy specialist when it came to the ten-foot-long alphorn routine!!

Guesting on Harry's *Highway* series on two occasions was another bonus, as was playing tennis in Cliff Richard's big event in Birmingham. I played against Frank Bruno! Very intense stuff! More laughs than points. He kept calling me 'Chicken legs'.

I made a video for schools pointing out the dangers of tobacco in the hope ...? One can but try.

As I was wallowing in this 'lap of honour' state, an award was proposed which was to be accompanied by quite a dilemma. The Royal Association for Disability and Rehabilitation (RADAR) were holding their 'People of the Year, 1992' awards at a prestigious lunchtime ceremony at the London Hilton, and I was one of many nominees to be welcomed. Other 'People of the Year' included flying instructor Robert Legg who had successfully 'talked down' a young man whose father-in-law had collapsed at the controls of a plane; the young man, Alan Anderson, was nominated for his courage in landing the plane with absolutely no prior knowledge of flying; the Right Honourable Betty Boothroyd, MP, first lady Speaker of the House of Commons; David Constantine, himself a quadraplegic, for his motivation in designing low cost wheelchairs in developing countries; the Right Honourable Baroness Chalker of Wallasey for her services to disabled people and developing countries; Sally Gunnell for outstanding achievements in athletics and her leadership at the 1992 Olympic Games; David Hempleman-Adams for his outstanding courage and leadership in taking the first-ever successful unaided expedition to the North Geomagnetic Pole; the late Dan Maskell for his outstanding contribution to broadcasting; James Partridge, who himself underwent extensive reconstructive plastic surgery, for launching Changing Faces, an initiative which aims to help facially disfigured people and their families; PC Jim Sullivan for his outstanding courage and bravery in throttling a ferocious, five-stone pit bull terrier which was terrorizing a playground full of children; Linford Christie for his leadership at the Olympic Games in 1992 and for being Britain's finest-ever male sprinter; Chris Holmes for his achievements at the Paralympic Games in Barcelona; and Tanni Grey for her outstanding achievements at the 1992 Paralympic Games.

Again, it was a big thrill to be included in such an auspicious assembly. The date was set for 11 November and, so far, all was cosy. I was then informed proudly that Brian Redhead would perform the introductions, Ned Sherrin would be a guest speaker and the guest of honour would be Baroness Thatcher. *This* was my dilemma. I must explain my state of mind at this time. Politics were never an important part of my life. I am far too naive to understand all the ramifications and count myself a bystander, mildly interested but not too involved. I've always been confused by the election the election promises that fizzle out and, like many, don't trust 'em. I rather liked Billy Connolly's remark at the London Palladium: 'The mere fact that anybody *wants* to be a politician should BAN THEM FOR LIFE!' All frivolous stuff but come to think of it, have you ever seen a politician kiss a baby *after* the election? (Not the ones they're caught kissing.) Lady Thatcher had done great things for our country according to the pundits, and she also had her critics. I had no real opinion apart from being worried by her often patronizing attitude.

After she was ousted from her long-standing reign, she seemed to go a little berserk in a back-seat driver mode. Natural, I suppose. Then one day, I heard a piece on the radio which I thought was a spoof on Mrs Thatcher by Spitting Image. It was a recital of the Gettysburg Address originally delivered by Abraham Lincoln on 19 November 1863. There was a lush orchestral backing and it was very funny ... until it slowly dawned on me that it wasn't a spoof. 'We'll fight them on the beaches' – fine! but the Gettysburg *Address*? The ladder wasn't reaching the loft any more. Shortly afterwards I heard the radio telling us that she had signed up with Philip Morris, the tobacco magnates for which she was to receive a gross amount of money. My first reaction was that of incredulity, then disappointment, then anger. I had read of the greed-ridden tactics of some tobacco companies in the developing countries which saddened me deeply, knowing the eventual suffering which would be caused, and I just couldn't believe that she could sign that kind of contract. I was sickened to think that more and more *money* was able to draw a veil over her conscience.

So – a dilemma – do I turn down the award, or do I confront her with the situation on the day? A confrontation would be selfish considering all the other recipients and a turn-down would be a total non-event, so I thought I would play it as it comes.

The reception was very pleasant and we all chatted happily

but my heart was thumping in anticipation of the 'Arrival'. We were eventually told to 'line up' and receive our guest of honour. I was, luckily, last in line as the entourage arrived through the majestic double doors, and eyes and cameras were swung in this direction. It was now perfectly clear what I should do. All attention was on the lady as I gently slid behind the banks of photographers. I just wanted to miss this bit and that is the truth. I don't know if I was scared or just didn't want a fuss, but I knew I could not shake the hand that signed such a contract. I would have had to cancel my chrysalis and remain a crawler for the rest of my life. I was happily concealed behind the photographers as they flashed away. 'Over here, please.' 'Everybody look this way.' 'One for the red sweater.' One chap fell back and, as he picked himself up, he saw me and said, 'Come on, Roy, get in the group.' I waved a kind of shush wave. 'It's OK. I'm not needed for this one.' The session ended and the party broke ranks and mingling resumed. I felt relieved to have escaped the crunch without any fuss. However, a journalist had seen my reticence to join the group and asked why.

It was headlines the next day. Roy Castle Snubs Margaret Thatcher, etc. Local radio stations chose it for phone-ins and the mail flooded in. A vast majority supported me though there was the odd reproof: 'What about the Tommies during the war, just before they went over the top? They needed a fag to fight for the likes of you!' I had no reply apart from 'What did they do before fags were invented?'

('Come on lads! Over the top!'

'We can't. Walter Raleigh hasn't turned up with the fags yet!')

Once I finally go over the top, I shall give Raleigh a sorting out! Then again, I hope I shall be in the other place. I don't suppose he'll need matches where he's gone. *And* he can roast his potatoes with consummate ease – *and* they won't be raw in the middle.

Whilst writing this part I have been watching the 50th Anniversary of D-Day and bow unreservedly. Ten thousand brave young men perished that day alone. Multiply that by families and friends, then calculate the indescribable grief. Pride quickly took the place of that grief and from folks like me, a twelve-year-old at the time, boundless gratitude.

Christmas 1992, the Christmas I thought I wouldn't see, was again Cheshire Cat time and we, as a family, took part in the Sunday morning programme for BBC TV *This is the Day* – LIVE! Our house was crammed with cameras, cables and technicians. Hardly room for *us*. My cup runneth over. I won't indulge any more, apart from the fact that I was included in the New Year's Honours List. OBE – according to the family, Old Boy's Ego! Having had no thoughts whatsoever of receiving this type of honour, I had always had an indifferent attitude to the whole affair. How fickle we are. I was thrilled to see that Leslie Crowther was also included, as I don't know anyone who has done more charity work and I had been distraught to hear about his tragic accident. We were both acclaimed in a good light by the media as 'deserving' alongside the usual derisory remarks encompassing the 'automatic' list.

The sixteenth of February 1993 was the day I was 'summoned' to the Palace. The invitation allowed me to take my wife plus two other family members. Daniel was home but Julia was working and living in Peru, so Antonia was next in line. Benji had to be left out. He didn't seem to mind. 'I'll watch it on the news!' It turned out that Anto had a heavy day at her theatre and couldn't make it *and* do her work properly, so her pink ticket was going begging. Ben was 'coaxed' into taking her place even though the name on the invitation was Antonia. He was wearing his hair rather long at the time. 'If they challenge me I shall say "My father wanted a boy!".'

A press photographer wanted to get an early shot for reasons known only to himself, and came to our house before we left for the ceremony. It was not compulsory to wear a morning suit and grey topper which was a relief to me but, I feel, a disappointment to the photographer who was looking for a bit of comedy I suppose. I'm glad he didn't suggest a 'blowing your own trumpet' type of embarrassing angle. We tried to do something lighthearted but the result was not a thing of beauty or character.

I drove us to the Palace in our highly polished Granada courtesy of the Fiona car-cleaning agency, and the repartee was bubbling as we anticipated the next couple of hours. We were lined up in specially arranged lanes alongside the Queen Victoria statue whilst our car was thoroughly searched, and awarded a special 'safe' sticker. We were then ushered through the main gates, through the first block and into another quadrangle where we were carefully parked and invited to enter the inner sanctum. Here, recipients were separated from the visitors and I followed the 'This way' signs. Shiny-helmeted guards brandishing unsheathed swords in front of their sombre faces were placed at regular intervals. I managed to get a wink from one of them – but he may have been recognizing David Coleman just behind me.

We were categorized into sections according to our M, O or CBEs and given a choreography lesson on how to approach Her Majesty, receive the medal, four steps back, bow, turn and move off. It was impossible to move into position too soon as a series of ushers' arms formed stop/go barriers that could have halted the Grand National. There were around three hundred of us as we gradually inched forwards down a side corridor until we reached the 'barriers'.

The final usher modelled for Toby Jugs and held me back until my name was announced: 'For services to show business and charity ...' Left-right left-right, turn and walk a few paces to the designated spot. Rather like finding your mark on a film set. Her Majesty slotted my medal into a specially prepared bar and said, 'Well done, it must be nice to make people laugh.' Then she looked at me seriously and asked, 'How *are* you now?' That floored me. I blurted, 'Very well, thank you, Ma'am.' 'Good.' And I was on my obligatory four steps backwards, bow, turn and away to join the rest of the audience.

It was about the time of the announcement that the Queen was to start paying income tax, so you can imagine the suppressed laugh when one chap was introduced: 'For services to the Inland Revenue'!

Her Majesty finally got through the gallant three hundred and the string and woodwind orchestra concluded their exhausting stint from the minstrel gallery.

More photographs in the quadrangle, then home to prepare for an immediate drive to Manchester where we were to attend a few interviews regarding our lives, faith and progress so far. Quite a day. It suddenly crossed my mind that it was nearly a year since I had received that fateful prognosis.

Daniel and Birthe were still with us and seemed to be getting along very well together and we were anticipating something of a more permanent situation on the horizon.

'Don't push.'

'Be patient.'

'Mustn't rock the boat. Could spoil everything!'

It was breakfast time and Fiona shouted upstairs, 'Do you want toast, cereal or a cooked breakfast?'

'We're coming down.'

They both joined us in the kitchen, holding hands and looking sheepish. Daniel smiled at Birthe, then at us and cleared his throat.

'We have an announcement to make.'

We all took an involuntary deep breath and waited.

'We have decided … we'd like a cooked breakfast!'

They were engaged shortly after that and arranged to be married in Norway at the YWAM base. It's amazing what a cooked breakfast can do.

The big event was on 20 March, and we all flew over to Hamar for a few days. The base provided us with friendly accommodation and we experienced their traditional culinary expertise and walked through fresh cold winds down lake Mjøsa through fields of brown grass which was just about to shoot as the winter snow blanket warmed and percolated through to the thirsty roots. The sky was blue and our cheeks were red as we returned to the busy base. Backpackers of all nationalities wandered in and out as the residents prepared the main hall for the reception the following day. Food was being prepared and the aroma was just too much for the widening nostrils of we Brits, having had our first two hours' worth of Norwegian champagne air.

Next day the wind had calmed and the sun shone across the lake as it burst through the windows of our little bungalow which was one of many scattered around the main building. Video-cameras were already recording events as we arrived at the main hall for breakfast and it was difficult not to over-react when you suddenly found yourself looking down a lens with a mouthful of Lapskaus.

The service was held in a small wooden Lutheran church in Hamar and, although fairly simple, was oozing with warmth and love. Anto and I turned up early as we were to play for the arrival of the bride.

Daniel timed the walk as we rehearsed the trumpet voluntary and hoped Birthe would walk at the same speed. Any slower and we would be in trouble. My lip would probably pack up and fizzle out. The guests started arriving and the chatter became more and more lively as the clock neared 2 p.m. Daniel joked around with his Norwegian best man who was an amateur conjurer. Fun with the ring was inevitable.

Signals were given to alert us of the arrival of the bride and the church diminuendo'd to an expectant hush.

I was really nervous as I launched into the trumpet voluntary but managed to start on the correct note. I was able to see Birthe as she walked majestically forward in the gown Fiona had made so lovingly. She looked stunning – *and* she walked quickly enough to get me out of trouble.

The ceremony was just beautiful with the Norwegian marriage service translated into English for us. Rings were exchanged with the slightest hint of fun and suddenly our first-born was married. My mind flashed back to that fifteen-year-old who fell on to the rocks on the Isle of Man and I remembered shouting at God to heal him or take him. Here he was, complete, happy, and now with a wife. I thanked God with all my heart.

The reception was like one huge family with masses of beautifully prepared local cuisine. The home-made gâteaux selection would have graced any five-star hotel and we chose to have a tiny piece of each one. Throughout the meal, friends would stand up and pay tribute to the newly-weds, mainly humorous interspersed with songs and poems. We laughed when everyone else laughed.

During the late afternoon we walked down to the lake again whilst the hall was transformed into a cabaret room. Many more guests this time and, after more gluttony, impromptu cabaret fairly rattled along. We finally crowded around Daniel and Birthe as they prised themselves out of our arms and into a modest limo and disappeared into the night on their way to a wedding-present hotel room in Hamar.

A few weeks later, we held a reception back home for friends and relations who couldn't get over to Norway. It amused us to be issuing invitations to Daniel's 'second marriage'.

During January and February I co-presented an afternoon TV

series for BBC 1. *Primetime* was aimed at the over-fifties and highlighted all kinds of benefits, tips, interviews and, occasionally, a musical guest. My co-presenter was Maggie Philbin and the series, although mainly serious, was a happy one.

It was at this time we had the saddening news of the death of the great footballing legend Bobby Moore after his own private battle with cancer. This rather unexpected revelation shook the whole sporting world and made me realize how complacent I was becoming again. My energy was good and, to all intents and purposes, I was back to normal even though the knowledge of the possibility of a return 'visit' was still a threat.

As Eastertime approached, Fiona and I had arranged to tour around the different Butlin's Centres to thank all the Spring Harvest gatherings for their love and prayers *and* the Get Well card. It was a tour which combined a sort of driving holiday dotted with tremendous welcomes from happy Christians who filled the 3000-seater marquees. We visited Minehead on three occasions, another three in Skegness, with Ayr and Pwllheli stretched in between. Fiona and I shared the driving and we clocked up three thousand miles during the seventeen days of being just us, driving as often as possible through sleepy country roads and toy-like villages as the hedges and trees were bursting into fresh life. Then the explosion of love and encouragement which sustained us as we drove on.

Shortly afterwards, the second Earl's Court Aerobathon was another massive turn-out and we smashed the world record with no problem. The computers were stopped at 15,000 and the whooping and hollering was still ringing in my ears as we negotiated the Hammersmith flyover.

On 24 May we had the first rehearsal of *Pickwick*, to be played at the Chichester Festival Theatre throughout the summer and we all turned up and gathered in the smaller

Minerva venue for the first read-through. I had never thought I would play the Festival Theatre, being on the other side of the tracks, so to speak, so this again was a big thrill. My contribution as Tony Weller (Sam's father) was just a cameo part but the duet with Sam in the second act was a little gem and went very well, so I felt I was making a decent contribution. (And, conveniently, was able to commute easily from our Bournemouth home.)

David Cardy played Sam and we shared a rather cramped dressing room, but got along like a garden shed on fire. The show didn't play every night in order to give Chichester and the tourists a chance of two visits in the week.

During the run I was suddenly surprised by my local Rotarians who presented me with the Paul Harris Award, the highest honour in the Rotary world. I was totally unaware of this and don't think I reacted with enough appreciation at the time but, as the significance of this special award gradually dawned, I think I made amends. It was given to me mainly for my involvement in our local Cheshire Home.

All in all, the summer slipped by very happily indeed. Packed audiences and lazy sunny days. I said to Fiona, 'I think I really *have* died and this is heaven.' Real quality time.

Towards the end of the run at Chichester I developed a bit of a cough which seemed innocuous enough as there was 'a lot of it about'.

It didn't get any better and I thought my immune system was perhaps a little slower to deal with it than normal. I continued with a few bits and pieces during the early autumn but the coughing bouts were worsening. During performances, the adrenalin seemed to keep it away, but once I came off, it was not a pretty sight. Sometimes I thought I would cough up my kneecaps.

I had managed to get through the twenty-second series of *Record Breakers* which was most gratifying, and I considered it another unexpected milestone snatched out of the ebbing tide. I know the gang were concerned for me towards the end of the ten recordings and made all possible efforts to help me along. Kriss Akabusi had joined Cheryl, Norris and me for a few of the shows and his bubbling enthusiasm fitted in beautifully. We had a lot of laughs and I'm sure you can imagine what it meant to me.

Another unexpected bonus was the Royal Variety Show on 15 November which included an excerpt from *Pickwick*. This incorporated an abridged version of my duet with Sam and I managed to get through it. I would have liked to have been in better shape but enjoyed this extra privilege as I remembered that first Royal Show 35 years ago when Harry dragged me back for that second bow. Here he was, encouraging me again as I sat huddled in our dressing room trying to stifle my wheezy outbursts.

Various prescriptions were administered for my cough, to no avail, and I began to find it difficult to swallow solid food. So on 19 November it was decided that I should have an exploratory endoscopy which entailed the dreaded tube being wormed down my gullet this time. The anaesthetic had to be as minimal as possible as I was performing the cabaret for the prestigious 'Wooden Spoon Ball' at the London Hilton, location of many mixed emotions. This one being yet another.

The endoscopy was rather different from its broncho equivalent as, like when in the dentist's chair, my dreamy conversation was limited to 'Aaahs' and 'Nnnngs' as the guided probe was expertly fed down my throat. I was quickly *compos mentis* and Fiona drove me home as we discussed the non-committal but apparently unalarming first impressions of the examiner.

The cabaret was a tremendous success as I incorporated trumpet, alphorn and finished with a tap-dance. I kept on thinking how bizarre the whole day was working out. Walking away from a thousand-strong standing ovation into a corridor-coughing routine which made the head swim.

Next day we were informed officially of the probe's findings which confirmed the previous afternoon's assumptions of nothing untoward. The swallowing problem was put down to *something* putting pressure on my oesophagus.

Monday 22 November

SCANNER! – Wexham Park Hospital. Back in the white gown with rear tie tapes. I only had to go through the hoop once and was given no idea of the result, so drove home with the familiar mixed feelings of hope and despair.

Tuesday 23 November

We were invited to see my specialist – or 'spesh' as we called him – who greeted us with what can only be described as solemnity. I felt the same dreaded anticipation as I had twenty months ago. His eyes were sad as he related the facts. 'The cancer has started up again and the prognosis is a little poorer than last time because the same intensity of treatment would not be advisable.' He told me how well I had done so far and assured me I had been one of his most successful patients – which was telling me something else altogether. Fiona and I exchanged glances as we asked his advice regarding the future. He basically intimated that we make the best of our Christmas together with the family.

He prescribed a week's course of chemotherapy capsules which 'may do some good ... I hope so. I'd like to see you again next week.' He tried to cheer us up with an 'all is not lost' parting comment, but we knew we were back in the scrummage.

This new development caused my having to pull out of a couple of concerts in Blackpool which alerted the media and so the whole procedure of collective interviews and photographs blazed through our home again, followed by the avalanche of love from well-wishers. The most quoted comment from this last session was, when asked if I was afraid to die, 'Billions have done it and we haven't had one complaint yet.' Frivolous, but what *can* you say to a question like that? Later I pondered the possibility of Marks & Spencers becoming Funeral Directors. That way, there may be a few returns (in green plastic bags).

The next few days brought back all the worst memories as I lolled around the place in a chemo haze. The capsules, known as bullets, were more like toy submarines and took ages to 'dive', but, as I approached the last of the five days, there was a distinct improvement with my swallowing. In fact, the day of my next appointment I ate a defiant plateful of fish and chips. My 'spesh' was delighted with the results and a new enthusiasm returned to his eyes which lifted my spirits considerably. A full course of capsules was prescribed to be taken at intervals over the next few months. One week on, then two weeks to recover. 'Oh, and you'll lose your hair again, but the other side-effects shouldn't be too harsh.' I was back in with a chance.

Pickwick was due to open in Birmingham on 11 December 1993 and Harry had kept my place open for the Christmas season if I felt I could handle it.

In one sense, I could take a chance as I would be covered by an understudy and this was acceptable to the management so, after a heart-to-heart with Fiona, we decided to give it a try. Might as well 'enjoy our Christmas'.

The nearest hotel to the Alexandra Theatre was the Forte Crest where I had performed at lots of functions when it was the Albany. They bent over backwards, providing us with a suite and converting a small ante-room into a kitchen with fridge, microwave and toaster. We added a blender and were self-sufficient. I paced out the distance from the hotel foyer to the stage door and it worked out at 164 strides on a good day. There couldn't be a more perfect situation under the circumstances.

Rehearsals were not too intensive as the cast had played a short season at Sadler's Wells which I had to miss as I was involved with *Record Breakers*. My part was taken over by none other than my friendly landlord of 1958/9, Don Smoothey. *His* cockney accent was genuine.

I shared a dressing room with my 'son' David Cardy again and we resumed the competitive banter we had developed in Chichester. The show was virtually sold out for the whole run and Harry was in great form. Still singing top Cs in his 73rd year. He always pulled me out of the finale line-up to take a special bow and the warmth of the audiences could have melted the Antarctic. Combine all this with three family days at home over the Christmas weekend and who's a lucky boy! I was enjoying!

Arrangements were made for check-ups at Mount Vernon Hospital in Middlesex on the odd Monday morning before our drive back to the theatre for another week.

Over these past months I had been prescribed various medications for the cough, ending up with methadone which I gathered was used to wean addicts off heroin. It didn't seem to be doing much good so I stopped taking it, but had no idea of the consequences. Nights were fitful again as I spent hours pacing around the hotel suite and my appetite dried up. Food was repulsive and despite all her efforts Fiona was finding it impossible to get me to eat. We had some prescription nutritional drinks which I could tolerate, but I took them more as a duty than a desire. The fear of suffocation returned and my nose was again an aggravation. I suppose I was doing cold turkey and didn't realize it. This was as bad a period as I had encountered throughout the whole illness and I just couldn't imagine there was a way out of it.

One night around 4 a.m. as I paced the floor, I wandered

out on to the balcony. There was almost no movement in the
orange-lighted streets as I looked over the rail and peered
down at the deserted pavement some 30 metres below. I was
tempted. It would all be so easy. Done with in a couple of
seconds. BUT. Apart from it being an unchristian thing to do,
what sadness and questions I would leave behind. I just
couldn't do that to Fiona and my family.

Besides, I was wearing my best new dressing-gown, given
to me by Harry and Myra for Christmas! I couldn't spoil
that. What if I changed my mind on the way down? A bit late
to turn it into a bungee jump!

It all seems quite absurd at this moment, but that fleeting
thought was a serious one.

In desperation I phoned my 'spesh' and he arranged for me
to see an ENT friend of his in Birmingham. Another session
in the scanner revealed nothing untoward and a follow-up
probe allayed any serious worries regarding my nasal
passages. 'A few nose drops may be of some help.'

Whether the nose drops did the trick or even had a
psychological effect or whether I was now coming out of my
withdrawal to methadone, I really don't know, but I began to
sleep more easily and food became a little more attractive. The
show was roaring along and we had another week and a half of
packed houses to look forward to before taking a two-week
break and then returning for a further two weeks in a
triumphant lap of honour. The backstage atmosphere was
bubbling along as it does with a popular show, especially with
Harry at the helm, so a request for everyone to assemble on
stage after the Wednesday matinée was intriguing but of no
great concern. Half expecting the announcement of a party
and a show of hands regarding where and what kind of food,
we assembled on stage and gabbled away until we were
hushed by a representative of the theatre.

We were totally stunned by the news that the 'Theatre is
bankrupt and must cease trading forthwith. Everything is

being done to save the situation but, by law, the box office is closed and tonight's performance will not take place.'

Nobody in the company had had any inkling of this development and the disbelieving hush seemed endless as the realization gradually dawned. I looked at Harry and he was as shocked as everyone else. How could it be possible for the theatre to cease trading with full houses ahead? What about the poor folks who had bought those tickets? It was all a bit weird.

We were all invited to a meeting the following morning and blame was not unlike pass-the-parcel. A previous production had cost them a packet along with a few other discrepancies which eventually came home to roost, so, even with our advance money already in the box office, the kitty was empty. 'Everything is being done to try and save the situation but, sadly, it will take some time.' It was pretty obvious our run was over, together with our triumphant return due to public demand. I was choked for our dancers and stage technicians who were left high and dry, with no wages and with landladies to pay. Equity would obviously come to the rescue and cushion the blow eventually, but, for now, the unexpected break was not a welcome one. I don't ever recall a seasonal run ending on a matinée before.

The show was due to tour for six weeks after the now truncated run at the Alex and we were assured that this was very much on, so this, at least, was some consolation. For us, it was swings and roundabouts. I was still struggling with my problems and a little floppo time could possibly be a good thing. I was due back in Birmingham a week later as we had organized the launch of an ambitious appeal to establish a lung cancer research station. I had been amazed to learn there was nothing of this intensive nature in the world. Ray Donnelly, the head lung surgeon in Liverpool and Chairman of the Lung Cancer Fund, made me wholly aware of this when I had helped him with a publicity campaign a few months

earlier. He was becoming more and more frustrated as he had
to explain to the bulk of lung cancer sufferers that 'nothing
more can be done'. Whilst the treatment was slightly less
harsh, the success rate hadn't improved since King George VI
died of it forty years ago. We were to have launched at the
Alex and all the invitations were already out. Graciously, the
Birmingham Hippodrome sprang to the rescue and the launch
went ahead followed by another grand event at the St George's
Hall in Liverpool the evening after. Rick Wakeman came
along and joined his son, Adam, with some keyboard duets
and the project was launched in tremendous style.
Archbishop Derek Warlock had been the recipient of a
successful lung cancer operation by Ray Donnelly and gave
the appeal his blessing as our Vice-President and our
President, Lady Pilkington, made the first substantial
donation. It was now down to the nitty-gritty task of
fund-raising in an already overcrowded cauldron. Everyone
equally important in their own field but, unfortunately, only
one public pocket which was already stretched.

The unexpected break proved to be fortuitous as Benji had
been invited to prepare an album of modern Christian music
together with a few original compositions. He could 'have his
head' regarding the treatment. A wonderful opportunity for a
20-year-old and he had been beavering away composing and
orchestrating since before Christmas. Kingsway Records were
going to produce the outcome and I was invited to guest on it
with the by now familiar 'If well enough' understanding.
Those extra few days allowed me time to familiarize myself
with some of the music and gently build up my tripe lip. I was
desperate not to let Ben down but feeling doubly trepidatious
about my contribution.

I actually thought I was dying the night before the session.
Maybe it was an involuntary act to provide me with an excuse
for the next day, but, as I'm no psychoanalyst, I wouldn't

know. Ben drove us down to the Eastbourne studios and we set up. The basics were 'laid down' and then we were invited to get involved. Modern recording techniques allowed me as many 'takes' as I needed but, of course, one has to get it right eventually, but with a tweak here and a tweak there, I got through the couple of days surprisingly well. Daniel joined us for a couple of tracks with a 'trad' feel and I found it difficult to play the trumpet and smile at the same time. The album was building very nicely and you can imagine the thrill I experienced when I went along to hear the Big Band session a few weeks later. It was a most unwelcome intrusion when I got a fit of the shakes and had to wrap up to try and keep warm for the rest of the evening.

Next day I was back in hospital for an antibiotic drip lasting four days. The 'bug' was examined and I was about to get pneumonia. *Olé*. Thanks for waiting!

During this drip period I had to miss Les Dawson's memorial service at Westminster Abbey, which saddened me as I had worked with Les many times and considered him a mate. He had phoned me early on during my illness and told me to 'Get *mad* with it! Don't muck about!' He had lost his first wife after a long struggle with cancer, eventually remarried and was blessed with Tracy and a lovely baby daughter, Charlotte. How could I possibly complain?

The antibiotics did the trick and I came out of hospital and into *Pickwick* for the six weeks' tour, beginning with two weeks in Woking.

After Woking, on the Sunday before opening in Sheffield, was the final Derby game between Liverpool and Everton. This was to be the last time they would meet in front of the beloved Kop before it was bulldozed into an all-seater affair as required by modern regulations. We were given the privilege of having a bucket collection for our 'Cause for Hope' appeal and I was invited to toss the coin before the kick-off. As far as we know, this was the first time a collection had been allowed at the venue.

We drove up in the early morning and squeezed in an appeal to the Lion's Convention North-West. They committed themselves to a year's fund-raising, which could result in quite a substantial amount. That was an exciting start to the day.

We visited the private boxes at Anfield as they prepared to have lunch with their guests. More donations and pledges. At one stage before the game, I had to walk past the already full Kop and someone started the chant 'There's only one Roy Castle'. What a thrill that was. What also impressed me was the fact that opposing fans stood together, some of them members of the same family, all equally fanatical about their respective team but showing no animosity whatsoever – only great humour and enthusiasm. Oh, that the world could get this message! Dream on, pal.

When I emerged with the two teams the noise was indescribable: 45,000 soccer fans giving us (and the Kop) a standing ovation. The referee whispered, 'How would you like to ref this game?'

'I'd rather have more chemotherapy!'

I tossed the coin and left the field to another ovation, taking my place in the stand.

Halfway through the match Fiona, who had never been to a soccer match in her life, leaned towards me and said, 'Is this my Mother's Day treat?'

I think she enjoyed it. As for me, I grinned all day and, I'm sure, all through the night too.

Next day we travelled to Sheffield for two weeks, then two weeks in Norwich, followed by a week of Music Hall in Telford, Halifax, Llandudno and Southport. We then drove back to Luton for a big Christian celebration: the main attraction, Luis Palau, was over from the USA. We were 'second top' and were to be interviewed about our life and faith. The new marquee had proved difficult to assemble and eventually died in a muddy field. It's amazing what old

Lucifer gets up to when he's about to lose a wicket. It had the opposite effect as everybody rallied to the call and two churches were used to accommodate the multitudes as we 'played' four times whilst being shuttled back and forth. The extra exhilaration of overcoming adversity doubled the enthusiasm and left old Nick with a smouldering tail. Had he been so clever, he would have waited until we were all in the marquee before he collapsed it. Shot himself in the hoof that time.

On numerous occasions, people had suggested my being baptized. I can't explain why but I really wanted it to be my decision and not feel as if I had been badgered into it by someone else. I had discussed it many times with Fiona and whilst it would please her enormously, she agreed it should be my decision in my own time. I have never been keen on going through rituals just to please other people. I felt that God and I had a perfectly good understanding and it was not necessary to make a public display.

However I did want to make my peace 'officially' and the perfect time came when my whole family was at home. Julia was on holiday from Peru, and Daniel and Birthe were visiting for a few days.

The ceremony was set up for Sunday 20 March and kept as quiet as possible as I didn't want to attract any media attention or the whole thing would have been for entirely the wrong reason.

I was to be the only 'customer' on this occasion and after discussions on procedure, I left my change of clothes in the vestry and joined the church orchestra. Ben on saxophone, Anto on keyboards and Daniel on trombone together with a few friends on bass, drums, guitars, clarinets, flutes and violins.

Daniel was also to be my helper and welcome me after I had taken the plunge.

The hymn I chose was 'Be Bold, Be Strong' which many people interpreted as 'Be *Bald*, Be Strong'.

The baptism was beautifully simple and I didn't know what to expect as I re-emerged a new man. There was certainly no blinding light or powerful surge through my body but a tremendous calm as I made my peace with my past and started afresh with my future. The whole congregation were singing their heads off as Anto took a few photographs of the ceremony. Daniel then handed me my specs and white fluffy towel before he joined Anto and Ben in the orchestra. I was supposed to go back into the vestry and towel off and change but I didn't want to miss this atmosphere so went and joined the musicians for the rest of the hymn. The whole experience was joyful as well as light-hearted. Everyone was smiling.

The next day, John Hughes our bass player was doing some decorating at Rock House, a home for the elderly which was attached to our church and received our service by way of close-circuit television. As John was slapping on the paint he heard one of the old ladies relaying news of the baptismal service to a friend who had missed it.

'Roy Castle was baptized last night, dear.'

'Oh yes?'

'Yes. It was very nice. He came out of the orchestra for the ceremony and all his family were there.'

'Family were there.'

'Yes, they all gathered round him when he came up and gave him his glasses and towel.'

'Glasses and towel.'

'Then his daughter went back to the piano and his two sons went to play their instruments and guess what?'

'Guess what.'

'Roy Castle went and joined 'em dripping away with his towel draped round him.'

'Towel?'

'Yes and blow me if he didn't look like Gandhi!'

Friday 6 May

We drove up to Manchester for another interview about our life and faith. It was held in a golf club and was to take the form of an informal dinner followed by the chat show.

We had a capacity turn-out and the atmosphere was bubbly and relaxed as we found our nominated places at the table and, once the other eight guests had been introduced, sat down. As we awaited the first course, we chatted to one side then the other and, during one of the lulls, I gently drummed the table edge with my two index fingers. Not really a nervous gesture, just something drummers do occasionally. It wasn't an attention getter, more of a 'what shall we talk about next' gesture. I didn't actually realize I was doing it but was suddenly aware that my left hand was a little sluggish. This concerned me and I tried it again – with more concentration. It still wouldn't keep up with my right hand. Conversation resumed but I was only partially listening. My mind flashed back to a few concerts I had done with Benny Green and Rosemary Squires in tribute to George Gershwin. Benny narrated the stories which led to our renditions of many of those wonderful compositions. Towards the end of the show, Benny told of Gershwin playing the piano when he suddenly had difficulty with an arpeggio which, hitherto, he had played with consummate ease. Shortly afterwards, he died of a brain tumour.

I knew this was a possibility in my case as I kept on quietly testing my left hand. I wasn't imagining it, the messages were not getting through.

I had been alerted to the fact that the cancer cells might seek refuge up there, so I can't say I was surprised, just disappointed. Old Nick's playing his joker!

My 'spesh' organized another scan which discovered two small deposits, so five visits to the zap machine were arranged.

Wednesday 25 May

I struggled with the chemo and radiotherapy treatments as we 'launched' our album, first at Ronnie Scott's Club in Soho then, later in the evening, at the Christian Resources Exhibition at Sandown Park. I was, again, deeply thankful that I had been spared to see it through.

As I look back on my career, I feel I have made so many mistakes and shudder to think how I could have been so stupid so often. I have never been able to see my goals clearly, and in giving most suggestions a chance, have come unstuck many times. I shouldn't have taken on *Billy* but hoped it might work. I shouldn't have taken on *Mr Polly* but thought this might be the big one. I should only have done the things that were perfect for me. Dickie Henderson once gave me some advice which was very powerful: 'Never let them raise you to your own level of incompetence.' I ignored that one many times, to my own distress. My determination to stay simple was fine until I mixed with the top bracket, and then I realized I was in the slow lane.

This then raises the question: 'What do you want out of life? What is success?' The answers are much clearer once you are told life's just about over. The simple, loving, caring things then score heavily, and the greed, selfishness and ego become millstones. I wonder what on earth goes through the minds of evil, indiscriminate people when they are told the bad news? You can't bribe a doctor to get you out of *this* one.

I feel I want to apologize to all the thousands of people who are praying for my healing. They say that when you're dying your life flashes by in front of your eyes. I've had to rewind mine three times. I feel I'm taking longer to die than James Cagney on the Cathedral steps. I am becoming aware of non-involved people getting bored with my situation – 'Do one thing or the other, mate! Stop it or pop it!'

Fiona has been magnificent. Strong when I have wilted and wholly encouraging when I have shown a little progress. These last few months she has driven me everywhere as I haven't felt one hundred per cent. It's a shame when it takes a crisis to realize such deep love and affection. Apart from our little hiccup over twenty years ago, we have treasured our happy relationship and shared faith.

I am thankful to have stayed around long enough to see our children grow up and become independent. These last two years have been difficult for all of us but we have also received many blessings. My doctors haven't given up on me yet, so who knows what the future holds? Maybe I won't live long enough to see the Research Centre up and running, but when it is, there'll be one big sunbeam shining all over it.

I have agonized over how I should finish this book. I certainly want to thank God for the life I have been given and for His promise of the life to come. I thank the medical profession for their care and expertise and all the friends who have showered me with love and encouragement. I ask forgiveness from all the friends I have not been able to mention as my concentration has slowly dwindled.

My final paragraph is for Fiona. Thank you for sticking with it and seeing us through into this happy and loving situation. As a wife and mother, I could ask for no better and I am at peace with whatever happens.

Epilogue
by Fiona Castle

When Roy finally set out to write his autobiography, neither of us had any idea of the interest it would generate. Roy had come to recognize that he was not successful when he deviated in any way from his performing talent. He had tried many times – but failed. These ventures included two previous books, children's books, records, a tap dancing school and his own children's theatre production of *Record Breakers*.

This book had been forming in his mind since he had confronted his first round of cancer. However, he couldn't summon up the enthusiasm to start writing. There were so many other commitments, including *Pickwick* with Harry Secombe. It was during this time, in early 1994, that Harry challenged him. He organized a meeting with his publisher, Jeremy Robson, and within days Roy had begun to write, longhand, his story. We were on tour with *Pickwick* and Roy was undergoing chemotherapy for the second time. He was therefore able to spend many hours writing, while he had little energy for anything else. Looking back I sense God's timing.

He started writing at the beginning of March and was given the deadline of the end of June to finish it. Had it been any later the book would not have been finished. As it was, he had to leave the inclusion of last-minute thoughts and anecdotes to his editor Louise Dixon and trust her to insert them where appropriate. She was brilliant! Louise said that they had never received a script that had needed so little alteration and which was so straightforward. Roy was too ill even to choose the photos or to read the final draft. I had gone through it with Roy, chapter by chapter, as he was writing it. Often he would read to me as I was driving him to the next venue on the tour of *Pickwick*. Much as I enjoyed the stories, I would have to open the windows and chew gum furiously and finally have to ask him to stop as he was lulling me to sleep with his quiet, gentle voice!

Jeremy, knowing how ill Roy had become, worked flat out to get an early publishing date so that Roy would be able to enjoy the success he had anticipated. To the end Roy didn't believe that it would be successful. One hand bound copy was rushed through so that Roy could see it before he died. This was the first time I read the final addition at the end of the book. I suppose he intended it that way as he would have known of my protests that he was over the top in his praise of me! It was too late.

When they discussed the title Roy laughingly suggested *Going Going*, so that someone could write the sequel – *Gone*. He was always able to laugh about his condition, making it easy for other people to be with him and laugh with him. He never knew just how much people appreciated him. I am now reaping this pleasure through thousands of letters received since his death, of different stories of how his life touched and affected others. I wonder if we as human beings realize how much one life can affect another. Never has that been more evident than in the life of Jesus Christ in whom Roy came to trust and who gave him the assurance throughout the final days of his life that he was not going to a lost eternity – but into His glorious presence. And what comfort to me now.

Many of the letters I received after Roy's death were in appreciation of the book. Comments like 'I couldn't put it down', 'I read it through the night', 'I kept waking my wife up with bouts of uncontrollable laughter'. I am so glad that even through the tough times his sense of humour shone through. People who came to visit him in the last weeks left saying he had cheered *them* up and made them feel better.

Before he died I was able to read the beautiful foreword to Roy, written by his trusted friend Harry, although with several pauses to wipe away the tears and pull myself together.

For my part I am grateful to Roy for the legacy he has left for future generations of our family. Without this book 90 per cent of the anecdotes, so rich in humour, showing the character of the man, would have been forgotten.

In January 1994 Roy willingly lent his name to an appeal to raise funds for the world's first Centre of Excellence to research lung cancer. I don't think he realized how involved he would become or what an impact it would have on his remaining months of life. When he was too ill, he undertook a gruelling train journey round the country to raise funds and awareness for the appeal. It was this I believe that brought Roy a great number of new fans. Somehow he managed to touch people who might never have seen him perform. Money has continued to pour into the Appeal and he is still remembered by such honours as winning the Radio 4 Personality of the Year award. Since his death I have found myself taking up the baton with as much determination, in order that future generations should not suffer the effects of this horrible disease. I am proud to know that this centre will bear Roy's name. He said that if he didn't live to lay the foundation stone, there would be a great big sunbeam shining down on it!

I have nothing but gratitude to God for the wonderful relationship Roy and I shared. I realize more and more how privileged I have been to share Roy's life for thirty-one years. What the future holds for me I do not know, but I do know that Roy would encourage me to get on with my life and make the most of every moment that's left.

His final words on the BBC TV programme *Fighting Back* will continue to ring in my ears: 'Don't whine – laugh!'

Fiona Castle
April 1995

Index